THE SEARCH FOR FORM

Studies in the Structure of James's Fiction

THE SEARCH FOR FORM

STUDIES IN THE
STRUCTURE
OF JAMES'S FICTION

by J. A. WARD

*The University of
North Carolina Press
Chapel Hill*

To my mother and father

PREFACE

The title of this book is taken from a passage in "The Art of Fiction": "Literature should be either instructive or amusing [it is commonly assumed], and there is in many minds an impression that . . . artistic pre-occupations, the search for form, contribute to neither end, interfere indeed with both."[1] Though in a negative context, the phrase "the search for form," aside from its advantages of brevity and precision, serves well to indicate what this book is about. First of all, the phrase crystallizes the purposes of James's own criticism and fiction. Reading, like writing, began and ended for him in the search for form, in the attempt to discover the relation of parts to each other and to the whole: "The study of connections is the recognized function of intelligent criticism."[2] Authorship, to James, simply means "composition"—the arranging, the placing, the structuring of materials; and "composition alone is positive beauty."[3]

The search for form is endless. Every novel, *nouvelle*, and tale requires the same effort; the form, when found, is always unique. The present study represents my own search for the forms of certain of James's works, as well as for those pervasive

1. "The Art of Fiction," in *Partial Portraits* (London, 1888), p. 381.
2. "Pierre Loti," in *Essays in London and Elsewhere* (London, 1893), p. 160.
3. *P*, p. 319.

but elusive principles of structure that inform the fiction and lie behind the technical dicta of the essays and prefaces.

This study proposes two theses. The principal one, set forth in the opening chapter, has to do with James's habit of building his works both from the outside in (that is, in accordance with some predetermined ideal of what the shape should be) and from the inside out (that is, in accordance with the organic development of the "germ"). The secondary thesis, taken up in Chapter Two, is the idea that most of James's structures are determined by logical and spatial conceptions of relationship rather than chronological ones. Thus, time and change, like plot and action, count for less in James than in most novelists; or, if they count for anything, it is for what they say about those elements in characters and situations that do not change. Though I believe the theses developed in the two general chapters to be neither narrow nor rigid, I have not hesitated to permit my general subject—structure in James—to divert me from the major arguments whenever it seemed necessary or profitable to do so. In the chapters devoted to specific works, many matters come up which have little direct bearing on the ideas elaborated in Chapters One and Two.

Several factors influenced my choice of works for special discussion. Above all I wanted a representative grouping, and so selected novels and tales as different from each other as was reasonably possible, and also loosely comparable to other works of the same class. I wished not just a chronological spread, but also a variety of "types" of Jamesian fiction: a *nouvelle*, an international novel, a Dickensian social novel, a "dramatic" novel, a novel of "the major phase," and so forth. The subject of my third chapter, *Watch and Ward*, requires a special explanation. Though it may seem too trivial an exercise to merit separate attention in a book that neglects *The Portrait of a Lady* and *The Ambassadors*, *Watch and Ward* offers unique advantages to the student of James's structures. It is the one novel in which James's emergent principles and methods are in direct clash with certain conventions of popular fiction that he was shortly to purge from his work. *Watch and Ward* is therefore an instructive preparation for understanding the fiction to follow. *The Europeans* is intended to represent the early international novel and also the comic novel of manners. "Madame de Mauves" represents the *nouvelle*. I confine my discussion of the "anecdote" and certain other Jamesian genres to the introductory chapters. *The Princess Casamassima, What Maisie Knew,* and *The Wings of the Dove* are my chosen illustrations of distinctive phases of James's later career. I add a chapter on *The Golden Bowl* less to analyze its own structural properties than to consider it as a nexus in which many of the characteristic methods and principles of earlier works achieve their highest development.

There is such a massive body of criticism of James's fiction that it becomes difficult to avoid redundancy. This condition chiefly accounts for my decision not to concentrate on those works most extensively scrutinized by others: *The Portrait of a Lady,* "The Turn of the Screw," *The Sacred Fount,* and *The Ambassadors.* (I have, however, freely drawn upon these, especially *The Portrait* and *The Ambassadors,* for purposes of comparison and illustration.) Previous critics have often spared me the task of marshaling evidence for certain ideas or interpretations that seem right to me; footnotes stand for pages of argument. Especially in the final three chapters, I have been able to confine myself to questions of basic form, with minimal attention to "interpretation."

The proliferation of James studies makes it necessary to justify the presence of even another book on an already crowded shelf. Though I doubt that anyone at all familiar with James would question the importance of my subject, I should point out its claims for distinctiveness. Most of the studies of James's method concentrate on techniques in themselves, rather than on their contribution to structural unity. Percy Lubbock's *The Craft of Fiction* is a brilliant apologia for the Jamesian dramatic novel.

Joseph Warren Beach's *The Method of Henry James* describes James's various methods and defines his critical terms: idea, picture, point of view, tone, etc. R. P. Blackmur's introduction to the collected prefaces is a helpful catalogue of James's principles and devices. Some more recent books have also increased our understanding of James's craft. Harold T. McCarthy's *Henry James: The Creative Process* and Walter F. Wright's *The Madness of Art* summarize James's theories of art and the artist, though in my estimation they too rarely rise above the level of paraphrase. Laurence Bedwell Holland's *The Expense of Vision* is a difficult yet rewarding book that takes us farther into the relation between the prefaces and the fiction and, though sometimes it abuses the critical tool of analogy, into the relation between the substance and the form of the novels. Finally, Krishna Baldev Vaid's *Technique in the Tales of Henry James* pays special attention to point of view and economy in James's shorter fiction.[4] Of all these (and others), Mr. Holland's approach is the closest to my own. Indeed, my references to his book in the chapter on *The Wings of the Dove* are a cause for embarrassment. The principal difference, I believe—aside from disagreements in judgment—is that I have concerned myself exclusively with the way James organizes his works, with how parts add up to a whole, whereas Mr. Holland ranges widely through many different aspects of "the Craft of Henry James." In a few places there is overlapping, but not in the main arguments. In searching out James's structures and trying to describe them, I have necessarily concentrated on the inner dynamics of

4. Percy Lubbock, *The Craft of Fiction* (New York, 1921); Joseph Warren Beach, *The Method of Henry James* (New Haven, 1918); Richard P. Blackmur, "Introduction," in *The Art of the Novel: Critical Prefaces* by Henry James (New York, 1934); Harold T. McCarthy, *Henry James: The Creative Process* (New York, 1958); Walter F. Wright, *The Madness of Art: A Study of Henry James* (Lincoln, Nebraska, 1962); Laurence Bedwell Holland, *The Expense of Vision: Essays on the Craft of Henry James* (Princeton, 1964); Krishna Baldev Vaid, *Technique in the Tales of Henry James* (Cambridge, Mass., 1964).

the works, on what James calls "the scheme." I have been as inductive as possible, drawing from the notebooks, reviews, essays, and prefaces, but finally studying the fiction as intently as I have been able. In so doing, I have tried to emphasize what James emphasized in his own criticism.

This last guideline would seem to minimize the relevance of those analyses of James's works concentrating on patterns of images and symbols. It is an approach given little support in James's critical and theoretical writings. Most of the structural and thematic analyses regularly appearing in the journals reflect the trend to convert images into symbols and symbols into structures, or else to identify the structures of some of the novels with their plots, which are assumed to have archetypal significance. In this preface I need only mention that the symbolic, allegorical, and mythic approach to structure—though often illuminating— is a subordinate one in this study, for reasons elaborated in Chapter Two.

Nor do I regard myself as the apologist for any critical system, unless it be that distinctively modified version of Coleridgean organicism that James seems to have advocated. Theorizing on the vexed question of form and content in literature is not directly relevant to my purposes. My terms and my principles are most often those of the notebooks and the prefaces, and when I speak of the structural strengths and weaknesses of certain works, the criteria are what I believe to be James's.

Three works used in this study are so often cited that all references to them are included parenthetically in the text:

I use *The Novels and Tales of Henry James*, the New York Edition (New York, 1907-9), 24 vols., as my text for all the works included in it. The references are to volume and page numbers.

The abbreviation "P" refers to *The Art of the Novel: Critical Prefaces* by Henry James, with an introduction by Richard P. Blackmur (New York, 1934).

The abbreviation "*N*" refers to *The Notebooks of Henry James*, ed. F. O. Matthiessen and Kenneth B. Murdock (New York, 1955).

ACKNOWLEDGMENTS

It gives me pleasure to make public my appreciation of those who, in a variety of ways, have helped me to write this book. I wish to thank the John Simon Guggenheim Memorial Foundation for its encouragement and generous support. For numerous kindnesses I am grateful to Mary E. Dichmann, W. S. Dowden, Richard Harter Fogle, Alan Grob, Walter Isle, Monroe K. Spears, and Frank Vandiver. Rice University subsidized the typing of the manuscript, and my graduate assistant, Richard McGuire, assiduously checked the quotations: to both I am much indebted.

Chapter One is reprinted in revised form from *PMLA* (June, 1965) by permission of the Modern Language Association. The editor of *The Personalist* has permitted me to use three paragraphs from an article in the issue of July, 1964. An earlier version of the third chapter ("The Double Structure of *Watch and Ward*") appeared in the Winter, 1963, issue of *Texas Studies in Literature and Language* © by the University of Texas Press, and I acknowledge the editor's permission to reprint. Editor Frank L. Hoskins has authorized the reprinting in revised form of "Structural Irony in *Madame de Mauves*" from the Winter, 1965, issue of *Studies in Short Fiction*. The chapter on *The Europeans*, © 1964 by The Regents of the University of California, is reprinted in revised form from *Nineteenth-Century Fiction,* Vol. 19, pp. 1-16, by permission of the Regents.

Thanks are due Charles Scribners' Sons and Paul R. Reynolds, Inc., for permission to quote from *The Novels and Tales of Henry James* (the New York Edition), *The Art of the Novel: Critical Prefaces,* and *The American Scene.* For permission to quote from *The Notebooks of Henry James,* edited by F. O. Matthiessen and Kenneth B. Murdock, I am grateful to the Oxford University Press.

Houston, Texas
February, 1967

CONTENTS

THE SEARCH FOR FORM

Studies in the Structure of James's Fiction

I · THE ORGANIC

AND THE

SCIENTIFIC

James's youthful ideas about the form of fiction are the germs of the principles expressed in the late prefaces. But his earliest dicta, in comparison to the late, are arid and formalist—dogmatically proclaimed, not experimentally discovered. They hint of an American Gallophile, infatuated with the rigid lines and harsh economy of the well-made play and the well-made novel. In 1874, James announced: "We confess to a conservative taste in literary matters—to a relish for brevity, for conciseness, for elegance, for perfection of form."[1] He never renounced such a taste; "brevity" and "perfection of form"—more frequently "economy" and "composition"—are as prominent, indeed as hieratic, in the prefaces as in the earliest reviews. But if James seems to have acquired his literary standards artifically and to have begun his career with a set of a priori principles to guide him, it was not long before he was to make these ideas his own

1. "Hugo's Ninety-Three," in *Literary Reviews and Essays*, ed. Albert Mordell (New York, 1957), p. 139.

by fully understanding their relevance to the craft of fiction. The early assumptions are not repudiated, but tested, clarified, and deepened. A reader of James's reviews of the late 1860's and early 1870's might have predicted a bright future for the literary critic, but he would doubtless have foreseen the eventual emergence of a literary theoretician, a dispassionate elaborator of inviolable principles. James, of course, became nothing of the sort. He came to disdain general ideas about the methods and modes of fiction, insisting that every novelist follows his own genius and that every novel dictates its own laws. There have been few more vigorous defenders of the experimental novel than James. There is a remarkable balance in his mature criticism between the general principle and the pragmatically discovered insight. Though the insistence on economy and order is never relaxed, the concepts become increasingly more flexible; with ease they accommodate notions of fiction that seem contradictory. James repeatedly exults in the freedom of the novelist: "The Novel remains still, under the right persuasion, the most independent, most elastic, most prodigious of literary forms" (*P*, p. 326). Indeed to James it is plastic enough and prodigious enough to allow for the reconciliation of the art of Scribe with that of Balzac and the principles of Coleridge with those of Flaubert.

It follows that the critic who searches James's writings to discover his conception of the structure of fiction encounters a unique set of difficulties. There is ample evidence of a neoclassicist James, whose critical lexicon is headed by terms like "logic," "law," "symmetry," "geometry," and "science," in addition to the ever-prominent "economy" and "composition." But there is the equally formidable romanticist James, for whom the indispensable terms are "germ," "organic form," "growth," "freedom," and "imagination." Clearly James had little of the academician's concern for the consistent and crystalline system. His criticism became increasingly pragmatic and ex post facto.

He employed whatever terms and ideas were available to suit his needs and match his performance. Nevertheless the problem remains: what in James's idea of the structure of fiction is neoclassical and formalist? what is romantic and organicist? what is uniquely his own?

Much of James's early criticism shows that he regarded form as the most important element in literature; and in most of these early reviews and essays such characteristic expressions as "admirably-balanced and polished composition," "delicate art," and "studied compactness" are employed without reference to subject matter.[2] Still it is exceedingly rare to find James issuing such a pronouncement as that which he delivers in his review of *Far from the Madding Crowd*: "We really imagine that a few arbitrary rules—a kind of depleting process—might have a wholesome effect. It might be enjoined, for instance, that no 'tale' should exceed fifty pages and no novel two hundred; that a plot should have but such and such a number of ramifications, etc. . . ."[3] In the same year, 1874, James wrote that "A brilliant work of art will always seem artificial."[4] But it is the rarity rather than the presence of such passages which gives the critic his clue. "Form" is not an independent concept to James. It is the ultimate criterion—"that which makes a book a classic"[5]—but it is not a mold to be superimposed upon substance or a linguistic embodiment of aesthetic precept. "Form" is the shape of a literary work in which there is "an unfailing cohesion of all ingredients."[6] Form is thus inseparable from substance, and,

2. "Howells's A Foregone Conclusion," in *ibid.*, p. 215.

3. "Hardy's Far from the Madding Crowd," in *ibid.* p. 295.

4. " 'The School for Scandal' at Boston," in *The Scenic Art*, ed. Allan Wade (New York, 1957), pp. 14-15.

5. "George Sand," in *French Poets and Novelists* (London, 1919), p. 180. James also wrote, "Everything in a picture . . . depends on the composition; if it be the subject that makes the interest, it is the composition that makes, or that at any rate expresses, the subject" (*William Wetmore Story and His Friends* [Boston, 1903], I, 15-16).

6. "Howells's A Foregone Conclusion," in *Literary Reviews and Essays*, p. 208.

insofar as it is dependent upon substance, it is also subordinate to it. These principles are seldom expressed by the youthful James, but they are his standards of composition at least as early as *The Portrait of a Lady*—as the notebooks unmistakably show.

However, one should not be tempted to discard the neoclassicist impression given by James's early essays and reviews—and indeed by his late notebooks and prefaces. Rather the problem should be more precisely phrased. In what way are "symmetry" and "harmony" inevitable effects of a unified representation? James delights "in a deep-breathing economy and an organic form" (*P*, p. 84); implicit in this and numerous similar remarks is the belief that such a form is geometrical. In other words, it is James's conviction that the form which best expresses an "idea" is necessarily of "the highest perfection and rarest finish,"[7] that it is "triumphantly scientific" (*P*, p. 117). The "organic" and the "scientific" are somehow one.

To James a novel or tale succeeds when it possesses intensity, coherence, and completeness. Intensity is the fullness and richness of texture that James found pre-eminently in Balzac. Coherence is total unity—the demonstration of the revelance of every part of the work to every other part. Completeness is the representation of the maximum of relationships logically involved in a subject. The standards are mutually dependent, so that a work deficient in one area is also deficient in the others. Implicit in James's threefold standard of excellence is the assumption that experience is most fully revealed when it is made lucid—that is, coherent. James's idea of coherence is more severe than that of most novelists; it is a concept repeatedly defined through the analogies of architecture, carpentry, and geometry. Though inseparable from substance, the form of a work can be discussed as an abstract entity, as when James speaks of the design of a work as a tapestry, a mosaic, or a geometrical figure, or when he

7. "The Future of the Novel," in *The Future of the Novel: Essays on the Art of Fiction*, ed. Leon Edel (New York, 1956), p. 36.

refers to *The Portrait of a Lady* as "a structure reared with an 'architectural' competence" (*P*, p. 52). James's embarrassment over his "misplaced middles," a failure in proportion caused by excessive preparation, follows from his conviction that coherence is necessarily symmetrical.

It is difficult to overestimate the importance of proportion to James. The term is close in meaning to "composition," "rhythm," and "harmony." James puts such stress on the idea of proportion that one critic equates James's entire concept of form with "the right distribution" of parts.[8] Virtually every one of James's novels and tales is marked by proportionate arrangement: of dialogue in relation to narration; of the internal and the external lives of the characters; of characters, locations, and "blocks" of material of all kinds.

James does not distinguish between the aesthetic form of a novel and the logical coherence of its rendered experience. Outward proportion ideally expresses the harmonious fusion of all the elements of the work: the artist's "synthetic 'whole' *is* his form. . ." (*P*, p. 118). The form lends to the fictional representation not only beauty, but also intelligibility; the novel is beautiful only in proportion to its intelligibility. Nevertheless, the considerable emphasis that James gives to exterior symmetry suggests his disposition to evaluate a successful novel both as a unified representation of life and as a beautiful object. The demand for proportion hints of some concept of "decorum"—even if the proportion is cause or effect of the full rendering of the subject matter.

One observes James adjusting his character arrangements and episodes so as to achieve a predetermined neatness and balance. The notes on *The Spoils of Poynton* show his effort to duplicate the precise structure of a play, wherein each act reaches its own climax. The outward shape also controls the action of *What*

8. René Wellek, "Henry James's Literary Theory and Criticism," *American Literature*, XXX (November, 1958), 316.

Maisie Knew; initially James planned for only one of Maisie's parents to remarry, but then he decided that "for a proper symmetry" (*P*, p. 140) both should do so. On the other hand, James rebukes Robert Louis Stevenson for caring less for his subject than for the form it shall assume: ". . . I remember no instance of his expressing a subject, as one may say, *as* a subject— hinting at what novelists mainly know, one would imagine, as the determinant thing in it, the idea out of which it springs. The form, the envelope, is there with him, headforemost, *as* the idea; titles, names, that is, chapters, sequences, orders, while we are still asking ourselves how it was that he primarily put to his own mind what it was all to be about."[9] Unlike Stevenson James does not construct his novels exclusively from the outside in. Rather he does so both from the outside in *and* from the inside out, guarding against excesses in both the natural development of the idea and the artificial arrangement of the form. The assumption is always that an idea is most fully developed when it assumes an orderly form. It is this assumption, more than any other, that is responsible for James's unpopularity with orthodox organicist critics. Edwin Muir, for example, deprecates James on the grounds that "If the situation is worked out logically without any allowance for the free invention of life, the result will be mechanical, even if the characters are true."[10]

"Logic" is one of James's essential terms. There is a logic to every given situation, which the novelist must discover and represent. It is not an imposed but an inherent logic. Muir presumably would object that a human situation contains no logic, that accident rather than necessity is the law of human conduct. But to James, for whom art "makes" rather than imitates life, "felicity of form and composition . . . mercilessly rests" on the exhibition of those "related" "figures and things" which are "*indispensable*" (*P*, p. 5) to the treatment of an idea.

9. "Robert Louis Stevenson," in *Notes on Novelists* (London, 1914), p. 12.
10. *The Structure of the Novel* (New York, 1929), p. 48.

The form of the achieved novel is felicitous, not because the various relations fall naturally into a form, but because the novelist contrives to make them seem to do so. "Really, universally, relations stop nowhere, and the exquisite problem of the artist is eternally but to draw, by a geometry of his own, the circle within which they shall happily *appear* to do so" (*P*, p. 5). The geometry—or the logic—is the author's own, and yet it is ideally inherent in the root idea. Without the geometry or the logic, the novel would fall short not only in "lucidity" and "roundness," but also in "completeness." Logic is thus a passage to reality, to the truth of things—not a distortion of experience by the imposition of a factitious clarity. This is the point of James's remarks on the creative process in his preface to *The Spoils of Poynton*: "[The novelist] remains all the while in intimate commerce with his motive, and can say to himself—what really more than anything else inflames and sustains him—that he alone has the *secret* of the particular case, he alone can measure the truth of the direction to be taken by his developed data. There can be for him, evidently, only one logic for these things; there can be for him only one truth and one direction—the quarter in which his subject most completely expresses itself" (*P*, pp. 122-23). Conversely, if the idea is logically developed—and thus its truth most completely expressed—the story will possess "a certain assured appearance of roundness and felicity" (*P*, p. 129). This aesthetic principle is the basis of James's idea of structure.

In many respects James's organicism seems identical with that of Emerson and Whitman. This is especially true of the belief that the form and the substance of a work are inseparable, that the shape follows directly from the germinating idea. Also James regularly refers to the creative process in organicist terms. It could easily have been Whitman who compared a "genuine poem" to "a tree that breaks into blossom and shakes in the wind."[11] Yet James was not such an extreme organicist that he

11. "The Poetry of George Eliot," in *Views and Reviews*, ed. LeRoy Phillips (Boston, 1908), p. 135.

would appear to abolish measurable form altogether. Nor did he assume that a geometrical or even a coherent form would magically emanate from free development. The novelist must constantly hold the finished shape of his work in mind even as he allows the germ of his fictional situation to develop freely: "I have ever failed to see how a coherent picture of anything is producible save by a complex of fine measurements" (*P*, p. 30).

It is not for nothing that James habitually uses the language of architecture in his considerations of fictional form. To James architecture, with its emphasis on proportion and symmetry, is virtually analogous to composition.[12] Architecture is both science and art; the architectural structure can simultaneously conform to the most exact geometric measurements and demonstrate the organic principle of free expansion. Certainly the theories of organic architecture of such contemporaries and near-contemporaries of James as Horatio Greenough, John Wellborn Root, Henry Hobson Richardson, and Louis Henri Sullivan comprise the best available parallel to James's theories of structure.[13] James's metaphorical account of the writing of *The Portrait of a Lady* perfectly illustrates the organic theory of architecture: "This single small corner-stone, the conception of a certain young woman affronting her destiny, had begun with being all my outfit for the large building of 'The Portrait of a Lady.' It came to be a square and spacious house. . ." (*P*, p. 48). The organic

---

12. At times James means other things by the term "architecture," such as an involved plot, an accumulation of detail, and magnitude.

13. See Richard P. Adams, "Architecture and the Romantic Tradition: Coleridge to Wright," *American Quarterly*, IX (Spring, 1957), 46-52. The relation of the organic theory of architecture to literary practice is implied in the following essays in Lewis Mumford's anthology, *Roots of Contemporary American Architecture* (New York, 1959): Horatio Greenough, "Form and Function," pp. 32-56; Louis Henri Sullivan, "Towards the Organic," pp. 74-82; Lewis Mumford, "The Regionalism of Richardson," pp. 117-31. James's own endorsement of organic architecture is suggested by his letter to the sculptor Hendrik Andersen: "Cities are living organisms that grow from within. . ." (*Selected Letters of Henry James*, ed. Leon Edel [London, 1956], p. 230).

theory of architecture stresses what is often absent or subordinate in organic theories of literature: that proportion, regularity, and geometry—in short, composition—are necessary attributes of the form that follows function. An organic pattern, unlike a mechanical pattern, develops logically from the controlling idea, but is no less considerate of outward appearance (thus the "building" of *The Portrait* is "square"). Organicism in architecture is opposed not only to order for its own sake, which is necessarily lifeless, but also to orderlessness.[14] Correspondingly, James has little tolerance for the bloodless symmetry of the well-made play, for example, those of such a "supremely skillful contriver and arranger" as Sardou[15] and those novels of Flaubert in which "we breathe the air of pure aesthetics."[16] But he is no less disdainful of inartistic novels, the "loose baggy monsters" (*P*, p. 84) of Thackeray, Tolstoy, Hugh Walpole, Arnold Bennett, and numerous others. Thus, to James, a synthesis of the natural and the artificial is not merely possible, it is of first importance—as he suggests in "The Future of the Novel": "[Many] see the whole business [of the novel] too divorced on the one side from observation and perception, and on the other from the art and taste. They get too little of the first-hand impression, the effort to penetrate—that effort for which the French have the admirable expression to *fouiller*—and still less, if possible, of any science of composition, any architecture, distribution, proportion."[17]

14. See, for example, John Ruskin, *The Stones of Venice*, Everyman's Library (London, n.d.), II, 163: "It is one of the chief virtues of the Gothic builders, that they never suffered ideas of outside symmetries and consistencies to interfere with the real use and value of what they did. [They were] utterly regardless of any established conventionalities of external appearance, knowing (as indeed it always happened) that such daring interruptions of the formal plan would rather give additional interest to its symmetry than injure it."

15. "Paris Revisited," in *The Scenic Art*, p. 40.

16. "Gustave Flaubert," in *Essays in London and Elsewhere* (London, 1893), p. 138.

17. "The Future of the Novel," p. 41.

James commonly approaches the writing of a novel as a set of problems to be solved and, as the prefaces regularly remind us, delights in the "charm of supreme difficulty" (*P*, p. 87). This disposition is no perverse obscurantism; rather it suggests the essential vitality and relevance of James's preoccupation with method. In general the difficulties that attract James (how to derive cogency from Maisie's point of view, how to fuse two stories in *The Tragic Muse*, how to prevent *The Wings of the Dove* from lapsing into morbidity) are attractive precisely because they require a delicacy of craftsmanship and, by the same score, insure that the artistry shall in no way be gratuitous, but essential to the representation of the subject. What the difficulties have in common is that they compel James to resolve the question of giving full weight to the demands of life without sacrificing the demands of art: to effect "the union of whatever fulness with whatever clearness" (*P*, p. 240).

James's creative energy thrived on the reconciliation of opposites. It is the unrelenting conflict of opposed intentions that gives James's prefaces and notebooks their dramatic interest. (Thus it is quite fitting that in both the prefaces and notebooks James should carry on dialogues with himself, for in effect different sides of his mind are competing with each other.) The central tension, that which includes nearly all the others, is the resolve to be at the same time natural and artificial, or organic and scientific. The following list, in which James's own terms are as much as possible used, catalogues and categorizes the subordinate antitheses:

The Organic Principle	*The Scientific Principle*
Incongruities	Congruities
Multiplicity	Unity
The novel	The drama
The explosive	The economical
The developmental	The anecdotal

The novel as independent form	The novel as genre
Imagination	Logic
Incompleteness	Roundness
Muddlement	Awareness

James, in spite of his fondness for principles, disdained schematic formulae; thus the headings of the above lists are not to be rigidly interpreted. The terms illustrating "the organic principle" reveal the novelist's impulse toward free expression and expansiveness, while those illustrating "the scientific principle" reveal the contrary inclination toward restraint and order.

Nearly all James's novels and tales may be read as a blending of the congruous and the incongruous, rather a fusion of incongruous parts into a unified whole. Actually most of the starting ideas for James's creations express some fundamental contrast or incongruity. In *The Princess Casamassima*, for example, James's "scheme called for the suggested nearness (to all our apparently ordered life) of some sinister anarchic underworld. . ." (*P*, p. 76). The pervasive incongruity of *The Wings of the Dove* is that of "a young person conscious of a great capacity for life, but early stricken and doomed" (*P*, p. 288). The "charm" of Daisy Miller is "incongruous" (*P*, p. 269); that is, incongruous with her vulgarity. Among other things, James's fictions combine Europe and America, the past and the present, the immediate house and the other house, the intelligent and the foolish, the artist and the Philistine, the sinister and the normal, and the good heroine and the bad heroine.

But "the precious element of contrast or antithesis" (*P*, p. 251) alone is valueless to James. Some fundamental "consistency" must be effected so that the divergent elements may "somehow hang together" (*P*, p. 75); they must be absorbed and unified by the whole. Such harmonizing techniques as consistency of point of view and singleness of tone are contributive but not essential to unity. For the novelist's overriding duty is to synthesize: "The novel . . . reports of an infinite diversity of matters, gathers together and gives out again a hundred sorts, and finds its order and its structure, its unity and its beauty in the alternation of parts and the adjustment of differences."[18] And in the preface to *The Golden Bowl*, James writes that among "the most exquisite of all good causes" are "the appeal to variety" and "a handsome wholeness of effect" (*P*, p. 239).

Now it is obvious that all novels to some extent are blendings of incongruities; some conflict must be resolved. James's divergence from the common habit is in degree rather than in fundamental approach. For one thing, his antitheses are more extreme and more pronounced. Indeed, James claims that his work is governed by the "law that antitheses, to be efficient, shall be both direct and complete" (*P*, p. 18). His principle of antithesis and contrast is responsible for some of the annoyance with James expressed by Maxwell Geismar, who maintains that absolute contrasts in fiction violate the character of human life.[19] The completeness of James's contrasts has also led critics to suggest the melodrama and the well-made play—both literary forms in which stark and simple contrast is a prime structural principle—as sources and analogues of many of James's works.

It may be more profitable, however, to relate James's idea of contrast to architecture rather than to other literary forms. The architectural analogy is not only favored by James and indicative of his larger conceptions of structure, but it is especially useful in considering the matter of contrast. Architecture, by definition, resolves contrary stresses and includes irregularities in a large harmony. James preferred a revealed to a disguised structure in architecture—in which respect he forecast twentieth-century functionalism. Likewise in his judgment of the novel he sought "traceable lines, divinable direction."[20] No structural lines in his works are more traceable than those formed by contrasts.

18. "The New Novel," in *Notes on Novelists*, p. 280.
19. *Henry James and the Jacobites* (Boston, 1963), p. 243.
20. "The New Novel," in *Notes on Novelists*, p. 262.

James was well aware of the dangers implicit in the architectural approach to fiction. The unrelaxed symmetry of character opposition, like the application of the principles of proportion and alternation of parts, can easily lead to an excessive and mechanical regularity. He speaks of the lifeless perfection of a poem by George Eliot: "George Eliot's elaborate composition is like a vast mural design in mosaic-work, where great slabs and delicate morsels of stone are laid together with wonderful art, where there are plenty of noble lines and generous hues, but where everything is rigid, measured, and cold—nothing dazzling, magical, and vocal."[21] In architecture as in fiction, James sought the sense of motion rather than static arrangement. He delighted in classical and Renaissance architecture, in which he found not only a finished form, but also an organic effect. In St. Clement Danes Church in London, for example, James noted the "very long high deep set of windows *springing* continuously from just above pavement to roof and *passing* behind gallery" (*N*, p. 328; italics mine). Though exceedingly regular, the structure gives the illusion of life and movement. It is not merely verbal extravagance that leads James in his travel accounts to animate so many of the buildings he describes.

To James a building possesses life when its various parts fuse so as to express a single idea. But the organic effect also requires the "tone of time" to complete the blending, to suggest that the relation of part to part and of part to whole is a process, dynamic and temporal, rather than an achieved fact. No doubt James in part is expressing the romantic idea of the picturesque, the cult of sensibility which insists that the beautiful is the handmaid of the mysterious. Whatever the case, age is an integral aspect of James's aesthetics of architecture. Numerous instances of this attitude might be cited from fiction as well as travel essays. The following, from *The American Scene*, is typical:

21. "The Poetry of George Eliot," in *ibid.*, pp. 135-36.

The older buildings, in the [Harvard] Yard, profit indeed, on the spot, to the story-seeking mind, by the fact of their comparative exhibition of the tone of time—so prompt an ecstasy and so deep a relief reward, in America, everywhere, any suggested source of interest that is not the interest of importunate newness. That source overflows, all others run thin; but the wonder and the satisfaction are that in College Yard more than one of these should have finally been set to running thick. The best pieces of the earlier cluster, from Massachusetts to Stoughton, emerge from their elongation of history with a paler archaic pink in their brickwork; their scant primitive details, small "quaintnesses" of form, have turned, each, to the expressive accent that no short-cut of "style" can ever successfully imitate. . . .[22]

If the implications of some of James's remarks are pursued, it seems that he felt that one way in which tone in fiction is achieved is through prose style. An effective style has a diffusive, blurring effect that, on the one hand, conceals the exact dimensions of a carefully constructed work and, on the other, gives a superficial unity to an ill-constructed one. Thus a distinct and charming style prevents a novel from *seeming* to be an ill-arranged assortment of parts, even though it may well be. At least the illusion of organic unity results from a "suffusion of the whole thing by the voice and speech of the author."[23] A tone may be satiric, as in Edith Wharton's *The Custom of the Country*, in which "the satiric light was doubtless the only one in which the elements engaged could be at all focussed together,"[24] or it may be one of "tragic, yet of exquisite, mystification" (*P*, pp. 172-73), as in "The Turn of the Screw"; but, if maintained, it unifies and vitalizes the work.

But a true organic unity can be achieved only by an application of the principle of the inseparability of parts. One part of a

22. *The American Scene*, ed. with an introduction by W. H. Auden (New York, 1946), p. 63.
23. "George Sand," in *Notes on Novelists*, p. 146.
24. "The New Novel," in *ibid.*, p. 242.

work—be it character, chapter, incident, scene, picture, or whatever—possesses tone insofar as other parts inhere in it. The principal effect of tone is the obscuring of separations, a benefit which only time performs in the work of architecture. In literature tone is most surely gained when parts are not fused merely from the outside—by style—but from the inside—by structure. This inward coherence can be gained only when the unity is dynamic rather than static.

The distinction between a static and a dynamic unity (and incidentally the difference between the potentiality of the drama and that of the novel) may be illustrated by the following quotations:

> The fine thing in a real drama, generally speaking, is that, more than any other work of literary art, it needs a masterly structure. It needs to be shaped and fashioned and laid together, and this process makes a demand upon an artist's rarest gifts. He must combine and arrange, interpolate and eliminate, play the joiner with the most attentive skill; and yet at the end effectually bury his tools and his sawdust, and invest his elaborate skeleton with the smoothest and most polished integument.[25]

the parts are not pieced together, they conspire and interdepend . . . (*P*, p. 151).

Parts which are not pieced together yet conspire and interdepend cease being independent parts; nor is their subordination to the whole merely the effect of a smooth and polished integument. It is a difference between the seams being concealed and there being no seams at all. The principle of dynamic unity explains the structure of many of James's works and accounts for many of the techniques he developed. Obviously the use of a single character's point of view as a compositional center is a way of insuring that the part be indistinct from the whole. More important, James constructs his novels not to represent char-

25. "Tennyson's Drama," in *Views and Reviews*, p. 181.

acters, but the relationships of characters; details exist not independently, but in relation to other details. In his prefaces to *The Wings of the Dove* and *The Golden Bowl,* James defends the technique of multiple point of view by the same principle. As the Prince's section "lights" Maggie's, so Maggie's "lights" the Prince's (*P,* p. 330). Correspondingly, "the play of the portentous" (*P,* p. 305) rules *The Wings of the Dove.* One "block" of narrative both recalls those which precede it and portends those which follow it. The technique of "multiplication of aspects" (*P,* p. 90), employed with especial rigidity in *The Awkward Age* and less insistently in many other novels, assures the interdependence of parts. Also there must be a mutual dependence of "picture"—narrative passages carefully "foreshortened"—and "scene"—distinct episodes dominated by dialogue. For example, *The Ambassadors* "sharply divides itself . . . into the parts that prepare, that tend in fact to over-prepare, for scenes, and the parts, or otherwise into the scenes, that justify and crown the preparation" (*P,* pp. 322-23). That unity is the ultimate intended effect of James's most characteristic techniques is clearly indicated in the preface to *The Awkward Age*: "The thing 'done,' artistically, is a fusion, or it has not *been* done— in which case of course the artist may be, and all deservedly, pelted with any fragment of his botch the critic shall choose to pick up. But his ground once conquered, in this particular field, he knows nothing of fragments and may say in all security: 'Detach one if you can. You can analyse in *your* way, oh yes—to relate, the report, to explain; but you can't disintegrate my synthesis; you can't resolve the elements of my whole into different responsible agents. . .'" (*P,* p. 116).

As was suggested earlier, James's conception of structure reflects the Coleridgean principle of the reconciliation of opposites. Not only does James seek repeatedly to synthesize divergent, or at least contrasting, parts into a dynamic unity, but he habitually describes the act of composition as a process in which tensions are resolved. The most comprehensive of these tensions has been discussed—that between free imaginative expansion and lucidity of design.

The most familiar evidence of this tension is what I have termed James's practice of building a novel simultaneously both from the outside in and from the inside out. He holds in mind some general controlling form, extremely symmetrical, even as he allows the "center" to develop freely. The notebooks and prefaces are full of instances in which James describes the tensions resulting from this encounter. In the preface to *The Awkward Age*, James provides an especially full discussion of the problem. He begins the preface with a confession of his repeated inability to impose a predetermined form on an unfolding subject. The very pages of *The Awkward Age*, he asserts, "emphasise the truth of the vanity of the *a priori* test of what an *idée-mère* may have to give" (*P*, p. 101). Inevitable "complications" expose the futility of the author's efforts "to surround with the sharp black line, to frame in the square, the circle, the charming oval, that helps any arrangement of objects to become a picture" (*P*, p. 101). Later in the preface, with no indication that he notices a contradiction, James makes the claim that the extremely diagrammatic preliminary scheme of *The Awkward Age* "holds . . . in spite of noted strains and under repeated tests. . ." (*P*, p. 109). Indeed there is no contradiction; James argues that the scheme is made even firmer and tighter by the considerable strains placed upon it, especially the strain to expand. He speaks of the "coercive charm" that such tensions lend to a "projected form"—"a charm that grows in proportion as the appeal to it tests and stretches and strains it, puts it powerfully to the touch" (*P*, p. 111). In effect the mechanical pattern merges imperceptibly with the organically developed subject.

As the notebooks make clear, James's initial schemes give detailed attention to plot. A desirable plot, to James, is marked by simplicity of action, a stressed contrast of characters, and a symmetrical design. The working sketch that James calls the "scenario" is an "intensely structural, intensely hinged and jointed preliminary frame" (*N*, p. 257). As the preliminary frame responds to the demands of character complexity and thematic richness, it necessarily loses some of its mechanical rigidity, but not, according to James, its final control.[26]

Often, though not always, it is the form of the drama that becomes the model in the scenario. And in this context of the tension between the restraint given by the a priori design and the pressures toward free growth given by the subject matter, it is helpful to consider James's curious attitude toward the drama. It has been insufficiently noted that, in spite of his considerable effort to succeed as a playwright and in spite of the obvious influences of dramatic forms and techniques on his novels, James finally judged the drama an inferior form—inferior precisely because of its virtues. One may easily be misled by James's numerous tributes to the Comédie-Française and by such remarks as "the drama is the ripest of all the arts. . . (*N*, p. 37). This very 'ripeness' proved inhibiting to James. Economy and precision are compelled by the restrictions inherent in the form, yet the rules for achieving these admirable ends are externally imposed. In addition, the drama proved too confining—as is made clear by James's impatience with novels employing excessive dialogue, by his preference for states of consciousness to exhibited action, and especially by his conviction that every literary idea seeks its own mode of expression which should be independent of a priori restrictions in technique and length. Though its freedom from timeworn conventions leads to carelessness and looseness in the work of such writers as Wells and Bennett, ideally the novel "can do simply everything, and that is its strength and its life. Its plasticity, its elasticity are infinite; there

26. In later chapters, especially that on *What Maisie Knew*, I attempt to show in some detail how this principle governs the structure of James's novels.

is no color, no extension it may not take from the nature of its subject or the temper of its craftsman. It has the extraordinary advantage—a piece of luck scarcely credible—that, while capable of giving an impression of the highest perfection and the rarest finish, it moves in a luxurious independence of rules and restrictions."[27] The dramatist, of course, lacks such an independence.

Nevertheless, the drama—and such novels as *Madame Bovary*, which approaches the scientific form of the drama—remains James's model of formal excellence. The drama indicates the aesthetic effects to be aimed at—balance, economy, lucidity, roundness—but the novel allows the artist many more ways of achieving the end. Thus the terminology of drama is as useful to James the critic as the "scenic method" and the "scenario" are to James the novelist. But "the dramatic analogy"[28] is imperfect. The drama supplies James with some of his methods and principles, but essentially the dramatic motive is at odds with the novelistic motive.

The same tension is evident in James's efforts to resolve the needs to be both expansive and economical. He writes that "Any real art of representation is . . . a controlled and guarded acceptance, in fact a perfect economic mastery, of that conflict: the general sense of the expansive, the explosive principle in one's material thoroughly noted, adroitly allowed to flush and colour and animate the disputed value, but with its other appetites and treacheries, its characteristic space-hunger and space-cunning kept down" (*P*, p. 278).

In practice James's short tales are the works in which the rule of economy suppresses the impulse toward expansion, and the *nouvelles* and novels those in which "the explosive principle" is given some authority. A simple comparison may clarify this point. "Madame de Mauves" is a good example of the kind of

27. "The Future of the Novel," pp. 35-36.
28. Joseph Wiesenfarth, F. S. C., *Henry James and the Dramatic Analogy* (New York, 1963).

carefully controlled freedom that the *nouvelle* form requires. One can see the resemblances between this story and the brief tale "Four Meetings," which contains potentially the complexity and fullness of "Madame de Mauves." The gain in "Four Meetings" is in economy, but the story remains so spare that the reader may properly judge it to be an insufficient rendering of the material. The narrator, for example, has the same general relation to the heroine, Caroline Spencer, as has Longmore to Euphemia Cleve. The nameless narrator of "Four Meetings," however, seems nothing more than a narrative device used to justify the four-part episodic structure that compresses the long history of Caroline's relation to Europe into "four meetings." His interest in Caroline is rather idle and uninvolving; unlike Longmore, he seems morally and emotionally neutral. More significant is the absence of any kind of growth or change in Caroline. She is progressively represented as a victim of her own gullible innocence and a victim of the smug opportunism of her wastrel cousin and the "countess." James devotes to her none of the close attention to interior development that he permits himself with Euphemia. In the short tale, the developmental impulse is simply suppressed. So it is that the *nouvelle* bears a closer structural resemblance to the novel than it does to the tale.

A strong implication of the prefaces is that there is really no such thing as a fictional subject incapable of complicated development. The concept of the "germ" emphasizes this capacity for growth. James nevertheless finds in certain types of situations a kind of built-in resistance to boundless elaboration. The problem is to discover the *donnée* that does not "require . . . developments" (*N*, p. 211) for fullness of treatment. Hence for his briefest tales James favors "the single incident" plot, which implicitly provides a "rigid limitation of subject" (*N*, p. 212).

Though the notebooks and prefaces give no definite evidence, it is tempting to surmise that one reason for James's preference for isolated and obsessive protagonists, especially in the *nouvelles* of the 1890's, is the economy that results from the representation of such characters as George Stransom of "The Altar of the Dead," John Marcher of "The Beast in the Jungle," and the narrator of "The Aspern Papers." The total consciousness of each of these "reflectors" is absorbed in a single restricted preoccupation, and their "relations" with others are necessarily most limited. (Actually the crisis in the life of each is brought about by the offered possibility of a human relationship, which they may accept or reject; of the cases mentioned, only Stransom finally abandons his isolation.) The *nouvelles* dealing with these lonely and obsessed men can thereby remain relatively brief without the author's resorting to severe foreshortening or arbitrary curtailment of developments. The "law of entire expression" (*P*, p. 144) is intended to govern the short as well as the long fiction; it is necessary that in the former the psychological and social subject matter be severely restricted.

But in all types of fiction "the explosive principle" must be adjusted to the demands of the economical principle. Thus it must be reconciled even with the inherent restrictions of the anecdote. The anecdote, according to James, is a single, completed action, "something that has oddly happened to someone" (*P*, p. 181). Since for its effect "the person whom [the anecdote] so distinguishes" must be represented in his relations with others, "the associational margin and connexion . . . may spread" (*P*, p. 181), even at a risk of the "anecdotic grace break[ing] down" (*P*, p. 182). In another preface James observes that for proper conciseness the anecdote should be extended "as much as possible from its outer edge in, rather than from its center outward" (*P*, p. 233). The key phrase is "as much as possible"; it reveals the difficulties, indeed the merit, of the form. Development cannot be altogether prevented. Through foreshortening the temptation to allow the "associational margin" to "spread" may appear to be resisted, but it is merely concealed; thus the form of the anecdote—the external mold—is unviolated, while the maximum of expansion has been permitted. Of "Greville Fane" James remarks, "the subject, in this little composition, is developmental enough, [that is, it contains what James found to be essential for every feasible subject: a "germ" requiring expansion and elaboration] while the form has to make the anecdotic concession; and yet who shall say that for the right effect of a small harmony the fusion has failed" (*P*, p. 234). The fusion is that of the organic and the scientific processes.

Another expression of these opposing tendencies is James's curious practice of categorizing his works. On the one hand, there is his insistence that the novel is free: "A healthy, living and growing art, full of curiosity and fond of exercise, has an indefeasible mistrust of rigid prohibitions."[29] It is difficult to reconcile this position with James's fondness for labeling his works. " 'Kinds' are the very life of literature," he writes; "and truth and strength come from the complete recognition of them" (*P*, p. 111). He recognizes a number of "kinds," or genres, of fiction. Though most of these are of his own invention—like the anecdote, the picture, and the *nouvelle*—each has its own structural laws, its required method, its special advantages and special disadvantages. James habitually conventionalizes his unique structural and technical methods.

The word "law" gives evidence of the same ambiguity. A Jamesian "law," for example, "the law of entire expression" (*P*, p. 144) and "the law of successive Aspects,"[30] has the rigidity of a law of biology. Yet only the imagination of the artist can detect it and know when and where it should be applied. "Imagination," a mysterious reshaping power, is the contrary of "logic." Yet the two activities of the artist's intelligence are inseparable. Fictional creation is "an act essentially not mechanical, but thinkable rather—so far as thinkable at all—in chemical, almost in

29. "The Future of the Novel," pp. 224-25.
30. Notes to *The Ivory Tower*, ed. Percy Lubbock (London, 1917), p. 268.

mystical terms. We can surely account for nothing in the novelist's work that hasn't passed through the crucible of his imagination, hasn't, in that perpetually simmering cauldron his intellectual *pot-au-feu*, been reduced to savoury fusion. . . . It has entered, in fine, into new relations, it emerges for new ones. Its final savour has been constituted, but its prime identity destroyed —which is what was to be demonstrated. Thus it has become a different and, thanks to a rare alchemy, a better thing" (*P*, p. 230). The echoes of Coleridge's secondary imagination are unmistakable. Likewise the Coleridgean "fancy" means much the same as the Jamesian "logic." There is no mysticism or "rare alchemy" in the contriving of *ficelles* to assist in the representation of a *disponible*, in the proper placing of "middles," in the invention of contrasting characters to "thicken" relations, or in the elimination of all that does not contribute to the "close little march of cause and effect" (*N*, p. 251). In the main, James understands imagination to be the "ciphering out" or seeing of a subject, and logic to be the coherent expression of it.[31]

There remains a further instance of the clash between the open principle and the closed principle: James's remarks on the question of completeness in fiction. James aims for "roundness" in his works, for the effect of a total finish. The favored term "perfect" may be hyperbolic, but there is much to suggest that James regards the novel to be capable of attaining the "highest perfection and rarest finish"[32] of a vase or a piece of furniture. Yet at times James holds to the organicist position that the work of art can never be judged finished, perfect, or complete. His revisionist habits surely demonstrate this. The novelist is never "disconnected" from his work: "if he is always doing he can

31. Dorothea Krook, *The Ordeal of Consciousness in Henry James* (Cambridge, England, 1962), writes that "in James the philosophic, analytic passion is all of a piece with the poetic and the intuitive: they can be distinguished but never divided" (p. 413). To Professor Krook this quality accounts for the singularities of James's late style (pp. 390-413).

32. "The Future of the Novel," p. 36.

scarce, by his own measure, ever have done" (*P*, p. 348). And though the artist's problem is to make relations appear to end, it is a characteristic of James's novels, especially the later ones, to be incompletely resolved. From Isabel Archer to Merton Densher, a large share of James's protagonists are left at the end in partially undetermined states, so that the reader's attention turns not only to the completed action, but also to the unrecorded and uncertain future.[33]

James's remarks on "The Turn of the Screw" are typically paradoxical. "['The Turn of the Screw'] was to aim at absolute singleness, clearness and roundness, and yet to depend on an imagination working freely, working (call it) with extravagance. . ." (*P*, p. 172). Surely it is the imaginative "extravagance" of "The Turn of the Screw" that makes it such a provocative and ambiguous story; its verbal suggestiveness, its calculated "mystification" (*P*, p. 173), and its hint of unspoken, if not unspeakable, meanings—all resist the logical definition which a clear and round structure would seem to insist upon. Critics have frequently remarked that in James's late novels the area of the unmentioned seems to increase in magnitude as the network of relationships surrounding it increases in complexity. Robert M. Adams expresses a familiar consternation: "Much of James's fiction involves a series of games and inferences by which a complex confusion of half-meanings and guesses is accumulated around a void which—for all one can tell—might by a perfectly simple, natural statement of fact."[34] In part James is in reaction against the Victorian novelist's habit of gathering all the loose ends of a novel into a fully obvious, if untidy, knot, giving the effect that everything worth knowing about the situa-

33. Viola Hopkins, "Visual Art Devices in Henry James," *PMLA*, LXXVI (December, 1961), 561-74, shows that "The irresoluteness of James's endings is suggestive of the Mannerist style—the struggle to repose which lacks a final triumph" (p. 573).

34. *Strains of Discord: Studies in Literary Openness* (Ithaca, New York, 1958), p. 198.

tion has been spelled out. Paradoxically, James, who sought the logic of every case, had an uncommon respect for the resistance of life to final arrangement. Thus Christina Light remains a "*disponible* figure" (*P*, p. 73) at the conclusion of *Roderick Hudson*, and so indeed do most of James's major characters. It would be impossible to say the same of the characters of Dickens.

At the conclusion of a successful James novel, the reader senses that he has been shown as much as he could possibly be made to see of the essential moral and psychological situation (not, of course, of the superficial data), but that there remains an element which is not merely unknown but unknowable. What Mark Schorer says of *The Good Soldier* applies as well to James's late novels: "The mechanical structure . . . is controlled to a degree nothing less than taut, while the structure of meaning is almost blandly open, capable of limitless refraction."[35] In part the effect is gained by James's preference for "the muddled state" (*P*, p. 149). The fact that even the most perceptive of his protagonists struggle with ignorance is evidence enough of James's conviction that the full truth of everything can never be known. Dorothea Krook has emphasized the relativism implicit in James's key technical terms, particularly "aspects," "conditions," and "internal relations." The "truth" of a given situation is wedded to "the world of appearances. . . . These appearances exist only in the consciousness, indeed *are* the content of consciousness. . . . The world of art . . . is a beautiful representation of the appearances present to a particular consciousness under particular conditions, and the artist's overriding task is accordingly to exhibit in the concrete, with the greatest possible completeness and consistency, as well as vividness and intensity, the particular world of appearances accessible to a particular consciousness under the specific conditions created for it by the artist. . . ."[36] Thus ambiguity is central to each situation, and

35. "An Interpretation," *The Good Soldier* by Ford Madox Ford (New York, 1957), p. vi.
36. *The Ordeal of Consciousness in Henry James*, p. 399.

the novelist's task is not to resolve the ambiguity but to dramatize it. A work of fiction possessing clarity and roundness, even perfection, renders life not by solving all the problems and answering all the questions inherent in the fictional situation, but by exhibiting the problems and the questions.

Coherence is not a cancellation of one or more of the heterogeneous elements or a last-page revelation that the opposition has been illusory. Form exists to reveal and to suggest a tissue of implications, extensions, and connections in the central set of relationships which comprises the subject; insofar as this form is ordered and restricted will these meanings and suggestions be manifest.

II · PICTURE AND ACTION

In a book review written in 1864, James mentioned in passing that "the soul of a novel is its action. . . ." A few pages later he added, "All writing is narration. . . ."[1] Like many of his youthful proclamations, the comments are interesting mainly because they indicate how radically James revised his literary principles in later years. For the earliest of the extant notebooks, those covering the 1880's, make it plain that James grew to regard the novel as essentially nonnarrative. Even when the concept of action is defined in the broad Aristotelian sense, the impression remains that the temporal dimension of fiction was of subordinate interest to James.

Of course he was reacting against the Victorian idea of "plot." In "The Art of Fiction" he ridiculed the popular notion that "a good novel" is "full of incident and movement, so that we shall

1. Review of Harriet Elizabeth Prescott, "Azarian: an Episode," in *Notes and Reviews*, ed. Pierre de Chaignon la Rose (Cambridge, Mass., 1921), pp. 25, 27.

wish to jump ahead, to see who was the mysterious stranger, and
if the stolen will was ever found. . . ."[2] James's organic conception of fiction led him to insist that "Character . . . is action,
and action is plot. . . . We care what happens to people only in
proportion as we know what people are."[3] Also his principle of
intensity made him wish to "get everything out of [an action] it
can give."[4]

Still there is nothing unique or extravagant in James's denun-
ciations of the heresy of plot. Dozens of nineteenth-century
novelists implicitly repudiated the notion that "story" is somehow separable from "character." Though Dickens might offend
in this respect, James found Trollope, who offended in many
other ways, to be liberated from the bondage of plot.[5] James was
no doubt correct in judging the relative plotlessness of his works
responsible for his diminishing popularity,[6] but there are more
important reasons for his repeated insistence that action is of
secondary importance in the work of fiction.

James rarely conceived the idea of a story in terms of event.
In his preface to *The Portrait of a Lady,* he wrote, "I might envy,
though I couldn't emulate, the imaginative writer so constituted
as to see his fable first and to make out its agents afterwards . . ."
(*P,* p. 44). In his notebook remarks on "The Real Thing," James
—typically—shows that the story came to him entirely as a static
situation: "The little tragedy of good-looking gentle-folk, who
had been all their life stupid and well-dressed, living, on a fixed
income, at country-houses, watering places and clubs, like so
many others of their class in England, and were now utterly unable to *do* anything . . . could only *show* themselves, clumsily,

2. *Partial Portraits* (London, 1888), p. 382.
3. "Anthony Trollope," in *Partial Portraits,* p. 106. James singles out
The American as his most excessively plotted novel. See *P,* pp. 22-39, and
Selected Letters of Henry James, ed. Leon Edel (London, 1956), pp. 147-
148.
4. Quoted from a letter to Horace Scudder in *N,* p. 251.
5. "Anthony Trollope," in *Partial Portraits,* p. 106.
6. ". . . I'm often accused of not having 'story' enough. . . ." *P,* p. 43.

for the fine, clean, well-groomed animals that they were. . . " (*N*, p. 102). The problem of converting the situation to a short tale is one of "straighten[ing] out the little idea. It must be an idea—it can't be a 'story' in the vulgar sense of the word. It must be a picture; it must illustrate something. . . . One must put a little action—not a stupid, mechanical, arbitrary action, but something that is of the essence of the subject" (*N*, p. 103). Thus the developed idea becomes not a story, but a picture. The action is illustrative, not of interest in itself; more important, it is a revelation of some meaning inherent in the root idea. In "The Real Thing" the action leads to and culminates in the ironic turnabout, whereby the gentlefolk exchange places with the lower-class models—an event that signifies a good deal about both the emptiness of upper-class social rituals and the aesthetic distinction between copy and imitation.

Repeatedly James's notebooks show his efforts to supply the animating action for an idea or a picture. He looks for "episodes" to "illuminate" (*N*, p. 130); he has "only an idea—and everything is wanting to make it a story" (*N*, p. 155); he must "enlarge" an idea in order to "get an adequate action" (*N*, p. 165). Likewise the prefaces show that James looked upon his finished works not as narratives but as static compositions—such as architectural constructions, mosaics, portraits, and pictures. The analogies to the visual arts are not to be taken lightly. James habitually discussed the relationships between parts of his novels in spatial rather than chronological terms, as when he spoke of one part "lighting" another or of the "aspects" of a situation.[7]

The subordination of action to picture is implied in several

7. Though it includes no mention of James, Joseph Frank's important essay, "Spatial Form in Modern Literature" in *Criticism: The Foundations of Modern Literary Judgment*, ed. Mark Schorer, Josephine Miles, Gordon McKenzie (New York, 1948), pp. 379-92, is obviously relevant to the present study. Mr. Frank discusses those twentieth-century writers (Joyce, Barnes, Eliot) whose spatial conception of form brings about a total—or near-total—disregard for chronological sequence. For James, chronological coherence is not ignored, but subordinated.

of James's technical principles. What is the effect of foreshortening if not to convert narrative to picture? The foreshortened passage not only gives a dramatic unity to a sequence of disconnected events, but also produces the effect of simultaneity. It depicts a string of episodes as a pervasive condition, unified either by the author's narrative voice or by the organizing central intelligence. In a passage from *The Spoils of Poynton* we see a good illustration of the foreshortening technique:

This was the first [Fleda] had heard of Mona's hatred, though she certainly had not needed Mrs. Gereth to tell her that in close quarters that young lady would prove secretly mulish. Later Fleda perceived indeed that perhaps almost any girl would hate a person who should be so markedly averse to having anything to do with her. Before this, however, in conversation with her young friend, Mrs. Gereth furnished a more vivid motive for her despair by asking how she could possibly be expected to sit there with the new proprietors and accept—or call it, for a day, endure—the horrors they would perpetrate in the house (X, 18-19).

Foreshortening is, of course, a way of reconciling the principle of dramatization with the principle of economy; it is rendered summary. It is equally important that foreshortening converts separate events into what James calls a picture: the emphasis being neither on consecutiveness nor on nonconsecutiveness but on singleness of effect. Thus in the passage quoted above, the three sentences take up in turn a present episode, a future episode, and a past episode, but what is stressed is Fleda Vetch's general vision of Mona Brigstock.

The effect of temporal progression is further diminished by one of James's most familiar techniques: the device of first leaping forward in time, often to a meeting between characters, then retreating to present the necessary preliminaries, all the while holding the meeting in abeyance. Chapter IV of *The Spoils of Poynton* well illustrates the method. It begins: "A week later Owen came down to inform his mother he had settled with Mona

Brigstock; but it was not at all a joy to Fleda, aware of how much to himself it would be a surprise, that he should find her still in the house. That dreadful scene before breakfast had made her position false and odious; it had been followed, after they were left alone, by a scene of her own making with her extravagant friend" (X, 33). In the second sentence James shifts from the past tense to the past perfect tense, in effect merging the two times. Two-thirds of the chapter is made up of foreshortened retrospection; the final third gives to the whole the effect of circularity, as the initially announced meeting between Owen and Fleda is allowed to proceed.

When James resumed the writing of novels after his experience in the theater, he formulated the principle of the alternation of picture and scene: that is, the alternation of foreshortened narration, made concrete and immediate so as to resemble a picture, and dramatic scene. Each technique tends to convert an episode or a series of episodes into a single presentation. Relationships between incidents are not sequential, but—as James puts it—logical. Incidents are occasions in which aspects of a situation are exhibited; and the situation is looked upon as static, not fluid. As Francis Fergusson observes, James regards a fictional subject "as a metaphysical or moral entity rather than as a sequence of events."[8]

A major result of this conception is James's developed system of cross references: the parallels, analogies, contrasts, balances, and recurrences that complicate and, at the same time, clarify the "relations" which are the subjects of his fiction. The detailed examination of this technique is one of my major tasks in subsequent chapters. But, in general, the form of a James work functions to reveal the maximum number of relationships logically contained in a subject with the maximum of clarity and economy —that is to say, the form, because it makes relationships manifest,

8. "James's Ideal of Dramatic Form," *Kenyon Review*, V (Autumn, 1943), 501.

gives intensity and coherence. The ideal result is the novel in which everything refers to something else. Of *The Awkward Age*, a complex instance of the method, James writes, "We are shut up wholly to cross-relations, relations all within the action itself; no part of which is related to anything but some other part—save of course by the relation of the total to life" (*P*, p. 114).[9]

In the novel of relations time obviously counts for little. Causation and sequence are less important than analogy and contrast. Yet it is difficult to imagine how any novel can represent experience independently of time. Thus James makes concessions to the temporal dimension. Yet it seems to be of little interest to him. To understand this point, it must be kept in mind that James holds a unique view of the idea of change—that is, of the change in status or emotional or mental condition of a character brought about by a set of experiences. R. S. Crane

9. A speculation may be in order. James's preoccupation with relations and internal analogies perhaps derives in part from a nineteenth-century American literary tradition—both an aesthetic tradition and a philosophic tradition. Melville's doctrine of "linked analogies," that passion for searching out the connections ultimately binding all the elements of existence, and Emerson's theory of "correspondences," his belief that earthly facts reflect spiritual facts, have a kinship with James's theory of fiction: "The painter's subject consist[s] ever, obviously, of the related state, to each other, of certain figures and things. To exhibit these relations, once they have all been recognized, is to 'treat' his idea. . ." (*P*, p. 5). The theory led Melville and Emerson into symbolism—the representation of the microcosm as an emblem of the macrocosm—but it led James in the opposite direction. James sought to make his novels as self-contained as they could possibly be made to be. James's "linked analogies" and "correspondences" contribute to this end, not to the identification of the natural and the supernatural orders. The James hero, like an Ahab or Ishmael, is directed by his maker to try to comprehend his world: to discover a unity that contains the bewildering multiplicity of his experience. In Melville, the protagonist's mind tragically fails, confronting the ultimate blankness of things, but this failure does not detract from that basic resemblance he has with the James seeker, who is also engaged in piecing together "relations." Likewise, it is in this respect that such a novel as *The Ambassadors* is close in spirit and intention to *The Education of Henry Adams*.

describes the plot of *The Portrait of a Lady* as one in which "the principle is a completed process of change in the moral character of the protagonist, precipitated or molded by the action, and made manifest both in it and in thought and feeling. . . ."[10] Such a reading does not severely distort the form of *The Portrait of a Lady* or of any James novel. Reversals of position and attitude are evident from *The American* through *The Ambassadors*. Yet the view that the structure depends upon some peripateia effected in time takes little account of certain important technical devices that would seem to minimize the importance of change.

When James composes a novel he is not so much interested in dramatizing what will happen to the protagonist as he is in dramatizing who the protagonist is. Yet the only way he can reveal a character's identity is by showing what happens to him. Thus Isabel Archer at the end of *The Portrait of a Lady* is to be thought of as a full revelation—a portrait—of the young woman imperfectly glimpsed in the first chapter. For its full exposure Isabel's character requires a set of relationships. The formation of these relationships is the action of the novel. Action is thus at the service of relations, which, in turn, serve to reveal character. The "developmental" element clarifies the central situation; it does not extend or alter it. James acknowledges Turgenieff to be the originator of the idea: "[The fictive picture] began for him almost always with the vision of some person or persons, who hovered before him, soliciting him, as the active or passive figure, interesting him and appealing to him just as they were and by what they were. He saw them, in that fashion, as *disponibles*, saw them subject to the chances, the complications of existence, and saw them vividly, but then had to find for them the right relations, those that would most bring them out. . ." (*P*, pp. 42-43).

To hold to his conception of portraiture, James relies to an unusual extreme on foreshadowing devices (what he calls "the

10. "The Concept of Plot and the Plot of 'Tom Jones,'" in *Critics and Criticism*, ed. R. S. Crane (Chicago, 1957), p. 66.

play of the portentous" [*P*, p. 305]) and on their opposite, re-
minders of prior events. The future is implicit in the present and
the present recalls the past. In *The Portrait of a Lady* many
examples suggest themselves. Most obviously, Isabel's principal
interest in the first half of the book is in what the future shall
hold for her; and in the second half, as the dominant characters
of the early stages rejoin her, her mind, with the reader's, recollects her beginnings. In addition to her general preoccupation
with her destiny, other details of Isabel's early history point
toward the future: her hopes for encountering the ghost of
Gardencourt; her awareness that she cannot escape unhappiness;
the presence of Ralph Touchett, whose own failure prophesies
Isabel's; the appearance of Madame Merle, whom Isabel shall
replace as Osmond's lover and Pansy's mother. The Countess
Gemini is almost wholly a foreshadowing device. In turn, Pansy
recalls the early Isabel, as do the return to Gardencourt, the
death of Ralph, and the final proposal of Goodwood.[11]

One effect of the formal circularity is to emphasize the unity
and continuity of Isabel's life, and thus to give added support to
her own determination to respect the sacredness of her early
decision. Like Strether, Isabel resists the notion that her life is
capable of fragmentation, that the present and the past are in
any real sense separable. This close association of the different
periods of her life is strongly enforced by the technique of the
novel, which insures that both Isabel and the reader shall regard
her story as a portrait rather than as a chronicle. Isabel does not
so much grow or develop as discover; she discovers, in the realm

11. See Laurence Bedwell Holland, *The Expense of Vision: Essays on
the Craft of Henry James* (Princeton, 1964), pp. 50-52, for a more detailed
analysis of the prefigurative and recollective techniques in *The Portrait of
a Lady*. Mr. Holland stresses the close relationship of the very first and
the very last scenes: "The novel is virtually framed by these two scenes
which begin and complete the pattern of its events and stand so close in
the foreground for the reader, the one encountered first in anticipation
and initiation, the other encountered first in the retrospect of memory" (p.
50).

of experience as opposed to the realm of thought, what it really means to take one's self seriously and to be governed by a belief in freedom and personal destiny.

Even in so simple a story as "Daisy Miller," the technique shows that James's goal is portraiture rather than narration. The work falls neatly into parallel halves. Rome replaces Vevey in the second half, but the episodes and character arrangement are nearly duplicated. Giovanelli, Daisy's escort in the second part, balances Winterbourne in the first part; the visit to the Coliseum parallels the earlier visit to Chillon, each occasion acting as the climax to the section in which it appears. The subject in each half is Daisy's innocent disregard for conventions, but the second half is a deepening of the first half rather than an extension of it. Daisy's conduct in Rome has more serious consequences than her conduct in Vevey. The recurrence of pattern shows not that Daisy's life is markedly different, but that with the change of setting—from the relative freedom of the Swiss watering place to the greater rigidity of the American colony in Rome—a graver dimension of the original situation is revealed. In Part One, innocence is charming; in Part Two, innocence is charming and destructive. Part Two recalls Part One, as Part One forecasts Part Two.

The ironic theme of "An International Episode" also derives from a functional two-part organization. There is a sense of duplication as we successively focus on two English visitors to America and on two American visitors to England. The characters who are the travelers each progress from the capital city (New York and London) to an upper-class retreat (Newport and Branches Castle). However, the Americans never visit the castle. For the basic contrast that produces the theme of the story is that the English are cordially received by the casual society of Newport and the Americans rudely snubbed by the English aristocrats of Branches. But apart from this main difference, the two halves have much in common. Both the American and the English worlds are matriarchies, since Mr. Westgate, an executive, and the Duke of Bayswater, a sportsman, are detached from the business of society and marriage that so occupies their wives. Furthermore, on each side there is a free spirit—Bessie Alden and Lord Lambeth—and a supporter of the class system—Mrs. Westgate and Percy Beaumont. The story follows a very rigid scheme, whereby the characters reverse their positions in the second half yet go through much the same action as before. Were it not for the variations among the balanced character types (Bessie is bright and Lambeth dull, though they have in common a dislike of the social rigidities) and the casual informality of the prose, "An International Episode" would be so mechanical as to be unconvincing.

The method is not that of the diptych, in which two aspects of an occasion are seen, but that of perspective painting, in which the viewer is made to see progressively more dimensions of the immediate scene. The technique stems from James's "incorrigible taste for gradations and superpositions of effect; his love, when it is a question of a picture, of anything that makes for proportion and perspective, that contributes to a view of *all* the dimensions" (*P*, p. 153). It is the method not only of such early works as "Daisy Miller," "An International Episode," and *The Portrait of a Lady*, but of *The Golden Bowl*, a novel in which the second half requires that the values and attitudes of the first half be radically revised. In effect, the Prince's judgment of the nature of marriage—the subject of the novel—is deepened by the addition of Maggie's judgment,[12] just as the reader's early estimate of Daisy Miller's innocence and freedom in the first part of the tale is deepened—not corrected—by the second half.

Most of the subsequent chapters in this study take up in detail specific applications of the pictorial method. The prominence and delicacy of character parallels in "Madame de Mauves," the use in *What Maisie Knew* of a single domestic arrangement—

12. See Chapter Nine.

Maisie in the midst of two adults—that prevails as the actors change, the striking procedure of *The Wings of the Dove* and *The Golden Bowl*, in which one character follows much the same course of action as another character—all these practices are modes of repetition, producing variations on a single motif, with each variation reflecting on the others. The methods give substance to James's idea that for a picture—of a character, a social situation, or a cultural institution—to be revealed with any fullness it must be rendered from more than one perspective.

This result is usually effected not by movement in time (though this is inevitable), but by movement in place (as in "Daisy Miller" and most of the international tales) or by the transference of the point of view from one consciousness to another. The dominant spatial transference in James is of course the movement from America to Europe, which James regards not as a growth or a development but as the establishing of the proper conditions (or relations) for the exhibition of the central character's identity. The method that James calls "the planned rotation of aspects" (*P*, p. 182) also places a subordinate emphasis on time. As Georges Poulet observes, James "invents a new kind of time, what one might call aesthetic time. It consists in establishing about a center a moving circle of points of view, from one to the other of which the novelist proceeds."[13]

The fusion of present and past into a single timeless structure no doubt reflects both philosophical and literary convictions.

13. *Studies in Human Time*, trans., Elliott Coleman (Baltimore, 1956), pp. 351-52. See also Ian Watt, "The First Paragraph of *The Ambassadors*: An Explication," *Essays in Criticism*, X (July, 1960), 250-74, for a brilliant analysis of the stylistic, syntactical, and grammatical techniques James employs to subordinate action to idea. Mr. Watt shows that James's late prose gives the effect of a "timeless idea based on the report of . . . chronologically separate events . . . ," of "characters and actions on a plane of abstract categorization . . . ," of a "mental continuum" which easily absorbs disconnected happenings. Also relevant is Hisayoshi Watanabe, "Past Perfect Retrospection in the Style of Henry James," *American Literature*, XXXIV (May, 1962), 165-81.

James's more perceptive characters are unusually liberated from the contingencies of time. The same high regard for maximum awareness or intensity of consciousness stands behind James's view of the novel as picture rather than as action.

For this reason the critic is generally on safe grounds in equating the structure of a James novel with the structure of the "world" represented in that novel. As I try to demonstrate in my chapter on *The Princess Casamassima*, the effort of both James and Hyacinth Robinson is to comprehend the immensely fluid and complicated London scene, and ultimately the novel itself reveals the form of this subject. This form is not identified with an action, but with a pattern of relationships that gradually assumes coherence.

Narrative movement subserves the major objective of "completeness and seeing things in all their relations" (*N*, p. 206). Thus it is of significance that James, in his preface to *Roderick Hudson*, confesses his difficulties in suggesting the passage of time (*P*, pp. 12-15). Time exists; therefore it must be represented, but not in the manner of Tolstoy or Arnold Bennett, in whose works the effect of fluidity diminishes the effect of a logical pattern of relationships.[14] Unlike several of his contemporaries, James was uninterested in the theme of transience—Thackeray's great theme. George Marcher and Lambert Strether may regret the lost opportunities of life and yearn for what might have been, but the interest of their dramas is in the permanent psychological conditions which either cause the privation in their lives or make it meaningful to them. Nor does James represent experience as a succession of aesthetic moments, like the "epiphanies" of Joyce or the "still points" of Lawrence and Virginia Woolf. Perception and intensity of awareness are of supreme importance in James,

14. See Walter F. Wright, *The Madness of Art: A Study of Henry James* (Lincoln, Nebraska, 1962), p. 44: *"Fluidity* is a general term to describe a series of events which do not seem to have inevitable relation, either because there is no sense of cause and effect or because there is no central focus or harmony of tone."

but his enlightened vessels of consciousness seldom exult in isolated ecstatic moments. For them as for the reader, the illumination is an understanding of the complete pattern of relationships surrounding the central situation—an illumination that has little to do with the conditions of time.

Action is subordinate not only to "idea" and "situation," but also to character. As Yvor Winters has observed, James gives unusual emphasis to the free will of his characters.[15] In this respect, it is worth noting that James's characters literally make the structures of the novels in which they appear. James speaks of Maisie Farange as in large measure constructing her own relationships: "Instead of simply submitting to the inherited tie and the imposed complication, of suffering from them, our little wonder-working agent would create without design, quite fresh elements of this order—contribute, that is, to the formation of a fresh tie, from which it would then (and for all the world as if through a small demonic foresight) proceed to derive great profit" (P, p. 142). James's adult heroes and heroines create their own relationships with less difficulty than little Maisie, but even Maisie has a greater control over her situation than the characters of most novelists. When James writes, "What is incident but the illustration of character?"[16] he means more than the truisms that character can be manifest only in action and that a person cannot be truly understood until he is tested by experience. He means that incident is a direct expression of will, a virtual synonym of personality. The total action of *The Wings of the Dove* may properly be judged the result of the separate early decisions made by Kate Croy—to become engaged to Merton Densher and to live with Aunt Maud—and by Milly Theale—to search out the possibilities of experience in London.

It follows that in the typical James novel the only significant events are those in which character relations are formed. As

15. "Maule's Well; or Henry James and the Relation of Morals to Manners," *Maule's Curse* (Norfolk, Conn., 1938), pp. 187-216.

16. "The Art of Fiction," in *Partial Portraits*, p. 392.

James puts it, the "evolution of the fable" is dependent upon the "needful accretions" and "right complications" of relationships (*P*, p. 52). Early novels like *The American* and *The Portrait of a Lady* have a large allowance of "plot," even of melodramatic intrigue, but in a good number of James's novels from the 1890's on the generalization holds true. *The Awkward Age*, as an obvious example, is essentially a complex pattern of pairings and matchings: each chapter is a meeting of characters, in which one sees his position altered as he learns more of the attitudes of another. Few happenings affect the material welfare of the characters: Mr. Longdon's proposal to give Van money, the marriage of Mitchy and Little Aggie, Mrs. Brook's calculated destruction of Nanda's reputation. Whatever else engages Mrs. Brook's circle —such as the sexual activities of Cashmore, Aggie, the Duchess, and others—enters the novel only indirectly, as subjects of veiled remarks and rumors. *The Awkward Age* is almost wholly talk, and the talk is all but entirely divorced from event. Action is made additionally subordinate by the preference of James's protagonists for renunciation and their distaste for aggression. The active figures—nearly all "fools"—are seen through the consciousness of the contemplative and usually passive protagonists, who, in turn, have as confidants those who are outside the action entirely.

In many of James's novels and tales the structure derives not from the external action, but from the developing awareness of the central consciousness. Thus such works as "Madame de Mauves," "The Beast in the Jungle," and *The Ambassadors* focus on the mind of the protagonist (or of the observer) in his search for truth. The pattern is that of the quest, but the exploration is inward and not objectified by the framework of a plot. The rhythmic design of "The Turn of the Screw" is indicated in the first sentence of the governess' manuscript: "I remember the whole beginning as a succession of flights and drops, a little see-saw of the right throbs and the wrong" (XII, 158). The governess' narrative follows a course from illusion to disillusion and from disillusion to illusion until the final terrible revelation. It is always a question of the children's being either angels or demons; of Bly's being either "a castle of romance" (XII, 163), or a castle with an evil " 'secret' . . . a mystery of Udolpho" (XII, 179); of the governess' being either capable or incapable of protecting the children. The structure is thus internal, stimulated by external events, but not represented or illumined by them. Albert Cook reaches a similar conclusion in his discussion of James's unique narrative method: "In James's novels the dramatized observer, or James himself as the postulated narrator, proceeds by analyzing what has already happened—a most unusual practice in narrative. This preoccupation with analysis of the past, paradoxically (for how can talk about the past get us ahead?) furthers the action. And the new stage is, in turn, only a version of the same tight set of relations which the perceptions of the characters demanded anew."[17]

The "events" in the forefront of the novels and tales often appear irrelevant or inconsequential: Mrs. Brook's circle leaves London to spend a weekend at a country house; Fleda Vetch meets Owen Gereth on a London street; Strether sees Chad Newsome at a Paris theater. Is there more to these meetings, movements, and occasions than the bringing together of characters in new arrangements? Or is there a significant level of action concealed beneath the surface, to be discovered only by close attention to imagery and metaphor? Critics have disagreed widely on this question. Interpretations of James's works have not been lacking in discoveries of religious, archetypal, and mythic patterns, of buried melodramatic struggles, of allegories and symbolic schemes of all varieties. On the other hand, some critics, insisting on James's "realism" and pre-eminence as a creator of character, maintain that James should be read only on

17. *The Meaning of Fiction* (Detroit, 1960), p. 145.

the psychological level, in which case his stories mean exactly what they say and no more.

James evidently regarded his highly figurative late style not as a way of suggesting additional levels of meaning, but as a way of gaining clarity, richness, and vividness. Language is "representational"; words convey "appearances, images, figures, objects, so many important, so many contributive items of the furniture of the world. . . " (*P*, p. 346). The fact that some of James's works have been read as versions of conflicting myths and symbolic patterns would indicate either James's disregard for metaphorical coherence or his indifference to the possible connotations of his language. No doubt both Christian and Freudian imagery may be found in "The Turn of the Screw;" *The Ambassadors* most likely offers parallels to both *The Golden Bough* and *The Secret of Swedenborg*. But James's resonances resist such imposed schemes. Even when James is acknowledged to be a symbolist— as no thoughtful reader of *The Wings of the Dove* can deny— some distortion or misplacing of emphasis results when his works are read as allegories. Nor is the figure in James's carpet an all-embracing internally consistent arrangement of metaphor. For one thing, James's language invariably inclined toward hyperbole: words like "abyss," "sacred," and "divine" recur in the notebooks and essays as well as in the fiction. The same is true of figures of speech. In the late novels in particular, the figures are often extravagant, even violent; they appear in the dialogue of characters as well as in the reporting of the author. But they serve to elucidate, dramatize, and melodramatize character and situation, rather than to equate them with something external. The graphic physical image is used to represent, literally, a psychological relationship or a state of mind. James's abysses and summits, rivers and boats, assaults and withdrawals, sacred founts and jungle beasts are inward. They dominate the language as late refinements of the principle set forth in "The Art of Fiction": "The only reason for the existence of a novel is that it does attempt to represent life. When it relinquishes this attempt, the same attempt that we see on the canvas of the painter, it will have arrived at a very strange pass."[18]

In *The Ambassadors* the prominent images of water, swimming, drowning, and boats are not to be interpreted through appeal to vegetation myth or Christian theology. The images function in the novel to show as urgent and potentially destructive the various crises that superficially appear not to be crises at all, but placid conversations and meditations. There is something in Strether's European experience like that of a shipwrecked man tossed about in the waves, sometimes falling under, finally being drawn into a boat and drawing others into his boat. When he observes Chad and Madame de Vionnet in a quite literal boat and their relationship is finally clarified, the metaphorical level of the novel merges with the explicit drama. The images constitute a fairly consistent pattern, but a pattern involving not very much more than the terrors of drowning. We need not search for recondite analogies for the explicit ones.

Because James's language is so rich in connotation, it contributes to the patterns of relationship that are central to the structures of all his novels. Such recurrent images as that of light and darkness in *The Princess Casamassima* and gold in *The Golden Bowl* are important not so much because they may suggest certain theological or mythic archetypes beyond the dramatic limits of the novels in which they appear—such as "good and evil" and "The Golden Age"—but because they establish certain connections among themselves. The pattern of light and darkness in *The Princess Casamassima* provides a figurative structure for some of the relationships between Hyacinth and the other characters. As for what it means—so I try to demonstrate in a later chapter—we need not go much farther than Hyacinth's own interpretation of his experience.

18. *Partial Portraits*, p. 378. Also see John Patterson, "The Language of 'Adventure' in Henry James," *American Literature*, XXXII (November, 1960), 291-301.

Likewise it is important to realize that the metaphorical and symbolic images are often created by the characters within the novels, not directly imposed by the author. Kate Croy defines the nature of her relation to Milly Theale when she calls her a dove, and Maggie and Adam Verver contrive the fantasy that they live in a Golden Age. In neither case are we to accept their valuations as "true." As *The Sacred Fount* and "The Beast in the Jungle" may remind us, we should hesitate to accept at face value the interpretations of those characters who depend upon grandiose surrealistic images to define the situations in which they find themselves.

The design of James's novels is not primarily a structure of verbal connotations. At times the design is revealed through action—events, movements, and gestures which objectify states of consciousness and moral and psychological relationships. In most cases the broad movements in James's fiction may be looked upon as initiations, aggressions, or searches, tracing the progress of a central character as he seeks access into (knowledge of) a social situation. The reverse is sometimes true; the central character who would retreat from experience is yet drawn into it. Most often we are given versions of the self's confrontation with the world, with the specific incidents that create the plot sometimes producing a pattern signifying the quality of that confrontation. Particularly in the works of the middle and late periods, James suggests coherent patterns in sequences of events, each of which taken alone seems inconsequential. The most common external action in *What Maisie Knew* is Maisie's traveling about in a carriage, to, from, and with her various parents and guardians; it is an action that perfectly represents Maisie's forlorn condition.[19] Fleda Vetch's characteristic movement is the effort to withdraw herself from the lives of the Gereths; she is frequently seen running away—to her sister, to her father, to

19. See Oscar Cargill, *The Novels of Henry James* (New York, 1961), p. 258.

any possible escape—and always being seized by one of the Gereths.[20] R. W. B. Lewis has written of the descent from heights to depths as the significant action of *The Wings of the Dove*.[21]

If such rhythmic movements are instances of what Kenneth Burke calls "symbolic action," their purpose is not to suggest analogies with external archetypes, but to contribute to internal cohesiveness. A rhythmic pattern serves the end of dramatizing relationships, not of outlining a sequential progress. Hence the pattern constitutes a picture rather than an action; that is, the rhythm is more repetitive than incremental. The rhythm of *The Spoils of Poynton* is nearly without variation: in effect Fleda constantly re-enacts the same role—that of the victim of a social trap ever seeking but never finding escape.

Of course, there are instances in James of what E. K. Brown calls "the combination of the repeated and the variable with the repeated."[22] The rhythm of *The Ambassadors* is both repetitive and progressive. But the outward action is almost wholly repetitive; the progressive is limited to the growth of Strether's knowledge. One motif contributing to the larger, densely complex, structure is made up of various dining scenes. Most of the stages in Lambert Strether's European education are marked by the taking of meals. In London, he takes Maria Gostrey to dinner before going to the theater.

Miss Gostrey had dined with him at his hotel, face to face over a small table on which the lighted candles had rose-coloured shades; and the rose-coloured shades and the small table and the soft fragrance of the lady—had anything to his mere sense ever been so soft?—were so many touches in he scarce knew what positive high picture. He had been to the theatre, even to the opera, in Boston, with Mrs.

20. See J. A. Ward, *The Imagination of Disaster: Evil in the Fiction of Henry James* (Lincoln, Nebraska, 1961), pp. 61-63.
21. "The Vision of Grace: James's 'The Wings of the Dove' "; *Modern Fiction Studies*, III (Spring, 1957), 36-37.
22. *Rhythm in the Novel* (Toronto, 1950), p. 17.

Newsome, more than once acting as her only escort; but there had been no little confronted dinner, no pink lights, no whiff of vague sweetness, as a preliminary. . . (XXI, 50).

The dinner crystallizes Strether's feeling that life can be more pleasurable than he has suspected. Later he recollects the dinner with Miss Gostrey as the first stage in his break with Woollett. But the meal in London is just the preliminary to numerous other meals, considerably more charming, in France. Dining at a restaurant in Paris with some friends of Chad, Strether feels that "the Paris evening . . . was . . . in the very taste of the soup, in the goodness . . . of the wine, in the pleasant coarse texture of the napkin and the crunch of the thick-crusted bread" (XXI, 104). It is in a restaurant that Strether first speaks to Chad, and the scene and the occasion serve to frame the gentility and charm of the "irreducible young Pagan" (XXI, 156-57). Not all of Strether's "recognitions" occur at meals, of course; the theater is used twice, and the most important illumination in the first half of the book takes place at the party in Gloriani's garden. But meals are by far the most numerous occasions for Strether's awakening of consciousness; and they are never perfunctory, never merely opportunities for conversation. Inevitably James relates them to the larger moral and historical experience of Europe. The beauty of Madame de Vionnet and the urbanity of Chad blend with the mood, decor, and sensuous appeal of leisurely repasts. As an example, when Chad asks Strether to visit Madame de Vionnet, he speaks "across their marble-topped table, while the foam of the hot milk was in their cups and its plash still in the air" (XXI, 235). It is a Keatsian rendering of a cup of coffee, and the fine sensory pleasure of the moment suggests the whole character of European life. It is to the viewpoint of the gourmet that Strether, the stiff New Englander, is gradually converted.

Strether's several dining engagements with Chad and Madame de Vionnet help to convince him that their relationship is "unassailably innocent" (XXII, 10). These meals, invariably informal and simple, suggest exquisite grace and refinement, as far as possible removed from ugliness and crudity. One luncheon, nearly pastoral in atmosphere, takes place shortly after Strether happens upon Madame de Vionnet in Notre Dame Cathedral, where he is naïvely led to believe in the woman's purity. The subsequent luncheon adds to the impression:

How could he wish it to be lucid for others, for any one that he, for the hour, saw reasons enough [for admiring and befriending Madame de Vionnet] in the mere way the bright, clean, ordered waterside life came in at the open window?—the mere way Madame de Vionnet, opposite him over their intensely white table-linen, their *omelette aux tomates*, their bottle of straw-coloured Chablis, thanked him for everything almost with the smile of a child, while her grey eyes moved in and out of their talk, back to the quarter of the warm spring air, in which early summer had already begun to throb, and then back again to his face and their human questions (XXII, 13-14).

The climax of *The Ambassadors* comes when Strether, after he has sacrificed his hope for the future by defending Chad and Madame de Vionnet, discovers that they are adulterers. This recognition scene, like the one in which Strether becomes convinced of the couple's innocence, occurs in a café by a river. The atmosphere is again pastoral and the implication is again of grace and innocence, of the simple and harmless pleasures of the senses. Sitting at the table in the country-side inn with Chad and Madame de Vionnet, Strether sees that the life of the senses, partly symbolized by the meal—"two or three dishes" (XXII, 262) and a bottle of wine—is far from innocent; passion and deceit lie hidden beneath the charm and beauty. And as Strether eventually understands, this ambiguity is central to the nature of Europe itself.

As James says in his preface, his intention in *The Ambassadors* is to demonstrate Strether's "process of vision" (*P*, p. 308). The "march of [the] action" (*P*, p. 308) consists chiefly in Strether's deepening perception, but the occasions are to a greater extent repetitive, not so much varied as deepened or "thickened." That is to say, his early experiences are partial mirrors of his later ones. The "meaning" of Europe expands as Strether progresses from one microcosm to another: from Chester to London to Paris; from Maria Gostrey's rooms to Madame de Vionnet's, the former suggesting a sensuous antiquity but carrying little of the richness of implication that Strether is to detect in the latter; from the charm of the Luxembourg Gardens to the exotic and rather dangerous beauty of Gloriani's garden. It would be an easy matter to mention further details in the novel which contribute to our sense of observing a picture whose surface continuously reveals a greater and more subtle depth. But as Strether's experiences and visions take on more complexity without essentially changing, his own capacity for unbiased perception grows. Each of Strether's insights is a discovery of the meaning of the whole of his and everyone's experience. The recurrence of situations demonstrates that the circumstance in which he is involved remains static. The "events" of the novel—like the announcement that Jeanne de Vionnet will be married, the arrival of the Pococks, and Chad's departure for England—are important not because they indicate a change in the situation, but because they show Strether the true nature of the situation, which, though unchanging, is revealed only gradually. Even the change in Chad's feelings about Europe and Madame de Vionnet is interpreted by Strether (and James) as a revelation of Chad's essential identity. Finally we see clearly what Chad has always been, as that ambiguity of surface and substance which has obscured his character from the beginning is resolved.

This mention of *The Ambassadors* brings to mind E. M. Forster's influential observation that the action of the novel approximates the shape of an hour glass—with Chad and Strether quite apart from each other at the beginning (as regards their relation to Europe), drawing together at the middle, and assuming opposite positions at the end.[23] The pattern is doubtless genuine. But the question arises: of what importance is it? A partial answer lies in James's ideal of roundness. The novel with the finished shape gives the illusion of completeness and the symmetrical structure is aesthetically pleasing. Yet it is obvious that in any novel an abstract structure of incidents can be of little importance in itself. The only merit of such a geometrical design can be that it assists the attentive reader in recognizing the important relationships in the novel—in this case the relation between the beginning, middle, and end—and ultimately of understanding the characters, who are defined by their changing relations with each other. But nothing could be more meaningless than to observe the peculiar geometrical figure that the events of a novel may resemble. Nor is there any apparent profit to be derived from assigning symbolic meanings to plot skeletons —at least to those of James's novels. One returns to the principle that James's works, when they succeed, derive their consistency and their coherence wholly from within. Every novel contains its own "logic." Neither figures of hour glasses nor patterns of fortunate falls are of much help in accounting for the placing of characters, the staging of scenes, or the arrangement of details.

James's guiding principle is the necessity of suiting action to idea. Thus the dominant occurrences in his novels are the meetings of characters, wherein one or more of the figures, with the reader, sees further into the idea. It often happens that these meetings additionally assist the reader's (not the character's) "process of vision" by assuming a rhythmic design that becomes a metaphor of the idea.

Since James habitually conceives of his ideas in static and spatial terms, his regular problem is to find appropriate actions— to show something happening which alters the welfare of his major characters and at the same time increases our understand-

23. *Aspects of the Novel* (New York, 1927), pp. 218-34.

ing of the original situation. Most often the plots center upon some reversal of fortune. They record falls from innocence to experience, withdrawals from illusion to reality and from isolation to involvement in society, and are accompanied by varieties of betrayal. The action of the novels and tales is invariably ironic, the irony sometimes tragic and sometimes comic. But James seeks not primarily to imitate an action—the plots being technical strategies rather than ends in themselves—but to discover an action that is an analogue of an idea. The main function of the action in much of James's fiction is to confront the protagonist with knowledge of himself and of his situation, neither of which has essentially changed from the start. The sharp turnabouts in the action of *The Portrait of a Lady*, "The Turn of the Screw," and *The Ambassadors* (to mention some random examples) follow upon the protagonists' insights into what always has been true.

James's idea of "illustrative action" (*N*, p. 197) lies behind one of his reservations about *The American*. He confesses that in *The American* the plot is largely irrelevant: that is, the "idea" of the novel is Christopher Newman's generosity of spirit, but the action is the intrigue of the Bellegardes, which is only indirectly related to Newman's case. The action is only responsible for Newman's situation; it is not an illumination of that situation (*P*, p. 36).

In his later novels James is more successful in matching action to idea, but the arbitrariness and factitiousness of plot in certain shorter works suggest that the problem remained acute when he worked in tighter confines. An extreme instance of James's inability to construct an organic plot is the short story "Sir Dominick Ferrand." Here the explicit subject of the story is "The idea of the *responsibility* of destruction—the destruction of papers, letters, records, etc., connected with the private and personal history of some great and honored name and throwing some very different light on it from the light projected by the public career" (*N*, p. 117). Unfortunately the unfolding of the tale fails to illuminate this central idea; it is mainly occupied with the thematically extraneous fortunes of the hero after he has destroyed the papers. His marriage and his coming into money have very little to do with the moral issue raised at the start. It is easy to understand why James rejected "Sir Dominick Ferrand" from the New York Edition of his works.

The notebooks show that James sometimes conceived his shorter tales as actions rather than as pictures. The "anecdote" is his term for an ironic action; the conception of the action precedes the conception of character. The anecdote compels a sudden and often drastic "climax," a rounding-off. In the extended fiction, on the other hand, the "developmental" is given freer play, so that the "climax" is less an event requiring a radical readjustment in character relationships than it is the point at which the protagonist achieves maximum understanding of the situation. Whatever "happens" in the climax of a novel follows from and is subordinate to the protagonist's achieved awareness. Hyacinth Robinson's suicide is a case in point. In many shorter tales (for example, "The Middle Years"), the climax is brought about by a sudden reversal of situation—such as a death—which precipitates a hurried recognition.

In some stories, there is barely any action; all is idea. In "The Great Good Place," the action does nothing more than give a temporal life to the curious *donnée*: George Dane's inexplicable withdrawal to a place of absolute peace. As Virginia Woolf remarks, "Something is wrong with the story. The movement flags; the emotion is monotonous. . . . The story dwindles to a sweet soliloquy."[24] What is wrong is simply James's failure to find an action to represent the idea.

In "The Altar of the Dead," on the other hand, the action is an effective embodiment of the idea. The idea is of "a man

24. "The Ghost Stories," in *Henry James: A Collection of Critical Essays*, ed. Leon Edel (New York, 1963), p. 48.

whose noble and beautiful religion is the worship of the Dead" (*N*, p. 164). The action places the man, George Stransom, in a relationship with a woman, who is herself devoted to the dead and worships at the same altar as Stransom. The hinge upon which the action turns is on the face of it arbitrary: Acton Hague, the man whom the woman specifically honors is also the one man in the world whom Stransom cannot honor, cannot forgive for a crime committed against him. Yet at the climax, Stransom, just as he dies, accepts Hague as one of "his" dead. This sketchy summary does no justice to the tone and persuasiveness of the story, but it may suggest that Stransom's involvement with the woman is not an extraneous story mechanically manipulated (as is the love plot in "Sir Dominick Ferrand"), but a way of extending Stransom's and the reader's understanding of the relation between living and dead; it is a relation in which wounded pride cannot be admitted.[25]

Still the action of "The Altar of the Dead" is essentially anecdotal. The final revelation is forced by the coincidence of the woman's love and Stransom's hatred for the same man and by the fortuitous death of Stransom. James's shorter works frequently rely on such unlikely (to James, "ironic") circumstances as means of rushing the climactic recognition.[26] The action in the novels is both more credible and less prominent.

25. "The Altar of the Dead" is an excellent illustration of the process by which James discovers the meaning of a fictional germ by devising an action for it—a process described and celebrated in the preface to *The Spoils of Poynton* (*P*, p. 122). The notebook entries on "The Altar of the Dead" suggest nothing of the moral complexity of the finished tale.

26. Such a complaint is made of "The Beast in the Jungle" by Allen Tate, "Three Commentaries," *Sewanee Review*, LVIII (Winter, 1950), 9.

On the other hand, the element of contrivance, especially in the shorter fiction, has led some critics to judge James a romancer or parabolist rather than a realist. Albert Cook is especially illuminating on this question: "James's plots are not romances, or fables, but fictions that resemble romances in their tightness. In James, plot is not a cipher of meaning, as it is in romance. His tightness is the aesthetic coherence of a fiction which knows its theme as fictive" (*The Meaning of Fiction*, p. 136). See

The principle of economy has even more harmful consequences in some of James's works. When he employs the consciousness of an outside observer as the reflector of the action, James is in part motivated by the desire to be brief. In his preface to *The Spoils of Poynton*, he explains that one of the advantages of concentrating on a central character's intelligent awareness of a situation is "the rule of an exquisite economy" (*P*, p. 129). The mind of the observer concentrates and organizes, rather than diffuses, the action. But another effect is to place the emphasis on consciousness rather than on action. The synthesizing reflector pictorializes rather than narrates: he is given not to the fluid reporting of incidents but to the assimilating of all the aspects of the entire situation.

The story told from the point of view of one character, particularly if the character is an observer and not an agent, sometimes turns into two stories: one of the situation which occupies the observer's mind and one of the observer himself, his own psychological, intellectual, and moral reactions. James says as much in his preface to *The Spoils*: "I committed myself to making the affirmation and the penetration of [Fleda's intelligence] my action and my 'story'; once more, too, with the reentertained perception that a subject so lighted, a subject residing in somebody's excited and concentrated feeling about something —*both the something and the somebody being of course as important as possible*—has more beauty to give out than under any other style of pressure" (*P*, p. 128; italics mine). Fleda is organically a part of the situation, indeed the center of the situation; thus in *The Spoils of Poynton* "the something and the somebody" are not really separate. *The Sacred Fount* is a different case altogether. There seem to be two unrelated subjects of this short novel. In the extensive criticism which the work has

also Krishna Baldev Vaid, *Technique in the Tales of Henry James* (Cambridge, Mass., 1964), pp. 214-48, for a view of "The Altar of the Dead," "The Beast in the Jungle," and "The Jolly Corner" as "fantasies that are also parables" (p. 214).

provoked most of the attention has been given not to the prima facie subject of the sacred fount of personality, but to the narrator, whose intense scrutiny of the situation involving the other characters is as prominent a part of the novel as the situation he observes. Whether this observer is a lunatic, an artist *manqué*, or a Hamlet-like figure reduced to a purely intellectual existence, his revelance to the real or presumed relations of the "active" characters is most tenuous and uncertain.[27]

Had James accepted the conventional narrative method of telling a story, the problem would vanish. But his preference for dealing with a situation that is essentially complete at the start and for concentrating the action in the inquiries and meditations of the onlooker requires that the observer rather than the observed receive the most attention. James's most debated tale, "The Turn of the Screw," is another instance of a work with two subjects: the (presumed) sinister relation between the ghosts and the children, and the response of the governess. Like the narrator of *The Sacred Fount*, the governess takes it upon herself to sort the evidence and to make a judgment as to what has been going on from the start. The "action" is mainly confined to her intellectual progress. Inevitably critical interest has been in the latter, and the question has been repeatedly raised: how reliable is her analysis? If the governess' analysis is reliable, her own role is secondary; but if her analysis is erroneous, the haunting of the children is secondary, if indeed real.

In a letter to H. G. Wells, James makes clear the source of confusion in "The Turn of the Screw":

Of course I had, about my young woman, to take a very sharp line. The grotesque business I had to make her picture and the childish

27. Since writing this comment, I have read Jean Frantz Blackall's *Jamesian Ambiguity and "The Sacred Fount"* (Ithaca, New York, 1965), a penetrating book which has the merit of emphasizing the structural problem of the novel and almost succeeds in finding a thematic connection between the obsessed narrator and the "sacred fount" theme that he constructs.

psychology I had to make her trace and present, were, for me at least, a very difficult job, in which absolute lucidity and logic, a singleness of effect, were imperative. Threfore I had to rule out subjective complications of her own—play of tone, etc.; and keep her impersonal save for the most obvious and indispensable little note of neatness, firmness and courage—without which she wouldn't have had her data.[28]

In view of the dozen of studies of the governess' "subjective complications," it can only be concluded that James's description of his tale is inaccurate. His remarks do, however, reveal his intention: to keep the governess subordinate to the "grotesque business" she detects and tries to end. In part James allows the "developmental" impulse to exceed the confines of the "*jeu d'esprit*" he has projected. It is one of many cases in which "the very simplicity of the action forces me . . . to get everything out of it that it can give" (*N*, p. 251). It would appear that in "The Turn of the Screw" this compulsion pushes James a little too far. As in *The Sacred Fount* the psychology of the reflector is so complex and intriguing that the reader is unable to accept the character as simply a reflector.

In most of his works James avoids the difficulty: by having the central consciousness himself an agent in the situation, as in the longer novels; by using the scenic method, with no "subjective complications" or "going behind"; by disallowing any introspection on the part of the reflector. The latter restriction rules most of the shorter tales narrated by or seen through the eyes of a relative outsider: for example, "Brooksmith," "The Death of the Lion," and "Mora Montravers."

But we have been considering those stories and novels in which, as Wayne C. Booth writes, James "gradually develops the reflector until the original subject is rivaled or even overshadowed."[29] It is a considerable irony that (according, for

28. *Selected Letters*, p. 182.
29. *The Rhetoric of Fiction* (Chicago, 1961), p. 341. Mr. Booth's chap-

example, to the preface of *The Spoils of Poynton*) the principle of economy would lead James to the creation of such complex reflectors. They may indeed compress and synthesize the experiences they observe, but they inevitably introduce certain "developments" and "relations" of their own. Regardless of the expressed motives of economy and intensity (in addition to James's disposition toward the subject of consciousness itself), it is just as important that the prominence of the reflector insures the conversion of the represented experience into a picture. The reflector is less an actor than a "central light" (*P*, p. 130); he is important to James principally for his capacity for "interpretation," "criticism," and "appreciation" (*P*, p. 129). The difficulties arise because, in the interests of verisimilitude, James must represent his central intelligences also as persons, and it is as persons that they sometimes assume a life distinct from the situations that they observe.

James's striving for condensation and intensity, his contempt for fluid narration—in short, his subordination of action to picture—is the source of most of his technical problems. At times James risks the effect of arbitrariness in positioning his char-

---

ter on "Henry James and the Unreliable Narrator" (pp. 339-74) is an illuminating discussion of James's "use of narrators [and reflectors] who run away, in effect, with the original subject, transmuting one idea into another very different though related idea. . ." (p. 345). In addition to citing numerous illustrations of this practice, Mr. Booth recognizes that the problem is considerably broader than the question of the narrator's or reflector's reliability. Especially in his remarks on "The Aspern Papers," Mr. Booth argues that the narrator is inconsistent, sometimes ironically exposing himself and sometimes directly expressing important attitudes of the author. My own emphasis in the present discussion is focused less on James's alleged failures in character consistency than on his failures in structural unity. The problem is basically whether in those stories in which the character of the reflector is stressed we should regard his outward experience as the subject of the work or as the phenomena to which his consciousness responds in a revealing way. Whereas Mr. Booth judges realism to be James's motive in disproportionately emphasizing the characters of his reflectors, I would give somewhat more weight to James's habitual preference of picture to action. This latter concern seems implicit throughout Mr. Booth's chapter, though not discussed as such.

acters, and at other times he pays excessive attention to the mind contemplating the action—both faults stemming from a lack of interest in story as story. But in the majority of his works there is a perfect adjustment of incident to idea, with the events of the story accommodated to the primary purpose of James's craft: the exhibition of human relationships, the truth and beauty of which are not contingent upon the temporal occurrences used by the artist to reveal them.[30]

30. Sometimes James uses the term "picture" to refer to the visual effect he wished to achieve in his work and at other times to the static effect. This chapter deals exclusively with the latter sense of the word—a subject neglected by James's critics. James's use of pictorial devices to produce visual effects has been ably discussed by F. O. Matthiessen, "James and the Plastic Arts," *Kenyon Review*, V (Autumn, 1943), 533-50; and Viola Hopkins, "Visual Art Devices and Parallels in the Fiction of Henry James," *PMLA*, LXXVI (December, 1961), 561-74.

III · *WATCH AND WARD*

Watch and Ward is one of the most curious first novels of any major author. The central situation of a twenty-nine-year-old bachelor's adopting a twelve-year-old girl and then preparing her for the eventual role of his wife is on the surface not only improbable, but at least mildly perverse. It seems a subject more suitable for an Elizabethan pastoral comedy or a Gothic romance than a late nineteenth-century novel of contemporary manners. James does not explore the abnormality of Roger Lawrence's adoption of Nora Lambert through the Hawthorne technique of using an extreme situation to dramatize intense moral states. Nor is the action so deeply grounded in the psychology of the characters as the perverse undertakings of later James characters like Christina Light, Rose Armiger, and Kate Croy. In fact, James treats Roger's enterprise as natural and normal; there is no suggestion that his calculated education of Nora is either immoral or neurotic. James develops a situation that might have originated in Hawthorne's notebook (if not in Charlotte Brontë's, or Freud's), but the novel is closer in spirit to Howells than to Hawthorne: the adoption situation is an occasion for domestic melodrama rather than for psychological or moral penetration.

In addition, the erotic overtones of the language are more pronounced than in any other novel of James's apprenticeship. In two key passages[1] (deservedly notorious for a novel written in 1870) and in the repeated references to Nora's long, thick hair, the heroine's sexual identity is clearly established, even though the author and the hero most often regard her with the extreme propriety required by the age. When we also consider the vague suggestion of sexual inadequacy in Roger, it becomes clear that there is a revealing (if far from cogent) level of meaning beneath the Howellsian surface. There can be little doubt that James has exposed much of his emotions and something of his frustrations in *Watch and Ward*.[2] And he has done so with considerable artlessness. The erotic motifs and the ineffectual and self-conscious nature of the hero lie outside the central theme of the novel. The young James reveals too little critical awareness of the feelings and attitudes latent in his subject. There is a set of undercurrent themes, abortive and cryptic, unassimilated in the surface theme, and quite irrelevant to the sentimental outcome of Roger's ordeal. For on the surface the interest of the story lies in Roger's overcoming adversity (in the form of the secondary characters) to win Nora's love and marry her. The apparent psychological interest is confined to the progress of Nora to womanhood (according to Victorian conventions) and to her

1. Both passages are quoted and commented on by Leon Edel in his introduction to the most recent edition of *Watch and Ward* (London, 1960), pp. 6, 8. Page references are to this edition.

2. Professor Edel shows a plausible connection between Roger's feeling of inferiority to his more dynamic rivals and the young Henry James's sense of being overshadowed by his father and his brother William. See Introduction, *Watch and Ward*, pp. 15-17.

recognition that Roger would be an ideal husband. But a deeper psychology also operates—particularly in Roger—though it has little to do with the contrived outcome of the story.

The undercurrent creates a secondary theme not closely related to the apparent theme. There is also a double structure in the novel. Because the novel is, in a sense, at odds with itself, tending to delve deeply when the sentimental plot requires it to be superficial, neither structure is successful. The forced melodramatic ending short-circuits the more credible psychological conflicts, so that we are left with the feeling that the deeper concerns of the novel have been arbitrarily evaded.

Quite obviously the novel develops according to standard Victorian formulae. Though James uses character and event economically, guarding against superfluous and digressive materials, he drastically restricts his characters by the unnatural tidiness of his plot. *Watch and Ward* illustrates the weakness of the closed or mechanical structure—a factitious arrangement of the various elements into a predetermined shape, specifically the resolution of a conflict by a conventional happy ending. In *Watch and Ward*, however, there are signs that James is moving in the direction of the open or organic structure—in which the form of the story is determined by the story itself and not by external rules. In James's youth a theory of organic form was very much in the air, but it had not been specifically and systematically applied to the art of fiction.[3] Not until James himself articulated his principles was a concept of the organic nature of the novel made available.

In *Watch and Ward* the clash is not so much between form and content as between two concepts of form: what I have called the organic and the scientific. In his mature fiction James customarily works toward some reconciliation of the symmetry

3. See Richard H. Fogle, "Organic Form in American Criticism: 1840-1870," *The Development of American Literary Criticism*, ed. Floyd Stovall (Chapel Hill, 1955), pp. 82-83.

supplied by an a priori frame and the natural form encouraged by the free development of the story. *Watch and Ward* is not James's only failure in achieving such a synthesis, but it is his gravest one. For the rigid outer design to be preserved, James must severely restrict and even distort the characters and situations that he seems interested in developing.

In *Watch and Ward* we can see the young writer fitfully, tentatively, and half-consciously exposing many of the themes and character types that in subsequent novels he comes gradually to understand and to subject to artistic control, but here he rather awkwardly imposes these themes and characters upon a set of commonplace plot devices. The major device is the happy ending. Another is the use of the secondary characters as obstacles to the happiness of the hero and heroine; these minor characters are made into a gallery of knowing and unknowing villains whose only function is to impede the success of Roger's plan and thus extend the story to novel length. Rather soon after *Watch and Ward*, James would use secondary characters not so much to block or further the action, but to form "relations" with the protagonist. As I observed in the previous chapter, these relations contribute to the revelation of the central character's identity and also become the materials that are seized upon and tirelessly interpreted by this character's intelligence. There is little suggestion in *Watch and Ward* that the secondary characters reveal anything important about Roger or even stimulate his intelligence. Roger, a rarity among James's protagonists, really possesses an autonomous existence; he is detachable from the characters who surround him.

The major flaw in characterization—to which I shall return—is that for James to place his figures in their predetermined final positions he must simplify and to some extent falsify them. He allows character to be subservient to plot. Considered in its most superficial aspect, *Watch and Ward* has a three-part structure: in the beginning, Roger discovers Nora and originates his idea;

in the middle, Hubert, his sophisticated clergyman brother, and George Fenton, a wastrel and confidence man claiming to be Nora's cousin, bid for Nora's affection and hence endanger Roger's plan; Roger himself is twice diverted from Nora by other women; in the end, however, Nora sees the two pretenders in their true venality and realizes that the only man who loves her is Roger. The plot may be reduced to a threefold movement: man adopts child, man loses child, man marries child. The climax involves a drastic alteration in Nora's feelings about Roger, a near kidnapping, and the rapid-fire exposure of the one-time suitors—clear evidence of James's commitment to the importance of a thrilling conclusion.[4] Also in the last pages the characters are neatly divided into the pure and the base; the base are not brought to ruin in this good-natured novel, but the pure are rewarded with permanent and unambiguous happiness.

Regarded solely as melodrama—and therefore judged merely for its facility with the conventions of story telling—*Watch and Ward* has a development that is in some ways skillful and in other ways awkward. The climax effectively draws the major characters together and logically (if superficially) resolves their conflicts. Nora's stages of development are crystallized in a series of dramatic incidents. James unobtrusively interweaves the private histories of Nora and Roger, so that we alternate from an emphasis on one to an emphasis on the other.

Yet the faults are just as obvious. The machinery for presenting Nora and Roger with their crises is cumbersome. Two intercontinental journeys and a major illness serve to expose the characters to outside influence, to offer them glimpses of life apart from each other. The ending is obviously a simplified resolution. James achieves an unnatural finality by reducing the four major characters to their simplest specifications. The difficulties latent

4. Editorial demands probably had much influence on the neat and happy endings of James's earliest fiction. See, for example, his 1867 letter to the editor of *The Galaxy* in *Selected Letters of Henry James*, ed. Leon Edel (London, 1956), p. 93.

in Roger's plan to marry Nora disappear in the end, and the whole relationship is brought down to the level of the sentimental love story: Roger generously allows Nora the freedom to choose or reject him, and Nora herself is forced by the most melodramatic circumstances to realize that Roger loves her. Hubert Lawrence and George Fenton are required by the plot to appear as simple frauds.

From time to time, ambiguity, or at least complexity, obscures all these characters, but in the end all are presented in extreme simplicity. To impress us that Roger's future with Nora will be cloudless, James must clarify the obscurities. The ambiguities are not resolved, merely ignored. Were James to keep his characters consistent, or—more accurately—to continue suggesting alternate attitudes that might be held about them, the slick ending would be impossible.

There is a misuse of technique in James's method of characterization. Insofar as *Watch and Ward* is an experiment in ambiguous characterization—and thus a precursor of the later works—the effect of the ambiguity is not to approximate actual experience, in which good and evil are mixed and human beings are not identified with simple moral abstractions, but to mislead us. By following James's hints, we form opinions of the characters; the conclusion shows some of these to be false. Obviously this effect does not imply that James has intended to mislead us. More likely the faulty ambiguity arises from James's attempt to include too much in a short, conventional first novel and from his inability to come to terms with the submerged conflicts in the story.

The most obvious instances of such an unsatisfactory ambiguity are Hubert Lawrence and George Fenton. The essential character of these two is crudely disguised, almost withheld, rather than gradually revealed. In the end both show themselves as loathsome, manifestly inferior to Roger in the eyes of both Nora and the reader. Though we suspect Fenton of being motivated by the lowest criminal instincts from the moment he appears on the scene, James complicates our attitude by suggesting another way of considering him. For he is described as a vigorous, dynamic, potentially wholesome man—a seedy Caspar Goodwood. In the introduction of Fenton in Chapter IV, James gives four distinct impressions of him: an objective observer's, Nora's, Roger's, and Fenton's own. Fenton's cynical evaluation of his chances to profit from his cousinship is the main fact—the damning evidence. But what in the end is the whole of his character is here but a part of his character. Roger envies him intensely and Nora feels drawn to him for his manliness, a quality stressed by the narrator: "His speech . . . possessed a certain homely vigour in which ears polite might have found their account. He was as little as possible, certainly, of Roger's circle; but he carried about him the native fragrance of another circle, besides which the social perfume familiar to Roger's nostrils might have seemed a trifle stale and insipid. . . . Considering his years,—they numbered but twenty-five,—Fenton's tough maturity was very wonderful. You would have confessed, however, that he had a true genius for his part, and that it became him better to play at manhood than at juvenility" (p. 78). With his diamond stick pin, his tattooed left hand, his long legs, and his Southwestern accent, Fenton is nearly a stereotype of the down-at-the-heels Mississippi gambler, perhaps a kin of Melville's confidence man or Twain's Arkansas royalty. But he also commands a kind of respect, from the reader as well as from Nora, for his masculinity, his self-possession, and his commitment to the real world. When Nora feels she is falling in love with him, we are intended to regard her as a victim of her own innocence. But Fenton's "tough maturity," his "certain manful hardness" (p. 95) are not to be overlooked in our judgment of him. His forcefulness is a positive quality, especially in contrast to Roger's timidity and fussiness. Even when Fenton agrees to accept a handout from Nora, he appears in a better light than Roger, whose jealousy provokes him to insult Fenton. While Fenton retains his dignity, Roger lapses from his characteristic mildness.

Like Fenton, Hubert Lawrence is unmistakably abominable in the end. When Nora offers herself to him, she finds that all along his attentions to her have been unserious. James establishes Hubert's shallowness early in the novel: "Hubert had apparently come into the world to play. He played at life, altogether; he played at learning, he played at theology, he played at friendship; and it was to be conjectured that, on particular holidays, he would play pretty hard at love" (p. 48). Without minimizing Hubert's superficial mind, his frivolity, his hypocrisy, and his casualness with women, James yet conveys the possibility that such faults are mere foibles. Not until the end are we sure he is a scoundrel.

Before then, the main emphasis falls on his superiority to Roger:

Hubert Lawrence was some four years [Roger's] junior; but Roger had always allowed him a large precedence in the things of the mind. . . . He was extremely good-looking and clever with just such a cleverness as seemed but an added personal charm (p. 47).
He was gentle without timidity, frank without arrogance, clever without pedantry (p. 104).
Unconscious as yet of her own charm, Nora was oppressed by a secret admiration of her companion, whose presence seemed to open a brilliant vista (p. 105).

Hubert's charm and urbanity are alternately meretricious and real; we are uncertain of his true character until he turns Nora away in his last appearance.

Roger is even more ambiguously presented. In the opening chapter, which shows Roger's proposal of marriage to Isabel Morton, he is broadly satirized. Our first impression is of a shy, nearsighted, balding, awkward, fastidious young man, quite ridiculous in a situation calling for social presence and self-assertion. The tone of the description accentuates the impression:

"In trifling matters, such as the choice of a shoemaker or a dentist, his word carried weight; but no one dreamed of asking his opinion on politics or literature. . . . The eye was excellent; small, perhaps, and somewhat dull, but with a certain appealing depth, like the tender dumbness in the gaze of a dog" (p. 20). It is noteworthy that in his first novel James regards what is to be his characteristic hero type (e.g., Rowland Mallet, Frederick Winterbourne, George Stransom, and Lambert Strether) with a degree of ironic detachment that is unique. Roger's successors are often vain, prejudiced, and fussy, but they are never so absurd or foolish as Roger.[5]

Still Roger has the author's full sympathy. The Prufrockian manner is gradually subdued, as James heightens the emphasis on his integrity and noble heart. In the end, even his faults are virtues. The men who possess the self-assurance, intelligence, and vitality that Roger lacks reveal their worthlessness. Nora's climactic discovery that "Roger was the only man in [the universe] who had a heart" (p. 236) leads us to reassess the importance of Fenton's manliness and Hubert's charm. Not only are these accomplishments worthless without love, but it seems that the very possession of such qualities precludes the capacity to love.

Thus the strong are made weak, and the weak is made strong. Roger, who in the beginning is ridiculous, and the two false suitors, who in the beginning are at least partly admirable, are shown to be the opposite of what they have seemed. In many of James's novels the technique of the reversal of roles is used skillfully and functionally, but here it is weak. It gives a form to the novel; the ambiguity abets the suspense; and the conclusion

5. In *The Novels of Henry James* (New York, 1961), Oscar Cargill tends to regard Roger Lawrence as a most decent and quite normal human being: "Roger's fault is his proprietorship . . . but it is a fault infused with his greatest virtue, unselfish affection" (p. 10). Such an estimate may agree with James's general intention, but it fails to account for the ridiculous aspect of Roger.

is more compelling because it is ironic. Yet the conclusion simply bypasses the problems which the earlier characterizations and character groupings have raised. The final division of the characters into the loving and the unloving is nearly an irrelevance to the deeper theme of the book.

Unless Fenton and Hubert are merely straw men for Roger to knock over—in which case the book is very bad—the theme is more complicated and more real than the superficial one—a rather banal instance of true love finding its course. The inner story is not about the developing awareness of love; rather it is a vague and incomplete sketch of the conflict between solitude and social existence, or between self-absorption and experience in the world. *Watch and Ward* is thus a tentative adumbration of the old Hawthorne problem of isolation and a forecast of one of James's major themes. But in this novel the conflict between the inclination to avoid life and the recognition of the need for full experience is resolved by a very comfortable (and unreal) compromise. The dilemma is solved only because the isolated preoccupation of the hero happens to be a woman and not a career in art or the workings of his own mind. More accurately, the woman and the work of art are one. Roger's ambition is nothing less than to create his own wife. So he has it both ways; through his solitary obsession he gains the means of having a full experience in life.

The artist theme will perhaps be more evident through a comparison of *Watch and Ward* and *The Portrait of a Lady*, in which the theme is fully developed. Nora is a crude forerunner of Isabel Archer, though her free choice of a husband has more pleasant results than Isabel's. As a virile man of affairs, Fenton is a Caspar Goodwood lacking wealth and integrity. Hubert remotely suggests Lord Warburton, though his urbanity is of a shallow order. Roger is a curious combination of Ralph Touchett and Gilbert Osmond. By temperament and by choice, for a time even by a grave illness, Roger is, like Ralph, detached from personal experience of his own. But he also resembles Osmond, who wishes to possess Isabel, to make her a part of his collection. In much the same way Roger wishes to mold Nora according to his preconceived idea of what a wife should be. Such parallels ignore some extreme differences between the novels, but they hint of a common theme. The main conclusion to be drawn is the absence of moral intensity in the earlier novel, particularly the absence of any suggestion of guilt in Roger. The characteristics of Goodwood and Warburton which command respect are minimized in Fenton and Hubert. We can conclude only that James has stacked the cards in favor of Roger, quite unfairly denigrating those men more active and socially able than he, and just as arbitrarily ignoring the very deficiencies in Roger that he finds significant in characters in later works.

After he is rejected by Isabel Morton, Roger decides to live as a recluse. The solemnity of his decision is ludicrous: "He would now, he declared, cast his lot with pure reason. He had tried love and faith, but they would none of him. He had made a woman a goddess, and she had made him a fool. He would henceforth care neither for woman nor man, but simply for comfort, and, if need be, for pleasure" (p. 29).

The doctrine of cynical hedonism which Roger voices to himself hardly reflects his temperament; nevertheless it serves to suggest a connection between him and Osmond, certainly a man who cares "neither for woman nor man, but simply for comfort, and if need be, for pleasure" and with one of James's least attractive centers of consciousness, the narrator of *The Sacred Fount*, the prime instance in James of a man who casts "his lot with pure reason." Tenuous as such resemblances are, they at least point to the pride implicit in Roger's chosen isolation from human society. They suggest that Roger is a vague prototype of the Jamesian egotist, the man who repudiates human involvement for the self.

Roger is not so much of the artist type as the aesthete type, a

forerunner of Osmond rather than Neil Paraday. Though he
is so unconscious as to be little more than a parody of the artistic
temperament, he wishes to control life, to give it a form that
exists only in art. He supervises the life of Nora Lambert, attempting to adjust her growth to his own ideal. "I have begun
at the beginning," he writes Isabel Morton; "it will be my own
fault if I have not a perfect wife" (p. 53).

Roger's insistence that his wife be perfect suggests two observations. First, the most important quality he wants in a wife is
that she be submissive to him—the weakest of men. The pride
which Isabel Morton injured can never again be tampered with.
The two women who temporarily distract Roger from Nora
have only one common characteristic: both submit to Roger's
will. The "lovely Teresita," whom Roger meets in Peru, is
"wholly without coquetry" (p. 56); she "smiled perpetual assent"
(p. 57). Though well-schooled in the ways of the world, Roger's
other charmer, Miss Sands, appeals to Roger because he feels
"there was . . . little to be feared from her" (p. 126). Quite evidently, Roger expects the same docility and agreeableness from
the little girl he has saved from a life of misery.

But Roger's demand for perfection may also remind us of
other James characters who have the same exalted requirement
of their wives. In *The American* Christopher Newman says he
wants for a wife "the best article in the market" (II, 49). Newman's robust good nature modifies the egotism implicit in his
grandiose ambition, but it does not conceal it. Isabel Archer's
exorbitant notion of what her husband should be leads her to
turn down a magnificent British nobleman. Less attractive
protagonists like John Marcher and Vanderbank feel they are
really too good for any woman short of perfection. Through a
crippling vanity Vanderbank rejects Nanda Brookenham and
Marcher remains blinded to the love of May Bartram. But
Roger Lawrence's insistence on perfection is not intended to be a

display of pride. Nothing suggests that James regards his marital ambitions with less than total approbation.

For the most part Roger is the gentlest of masters. But when he rebukes Nora for her affection for Fenton, his jealousy makes him seem cruel. He behaves much like Dr. Sloper towards his daughter in *Washington Square*. The comparison is apt: Dr. Sloper is a kind of frustrated artist in life; because Catherine is plain and slow-witted, he denies her affection.

Psychologically, however, Roger wants not to master life, but to combine adult experience—that of a father, a suitor, and a husband—with the security and ease he had known in childhood. His closest ties are with the persons and places of his childhood. He brings Nora to the country home in which he had grown up; he assigns the household duties to his late mother's maid. Roger almost tries to make Nora a duplicate of himself, both by attempting to obliterate the child's memory of her past and by providing her with a maximum of security and comfort.

Roger's system of educating Nora is simple: he tries to shelter her from evil and "to make her happy that she might be good" (p. 40). His control of her is largely negative, but James relies upon a metaphor to remind us of Roger's activity. He is regularly compared to a gardener fervently protecting a flower and encouraging its natural growth. But the scheme which Roger calculates for Nora turns out to be unhealthy. Quite ironically, Roger has little to do with the "blooming" of Nora. His main principle is to shelter her from the vulgar, menacing world. Though Roger diligently resists his inclination to keep the child completely to himself, he seldom lets her stray far from him. So it is with extreme reluctance that he agrees even to send her to school. But it is not Roger's protective security but a series of unplanned events that most effectively develops Nora into a perfection of womanliness. Experience in the world and not the comfort of Roger's hothouse forms Nora. Her travels in Europe immeasurably deepen her sensibilities. In Fenton and Hubert she encounters not merely worldliness, but a degree of human evil she had not suspected. In the end Nora is considerably deeper and wiser than the "perfect woman" stereotype Roger had intended to make of her.

Throughout his career James dramatized instances of men and women maturing through experience. Moral maturity comes only with a deep involvement in life. Though Nora's exposure is brief, it enables her to understand herself and the purity of Roger's affection. But James gives a rather sentimental version of the experience theme. For one thing, the exposure to evil causes no deep or lasting suffering in Nora. The knowledge she gains is ultimately ignored.

Roger himself is just as uninvolved in social experience in the end as in the beginning. Though he leaves his shell to retrieve Nora from Fenton, nothing suggests that his opinion about his way of life changes. James equips him with an unnatural vigor in his search for Nora, but significantly he assigns the active role to Nora, who forces her way out of Fenton's room while Roger seeks comfort from his brother. In effect the novel tests Roger's experiment in evading life and finds it successful. The irony of Nora's benefiting from a set of experiences that Roger tries to shield her from is merely implicit. James seems unaware that the meaning of Nora's story contradicts the meaning of Roger's story. Roger's South American journey and his encounters with Miss Sands, Teresita, Hubert, and Fenton have no more effect on him than to confirm him in his policy of evasion. Nora develops through her exposure to life, but Roger remains unchanged. James simply shows him as a good man, neither requiring nor receiving the test of experience.

James makes Roger's remoteness from life seem commendable by describing the world outside as almost unrelievedly base. There are two broad areas of experience which continually threaten to break in on Roger's private life. One is the dismal world of the poor, typified by Mr. Lambert, Fenton, Fenton's business partner, his landlady (presumably his mistress), and the nameless, abject creatures on the New York streets. The other is the upper stratum of Boston society, well-to-do, urbane, and shallow. Isabel (Morton) Keith and Hubert are triflers. Both in a sense provide debased parallels to Roger's regulation of Nora's life. Hubert tries to manipulate her, but with no sense of responsibility. Mrs. Keith also has a hand in her control, but she is a skilled marriage broker and social opportunist, who would fit Roger and Nora both into her plans. She is a shrewd pragmatist, well pleased with her comfortable widowed state.

In addition, those outside Roger's self-contained sphere are preoccupied with money, and if this preoccupation is not always sordid, it is at least vulgar. Roger's money is a concern to many people, but never legitimately. In the opening pages, even the appeal of Nora's desperate father is considered offensive. The man doesn't so much beg as threaten, so that Roger's irritation seems almost justified. After Lambert's suicide, the proprietress of the hotel begins to organize a collection for Nora as a means of getting rid of her. Fenton schemes twice for Roger's money. Money also figures importantly in the calculations of the upper-world, particularly when Mrs. Keith increases Roger's value in the marriage market after she learns the size of his bank account. Roger, on the other hand, is aloof from money, at times generous and at times prudent, but never conspicuously concerned with it. Such, James implies, is the proper attitude for rich and poor alike.

Basically, the lower-world is too vulgar for Roger and the upper-world too cynical. There is little reason to suspect that James's judgment differs. Nora, it is true, has a vague compassion for the suffering poor, particularly in her frightened walks through the New York streets. But Roger has no such feeling. His engagement with the sordid and the criminal takes a symmetrical form, but the form seems meaningless. Only in the beginning and the end does Roger become involved with the lower levels of society. In the first chapter he witnesses the ghastly tableau of Nora's standing above her father's bleeding corpse; and in the end he is forced to bargain with Fenton, who has kidnapped Nora. His later meeting with Fenton is comparable to his early meeting with Mr. Lambert. But if the novel ends where it begins—with a glimpse into the social depths—the structural pattern has little point. Nora, we might suppose, returns to the life of her childhood, recognizes its baseness, and willingly abandons it for Roger, purged of the vague longings for her own family roots that had disturbed Roger throughout. But Roger himself gains nothing from his two engagements with the vulgar and squalid—nothing except possibly the reassurance that he should never again have anything to do with the poor. Thus in the final chapters everything is made to support Roger's preference for solitude; the public life is not only unredeemable, but any involvement in it is a threat to happiness and integrity.

As Nora finally develops, she is tainted neither by the vulgarity of her father and cousin, nor by the shallowness of Hubert and Mrs. Keith. Quite miraculously, her inner character has perfectly emerged, profiting from contact with the world, but not in the least injured by it. And though Roger's plan has had little influence on the formation of this ideal wife, we are supposedly to regard her perfection as an indication of the rightness of his design for her. After all, she finds him the most desirable of men.

Ultimately the conclusion of the novel both cheapens and falsifies the inchoate yet potentially rich thematic materials beneath the surface. By contriving a conventional happy ending, James either evades the problems which the novel raises, or provides simple solutions to them. In order to represent Roger to advantage, James must overlook what he has clearly shown— that Roger is deficient in masculinity and wit, and that Nora profits from experience in the world. The interesting conflict between the world and the self is simply jettisoned, left submerged and unresolved by the author's apparent involvement with the hero and his subservience to a bad convention. The very weaknesses of *Watch and Ward* make it all the more remarkable that within a few years James would not only have broken off from such a convention to establish his own (or, at least, to work with more promising ones), but would have gained a sure critical understanding of his own feelings. Most important, it is remarkable that James would shortly have gained the ability to fuse a preconceived design with the emergent complexities of a subject.

IV · "MADAME DE MAUVES"

On the surface, James's international fiction of the 1870's does little more than straightforwardly contrast characters of different national origins. Though such a contrast dominates these works, James is concerned with more than national differences; nor are his characters only illustrative. James is interested not only in the relationship between America and Europe, but also in the relationship between individuals and their cultural backgrounds. Though most of the minor characters in the early works are "fixed"—that is, fully and unchangeably formed by their native environments—the major characters generally make some effort to understand and evaluate their formative influences and even to free themselves from them. Within the pattern, there are a number of variations. A significant body of characters—such as Roderick Hudson, Frederick Winterbourne, and Gilbert Osmond —deviate too extremely from their native American influences and lose stability and moral judgment. There are other characters, however, for whom national habits are narrowing and inhibiting. Some of these come to understand and rise above the restrictions of their cultures. Most often the circumstance which forces them to seek some degree of independence of mind is their falling in love with foreigners. One or both of the partners must go beyond the limited viewpoint of his own code for a satisfying marriage to be possible. Such American characteristics as the puritan conscience and provincial vulgarity come into conflict with such European characteristics as aristocratic snobbishness and sexual indulgence. The stories are generally read only as dramatizations of such conflicts, but most often—especially in the *nouvelles* and unmistakably in the novels—James is additionally concerned with the conflicts within the protagonists, who find that what they have always believed is at odds with the insights gained from personal experience.

"Madame de Mauves," published in 1874, well illustrates James's early intentions in the international theme, as well as the skill with which he elaborates the theme. The story seems intended to be a portrait of Euphemia Cleve, a young American girl whose sentimental impressions of the French aristocracy, derived from reading "Ultramontane works of fiction" (XIII, 225) in the Paris convent where she spent her girlhood, induce her to marry an impoverished nobleman, Count Richard de Mauves. Because Euphemia is wealthy, neither the Count nor his family raises objections to her inferior social position. But she has a rigid conscience; she is intolerant of the society of her husband, which she considers immoral and frivolous. Therefore M. de Mauves abandons her to his ancestral home in Saint-Germain while he spends most of his time in nearby Paris, enjoying himself with his friends and his mistresses. The story focuses upon Euphemia's relationship with Bernard Longmore, an American tourist who is successively curious about her, sympathetic with her, and in love with her. The crisis occurs when the Count's sister, Madame Clairin, suggests to Longmore that

he and Madame de Mauves become lovers—as a way of benefit-
ing from the ugly situation and, at the same time, of giving the
Count an excuse for his infidelity. Though at first appalled,
Longmore is tempted to take Madame Clairin's advice, but
Euphemia remains adamant and asks Longmore to leave.
Two years later, when he is back in America, Longmore learns
that the Count has repented of his loose ways and has begged
his wife to forgive him. But Euphemia has refused him, and the
Count, disgusted with his mistresses and unacceptable to his wife,
has put a bullet through his head.

The abrupt and rather improbable ending considerably lessens
the effectiveness of the story, but unless "Madame de Mauves" is
regarded as something more than a conventional contrasting of
American innocence and European experience, the ending must
either be irrelevant or completely perplexing. The ambiguity is
obvious in the conclusion, but it is subtly present throughout the
entire story—and not merely in our attitude toward Madame de
Mauves, but in our attitude toward nearly all the characters.
The story has a complex yet unobtrusive design, the total effect
of which is to reveal a rather intricate pattern in the character
relationships. The technique might be called structural irony.
The similarities rather than the differences between certain of the
Americans and certain of the French are revealed, so that we
come to revise our earliest judgment of the situation. In effect,
the reader is at first persuaded to evaluate human beings in terms
of national characteristics and later to see the shortsightedness of
such a criterion.

In a prefatorial remark on "the supposed 'international' conflict of manners," James notes that simple contrast between "the
fruits of a constituted order" (Europeans) and "the fruits of no
order at all" (Americans) is not a suitable subject. The opposed
sides have too little in common. "We may strike lights by opposing order to order, one sort to another sort; for in that case
we get correspondences and equivalents that make differences

mean something; we get the interest and the tension of disparity where a certain parity may have been in question . . . where the dramatic encounter is but the poor concussion of positives on one side with negatives on the other, we get little beyond a consideration of the differences between fishes and fowls" (*P*, p. 132). The remark does more, I believe, than support my contention that the theme of "Madame de Mauves" has to do not with the significance but with the insignificance of national differences. It suggests also that the real contrasts in the tale are not those emphasized by certain characters, but are rather those created by the structure. The irony derives from the wide separation between the apparently significant character arrangements and the truly significant ones.[1]

The early portions of the story foster most of these false—at best superficial—attitudes. Longmore's devotion to Madame de Mauves strongly influences our attitude toward the events. We accept implicitly his feeling that the American girl has been betrayed and exploited by the immoral and opportunist French family. To Longmore, Euphemia is "a sweet American girl who marries an unholy foreigner" (XIII, 220). His compatriot, Mrs. Draper, views the situation as a very simple case: "It's the miserable story of an American girl born neither to submit basely nor to rebel crookedly marrying a shining sinful Frenchman who believes a woman must do one or the other of those things" (XIII, 222); "As for M. de Mauves he's a shallow Frenchman to his fingers' ends. . ." (XIII, 269). To the Americans, Euphemia's

1. Elsewhere in this study I indicate some other instances of the method. In *The Wings of the Dove*, James devotes considerable effort to dramatize the parallels between Kate and Milly, though we are first impressed by their economic and national differences. In *The Golden Bowl*, the basic structure emphasizes the similarities between the Prince-Charlotte relation and the Adam-Maggie relation. In this novel the ethical distinction between adulterous lovers, on the one hand, and a father and daughter, on the other, carries about the same weight as the distinction between Americans and Europeans in "Madame de Mauves"—which is very little weight indeed, though the characters may think quite otherwise.

only fault is her susceptibility to the illusion which made her accept M. de Mauves's proposal: "She was romantic and perverse —she thought the world she had been brought up in too vulgar or at least too prosaic" (XIII, 222).

Such judgments are not wrong, but incomplete. The error of Longmore and Mrs. Draper consists in assuming that the codes of behavior they describe are inflexible and insurmountable. But since we are first introduced to Euphemia and her husband through the opinions of these Americans, we are conditioned to make a simple black and white evaluation of the pair. In addition, in the first half of the story, all the characters are completely absorbed in their national attitudes. Their behavior, their way of thinking, and their judgments of others are predictably typical of their native cultures. Later, however, the three main characters encounter problems requiring independent judgments; they are made to see the possibility of acting contrary to their deeply rooted beliefs. Longmore, Euphemia, and the Count have conflicts within themselves which make us less inclined to accept them as undeviating stereotypes. It turns out that Madame de Mauves is unable to rise above her restricting New England conscience, but Longmore and M. de Mauves both reach an awareness beyond the limits of their national codes. Contrast thus rules the story, but it is of a very different order from what we were led to expect. And it is a contrast that follows upon the demonstration of underlying similarities among the characters.

The story is not so much a conflict between America and Europe, as embodied in Euphemia and M. de Mauves, as it is a conflict between what James calls the imagination—a full and growing responsiveness to experience—and deeply ingrained habit. Exposed to alien habits of mind, the three central characters not only encounter different points of view but are led to re-examine their own.

Both Americans and French are guided by strong cultural

convictions, and they articulate them frequently; they refer to them as principles and exalted ideals, not just as customs or habits. Madame de Mauves submits to her misery out of "a lurking principle of sacrifice" (XIII, 299). Her renunciation of personal happiness is no mere instinctive response, but a highly conscious and formalized decision. Madame Clairin, the major spokesman for the French view, also idealizes her tradition. In her view a woman in Madame de Mauves's position should hide her misery and conduct herself discreetly. She eulogizes the long line of betrayed de Mauves wives:

Not one of them ever had the bad taste to be jealous, and yet not one in a dozen ever consented to an indiscretion—allowed herself, I mean, to be talked about. *Voilà comme elles ont su s'arranger.* How they did it—go and look at the dusky faded canvases and pastels and ask. They were dear brave women of wit. When they had a headache they put on a little rouge and came to supper as usual, and when they had a heart-ache they touched up that quarter with just such another brush. These are great traditions and charming precedents, I hold, and it doesn't seem to me fair that a little American bourgeoise should come in and pretend to alter them. . . . She should fall into line, she should keep up the tone (XIII, 289).

Curiously both codes are forms of stoicism. The American requires that happiness be suppressed for the sake of morality, and the French requires that sorrow be concealed for the sake of propriety. To the French, Madame de Mauves is just as selfish and abominable as she believes her husband to be.

Both Madame de Mauves and Madame Clairin are determinists, not only convinced of the inexorability and absoluteness of their ruling passions, but equally insistent that others adopt them. Madame Clairin tells Longmore that "we are as history has made us" (XIII, 290), and that the Count "wouldn't be my brother if he weren't" (XIII, 292) involved with another woman. Madame de Mauves, on the other hand, tells Longmore that she has "nothing on earth but a conscience" (XIII, 281), which she must obey without question. "Endless constancy was all her law . . ." (XIII, 318), Longmore concludes, and when she urges that he submit to her principle, he thinks, "He must assent to destiny" (XIII, 318). Madame de Mauves and Madame Clairin are alike assured that they are guided by irresistible forces, either by history or by the absolute law of conscience. Each imposes on experience a single, narrow rule. Accordingly, both are unbending and intransigent. They are "cold" women, for just as Madame Clairin gives Longmore "a moral chill" (XIII, 250), Madame de Mauves in the end is "ice" (XIII, 331). Both scorn sentiment, Madame Clairin because she prefers to act "scientifically" (XIII, 291) and Madame de Mauves because she considers "it would be a weary world" if people heeded Longmore's belief that "the one thing for one's mind to be fair to is the thing one *feels*" (XIII, 311).

Another similarity between the two women is that both drive their husbands to suicide. In a brief flashback we learn that Madame Clairin's husband, like Madame de Mauves, was a person unable to adapt himself to the ways of the gentry. Also like Madame de Mauves, he attracted the de Mauves family solely because of his money, for he was a socially undistinguished wholesale druggist. He adopted the aristocratic vice of gambling, lost heavily, and, terrified of his wife's anger, blew his brains out. His suicide is an obvious and rather sardonic parallel to that of Richard de Mauves, who likewise fails to adapt himself to an alien culture. The Count cannot win the affection of an American wife, and M. Clairin fails at learning how to be an aristocrat. In each case it is the absoluteness of the code—the French aristocratic and the New England puritan—which prevents the outsider from crossing his class lines. Clearly M. Clairin is a fatuous and ignoble illustration of the difficulty of changing social systems, but his effort, his failure, and the resistance of his wife parallel the experience of the Count.

Though the beliefs of Madame Clairin and Madame de

Mauves are in complete opposition, the two women act in much the same way. A similar resemblance underlies the behavior of the American Longmore and the French M. de Mauves, also very different on the surface. Unlike Euphemia and Madame Clairin, these men have changes of mind; each comes to revise his long-maintained principles. But neither simply exchanges his own national point of view for that of the other. Through his own experience each acquires a respect for a differing way of life. Each sees his situation in itself, without either an American or a European interpretation. It is for this reason that James inserts the otherwise irrelevant interlude in which Longmore observes a French artist and his mistress in the forest. The lovers may strike us as stereotypically French, but from them Longmore gains a vision of a way of life utterly free from inhibitions, restricted neither by American ethics nor by European class traditions. This is a "vision of unattainable bliss" (XIII, 305) for the "Puritanic soul" (XIII, 250) of Longmore; it helps convert him, not to an acceptance of Madame Clairin's cynical and immoral strategy, but to an admission of his passion for Madame de Mauves.

Richard de Mauves's conversion is, like Longmore's, thwarted by the resistance of Euphemia. It is the major irony of the story that the American and the Frenchman (on the surface the hero and the villain) come close to adopting each other's attitudes toward love, and that the pure and admirable Euphemia stands in the way of either's gaining happiness. M. de Mauves transcends his ancestral ideas to perceive a different kind of beauty and to feel a different kind of love. At the news of Longmore's decision to return to America, he loses all interest in his mistress and his routine pleasures. On the final page we learn that "he fell madly in love with [his wife]. . . . He was the proudest man in France, but he had begged her on his knees to be re-admitted to favour" (XIII, 331).

James himself takes no sides in the story; his position is

neither narrowly American nor narrowly French. He stands above the action, exposing it in its full irony and complexity.[2] If there is a moral conclusion to be drawn it is that rigid and abstract principles—be they based on ethical scruples or social propriety—are inadequate guides to conduct. In Lionel Trilling's phrase, the story is "a quest for reality."[3] A set of cultural illusions is challenged by concrete experience. The first illusion to be shattered is Euphemia's conception of the French aristocracy. But Euphemia's own constancy upsets her husband's belief that marriage is not to be taken too seriously. Finally Longmore begins to doubt that renunciation is a sublime virtue, as Euphemia believes it to be.

The secondary characters are symmetrically arranged to illuminate not only Madame de Mauves but also each other. The two men, Longmore and the Count, balance each other as rivals for Euphemia's affection, and also as converts to different points of view. They are flexible characters, while the two peripheral women—Madame Clairin and Euphemia's mother— are completely inflexible. The two women hold different opinions, but they are bound by them absolutely. They are rigidly national, so frozen in their types as to be caricatures of provinciality and social pretense. Mrs. Cleve, it is true, admires Europe, but she makes a false adjustment to foreign experience. Like many of James's American women, she repudiates a stereo-

2. Most recent critics agree that James is not altogether sympathetic with Euphemia. For example, see Philip Rahv, *The Great Short Novels of Henry James* (New York, 1944), pp. 3-5; Marius Bewley, "Henry James and 'Life,'" *Hudson Review*, XI (Summer, 1958), 167-74; and Christof Wegelin, *The Image of Europe in Henry James* (Dallas, 1958), pp. 43-45. For the view that Euphemia is completely innocent and admirable, see John O. McCormick, "'The Rough and Lurid Vision': Henry James, Graham Greene, and the International Theme," *Jahrbuch für Amerikastudien* (1958), pp. 158-69; and Benjamin C. Rountree, "James's *Madame de Mauves* and Madame de La Fayette's *Princesse de Clèves*," *Studies in Short Fiction*, I (Summer, 1964), 264-71.

3. "Manners, Morals, and the Novel," *The Liberal Imagination* (New York, 1950), p. 212.

type of America for a stereotype of Europe. Like Madame Clairin, she reduces ethical and personal values to the level of social convenience.

Both women sacrifice others to their narrow codes. Madame Clairin, who is Euphemia's classmate at the convent, maneuvers both Euphemia and the Count into the marriage. She is not only the most forceful apologist of the family, but she provides its strategy and its energy as well. Richard de Mauves is an unconscious and even gentle embodiment of the system. His infidelity is virtually urged upon him as a duty. In his docility he is somewhat like the Prince Casamassima in *Roderick Hudson*, and like the Prince he wears his ancestry and his good manners gracefully, but they are so pronounced in him that he seems to have no character at all. But James hints that the double obligation of his class—his sensuality and his formality—has corrupted a finer nature. Removed from such a tradition he would be a better man:

What his original faith had been he could hardly have told you, for as he came back to his childhood's home to mend his fortunes by pretending to fall in love he was a thoroughly perverse creature and overlaid with more corruptions than a summer day's questioning of his conscience would have put to flight. Ten years' pursuit of pleasure, which a bureau full of unpaid bills was all he had to show for, had pretty well stifled the natural lad whose violent will and generous temper might have been shaped by a different pressure to some such showing as would have justified a romantic faith. So should he have exhaled the natural fragrance of a late-blooming flower of hereditary honour. His violence indeed had been subdued and he had learned to be irreproachably polite; but he had lost the fineness of his generosity, and his politeness, which in the long run society paid for, was hardly more than a form of luxurious egotism. . . (XIII, 234-35).

The Count is—at least symbolically—a victim of his sister's aggressive adherence to the old family code. His wife is just as much a victim of her mother's social ambitions. If Madame Clairin arranges Euphemia's marriage, Mrs. Cleve condones it. Mrs. Cleve is the ultimate source of Euphemia's childish illusions about the aristocracy, for she abandons Euphemia to the convent, where the child's inexperience and isolation condition her to romantic fantasies. One suspects also that Euphemia's scorn for America—which she eventually regrets—has been derived from her mother, who spends most of her time traveling about Europe and deriding the vulgarity and barrenness of her homeland. In addition, Mrs. Cleve permits the marriage even though she predicts her daughter will be miserable. She is finally influenced solely by matters of propriety. At first she tries to dissuade her daughter, not so much because she foresees she would be unhappy but because the manner of the proposal is improper—informally American rather than formally European. But the Count's fine manners and his submission to her demand that he come to America to make his plea (a French nobleman reduced to humble supplication in New York) finally persuade Mrs. Cleve to allow the marriage. Thus James embodies the most oppressive characteristics of America and Europe in the two women who supervise the marriage.

M. de Mauves's dual character—his private identity and the class compulsions which overlie it—is not fully exposed until the end of the story when he makes an independent judgment. But throughout Euphemia is presented as a fine and generous nature oppressed by ethical restriction. She becomes increasingly unnatural; Longmore considers her perverse. We should not read the story as a condemnation of all inhibitions to sexual experience, but as the appraisal of an extreme case of moral rigidity suppressing natural emotion—in this instance the emotions of pain and of love. Euphemia's conscience stifles her consciousness. Isabel Archer, in a situation similar to Euphemia's, benefits from her suffering. Her emotions deepen; her consciousness widens. Unlike Madame de Mauves, she illustrates James's insistent belief in the importance of the mind's fully responding to experience. In a well-known letter to Grace Norton, James wrote: "Consciousness is an illimitable power, and though at times it may seem to be all consciousness of misery, yet in the way it propagates itself from wave to wave, so that we never cease to feel, and though at moments we appear to, try to, pray to, there is something that holds one in one's place, makes it a stand-point in the universe which it is probably good not to for-sake. . . ."[4]

Since her illusions of childhood have been shattered, Madame de Mauves wills to believe that "life itself is an illusion" (XIII, 278). She remains physically and emotionally a recluse; she evades reality. "I hate tragedy . . . ," she tells Longmore; "I'm a dreadful coward about having to suffer or to bleed. I've always tried to believe that—without base concessions—such extremities may always somehow be dodged or indefinitely postponed. I should be willing to buy myself off, from having ever to be *overwhelmed*, by giving up—well, any amusement you like" (XIII, 257).[5] Renunciation is a psychological support as well as a moral principle, just as artificial a barrier against experience as the aristocratic code of manners.

As is typical in James, the narrative is a journey to under-standing; we are totally absorbed in Longmore's developing recognition of the true character of Madame de Mauves. His physical movement—back and forth between Paris and Saint-Germain—parallels his intellectual movement; he gets ever closer to her, but her extreme reserve prevents him from fully under-standing her. Longmore is always uncertain about Euphemia. He sees in her an inner beauty, but the beauty is concealed. He continually tries to identify the source of her attractiveness. At

4. *The Letters of Henry James*, selected and edited by Percy Lubbock (New York, 1920), I, 100.

5. This sentiment looks forward to Isabel Archer's confession to Ralph Touchett that ". . . I don't wish to touch the cup of experience. It's a poisoned drink" (III, 213).

times it seems that her suffering heightens her beauty: "He began to regard his hostess as a figure haunted by a shadow which was somehow her intenser and more authentic self. This lurking duality in her put on for him an extraordinary charm" (XIII, 246). The self behind the stoic exterior draws Longmore on: "I've admired your reserve," he tells her, "your courage, your studied gaiety. But I've felt the existence of something beneath them that was more *you*—more you as I wished to know you—than they were; some trouble in you that I've permitted myself to hate and resent" (XIII, 259). Madame de Mauves resists the emotion of sorrow and eventually becomes numb—or hollow. It is not a question of scruples withholding her from adultery, but of fears withholding her from the experience of pain. The inner self which attracts Longmore becomes increasingly obscured until in the end Madame de Mauves is only a hard, unforgiving surface. We witness the formation of the puritan personality.

Longmore finds it unnatural and inhuman that Madame de Mauves never expresses her pain, her anger, or her jealousy. We learn indirectly that when she discovers tangible evidence of her husband's infidelity, she has a scene with him. At all other times, she evades the facts of her own misery and her husband's long absences. Her emotionlessness, her iron stoicism, and her refusal to respond to Longmore's compassion make her an enigma to him. Though in the beginning she appears delicate and sensitive, he eventually wonders whether she may be more self-righteous than good, more perverse than generous: "She struck him as having long resisted the force of cruel evidence, and, as though succumbing to it at last, having denied herself on simple grounds of generosity the right to complain. Her faith might have perished, but the sense of her own old deep perversity remained" (XIII, 257). "You're killing yourself with stoicism" (XIII, 277), Longmore tells her, when she continues to resist his sympathy. Hurt once by an illusion, Madame de Mauves has determined to believe in nothing. She especially distrusts her feelings; she shields herself from affection for Longmore, from her own pain, and in the end from the remorse of her husband.

Longmore, as an American in Europe, is engaged in the same kind of moral struggle as Madame de Mauves. He too mistrusts his own feelings, and in such a way that he is nearly a parody of Madame de Mauves and the New England conscience in general. He is excessively proper and delicate, and fitfully presented in a satiric light. When he wonders if he may be in love with Madame de Mauves (a married woman!), he is comically fastidious, embarrassed by his own thoughts. After deliberating whether to leave Paris for a museum tour of the Lowlands or to return to Madame de Mauves, he hesitantly examines his motives: "This inward ache was more than he had bargained for, and as he looked at the shopwindows he wondered if it represented a 'passion.' He had never been fond of the word and had grown up with much distrust of what it stood for. He had hoped that when he should fall 'really' in love he should do it with an excellent conscience, with plenty of confidence and joy, doubtless, but no strange soreness, no pangs nor regrets" (XIII, 270-71).

In contrast to Madame de Mauves, who becomes increasingly less tolerant of her (or anybody's) feelings, Longmore sets aside the abstract considerations of propriety and convention to admit of his zeal for Madame de Mauves. His first conscious decision is to abandon plans for his Belgian tour and return to Saint-Germain: "Nothing in his tranquil past had given such a zest to consciousness as this happy sense of choosing to go straight back to Saint-Germain. How to justify his return, how to explain his ardour, troubled him little" (XIII, 273-74). As Longmore opens his mind to the new experience (at first of pleasure, then of pain), Madame de Mauves determines to seal herself off from all experience.

Like M. de Mauves and Longmore, Euphemia has the capacity to overcome her cultural inhibitions. But she does not remain a free spirit; like her mother and Madame Clairin, she becomes hardened. These two pairs of secondary characters—the morally fixed and the morally supple—represent the two ways of life available to Euphemia. She can change or remain static; she can live or die.

Two other characters also help define the theme. Mrs. Draper serves mainly to introduce Longmore to Madame de Mauves; then she becomes his confidante. She is another rigid character; she judges the Europeans according to conventional biases.[6] The old Madame de Mauves, Richard's grandmother, has a different kind of significance in the general conflict between personal judgment and cultural predisposition. Like some other old European women in James's early fiction—particularly Madame Grandoni in *Roderick Hudson* and the Countess Gemini in *The Portrait of a Lady*—she is wise, skeptical, and ineffectual. From the beginning she sees that Euphemia's marriage will be an agony for her. At first her advice to Euphemia is like Madame Clairin's. Euphemia should adapt herself to the French way and reconcile herself either to suffering or to a total abandonment of morals: "If you don't take life as a fifty years' mass the only way to take it's as a game of skill" (XIII, 230). But the old woman, vaguely forecasting her son's reversal, has a change of heart.

6. It is Mrs. Draper who in the final scene tells Longmore of M. de Mauves's suicide. Mrs. Draper has heard of it from "a clever young Frenchman" (XIII, 330), who in turn has heard of it from Madame Clairin. Mrs. Draper doubts the interpretation put on the suicide by the Frenchman; she questions the authority of both the Frenchman and Madame Clairin. But her disbelief mainly shows the limitations of her national attitude. Since we have already seen evidences of Mrs. Draper's American bias, we tend to believe the French version, though of course we have no way of being certain. If James intends us to question the stated motives of M. de Mauves, as reported by Madame Clairin and the anonymous Frenchman (a position maintained by Charles Kaplan, "James' 'Madame de Mauves,'" *The Explicator* [February, 1961], Item 32), the story ends in epistemological chaos and we are left with no way of knowing what has happened. The reason for such an indirect account of the suicide is probably narrative economy.

Because she admires Euphemia's innocence, she is unwilling to see her sacrificed for the sake of the family fortunes. She tries to interfere in the marriage; but it is a meaningless, even irrelevant, interference. Madame Clairin writes a letter to the Count, telling him to come to see Euphemia; the grandmother appends a note to the letter: "If you've a particle of conscience you'll not come and disturb the repose of an angel of innocence" (XIII, 231-32). But as the Count later tells the old woman, "If you meant what you said . . . it would have been simpler not to have sent the letter" (XIII, 232). After the marriage is arranged, old Madame de Mauves can only advise Euphemia. But it is sound advice—perhaps the key to how Euphemia should have taken to her situation: "Whatever befalls you, promise me this: to be, to remain, your own sincere little self only, charming in your own serious little way" (XII, 239). The old woman has the obvious function of preventing the reader from making a general condemnation of the French. She also illustrates a kind of compromise between the private judgment and tradition.

Like the systematic arrangement of characters, the setting also is a means of defining and showing relationships among characters. There are three general locations in the story; all are described in the opening sentences: "The view from the terrace at Saint-Germain-en-Laye is immense and famous. Paris lies spread before you in dusky vastness, domed and fortified, glittering here and there through her light vapours and girdled with her silver Seine. Behind you is a park of stately symmetry, and behind that a forest where you may lounge through turfy avenues and light-chequered glades and quite forget that you are within half an hour of the boulevards" (XIII, 215). The tripartite scene—Paris, the formal park, and the forest—comes to symbolize the three possibilities of experience dealt with in the story: a civilized sensuality, an oppressive social formality, and a natural innocence. Paris is depicted in its conventional aspect as a capital of ordered and perfected pleasure. In spite of his puritan background, Longmore succumbs to its charm, though he feels "this is no world for you unless you have your pockets lined and your delicacies perverted" (XIII, 320). What we see of the Count's life in Paris is neither sordid nor vulgar. He needs sacrifice none of his grace or his dignity. The glimpse Longmore has of M. de Mauves's mistress in a Paris restaurant shows her to be "evidently very happy, and her happiness gave her an air of innocence" (XIII, 272); Longmore, indeed, "couldn't help admiring her expression of basking contentment" (XIII, 272). Paris is alive and gay; Saint-Germain is dead and morbid. The ancestral home and stately formal garden effectively symbolize the sterile formality of the old world. Euphemia is a prisoner of the place: "She lived in an old-fashioned pavilion, between a high-walled court and an excessively artificial garden, beyond whose enclosure you saw a long line of tree-tops" (XIII, 244).

In Paris and Saint-Germain, James symbolizes two different (yet inseparable) aspects of French culture: its high skill at pleasure and its decayed and corrupting traditionalism. In *The American* and *The Europeans* he makes the same general division. Valentin de Bellegarde and Felix Young, like Paris in "Madame de Mauves," signify the highly cultivated zest for life of the French, while Urbain de Bellegarde and the Baroness Eugenia, like Saint-Germain, signify the rigid social order. Both Paris and Saint-Germain oppress Euphemia: her conscience cannot endure the Count's sensuality, and her natural emotions are suppressed by the rigid code of manners of the family. But the walled-in formal garden—as well as the pervasive atmosphere of twilight gloom—has a double meaning; though its main function is to represent the restrictiveness of the traditional order, it also symbolizes Euphemia's own inhibitions, the smothering of her spirit by a morbid conscience. Thus at one point she tells Longmore, "France is out there beyond the garden, France is in the town and the forest; but here, close about me, in my room and

. . . in my mind, it's a nameless, and doubtless not at all remarkable, little country of my own" (XIII, 248).

Distinct from both Paris and Saint-Germain is the intervening forest. For both Longmore and Euphemia, it signifies freedom—from the restraints of conscience as well as those of social convention. The young artist and his mistress whom Longmore meets in the woodland are not so much symbols of an ideal life as symbols of a lost innocence. The lovers are totally unconscious and spontaneous; they exist outside all moral and social codes. Since the story so complexly deals with the injurious effects of civilized attitudes, this young couple, who are so untouched by civilization, have an obvious and important significance. But their function is not so much to represent "the positive values James wishes to give us," as Marius Bewley argues,[7] as it is to expose by contrast the almost necessary sickness and perversion of both the American and the French ways of life. To represent the inadequacies of civilization is not necessarily to advocate primitivism.

In its total effect, "Madame de Mauves" is a remarkably complex and carefully organized work of fiction. The relationships among the characters, the narrative development, and the setting work together to explore the delicate relationship between class and character, between cultural persuasion and private perception.

7. "Henry James and 'Life,'" p. 173.

V · THE EUROPEANS

Any analysis of the structure of *The Europeans* should begin with the observation that it is essentially a comic novel. For one thing, it owes much to the well-made dramatic comedies of such nineteenth-century playwrights as Dumas *fils*, Augier, and Sardou, and also to the narrative romances of Feuillet and Cherbuliez.[1] Not only do the wit, the grace, and the situation of *The Europeans* suggest such works, but also the rigid construction, the careful balancing and juxtaposition of character types, and the rigorously logical progression of events (rendered scenically) to an inevitable conclusion. Also James draws freely upon much older comic patterns, such as the conversion of a traditional society by a group of young intruders to a fresher view of life

1. See Oscar Cargill, *The Novels of Henry James* (New York, 1961), pp. 67-68. James's admiration for the French dramatists of the 1870's is amply reflected in his essays on the Parisian stage collected in *The Scenic Art*, ed. Allan Wade (New York, 1957). Leon Edel, *The Complete Plays of Henry James* (Philadelphia, 1949), discusses the general influence of the well-made play on James's novels (pp. 34-40).

and the triumph of the young lovers over the objections of their obtuse and narrow-minded elders.[2] In addition, *The Europeans* uses such venerable devices as the comic intrigue and the complicated and neat rounding-off. The atmosphere is pastoral, and the spirit is predominantly gay.

The clash of opposing social groups provides the central comic situation, and since the clash is for the most part resolved harmoniously, the prevailing view of life in the novel is comic; that is, faults exist to be laughed at, and errors exist to be corrected. In *The Europeans*, James gets closer to a purely comic vision of the international conflict than in any other novel, but it is a mistake to force the work into an exclusively comic pattern. Finally the novel is *sui generis* in its design. It has a conventional comic foundation, but the total effect is something different. James's conception of structure in this novel is organic, so that while he uses many of the usual motifs and compositional devices of comedy, he rejects those demands of a mechanical form that either misrepresent or have no bearing on the idea he wishes to develop.

The New England setting is of first importance in the comic mood of *The Europeans*. Though James frequently uses Europe for comic and satiric purposes—as when he exposes the provincialism of Henrietta Stackpole against the background of St. Peter's Cathedral—he never makes it the setting of a predominantly comic story. Even in the stories in which James invests Europe with the picturesque coloration of travel literature, he is unwilling to isolate the beauty of the past from the evil he usually associates with the past. But America in *The Europeans* is mainly a pastoral scene—a Forest of Arden or "green world" suggesting the Golden Age not only to Felix Young, but also to the reader. Here is a world in which evil can exist only as

2. Here and elsewhere in this chapter I am indebted to the analysis of comic modes in Northrop Frye, *Anatomy of Criticism* (Princeton, 1957), pp. 43-52, 163-86.

something temporarily disagreeable. If the pastoral scene makes the gloom of the Americans additionally quaint and groundless (they are seen as Calvinists in Eden), it also provides an atmosphere in which young lovers can achieve bliss and in which innocence can never be sullied. The setting also colors our estimation of the Europeans; it prevents us from associating them with any Old World corruption. The casual, semi-rural Arcadia that James wishes us to accept as a Boston suburb of the 1840's[3] is in every way congenial to a humorous treatment of the international theme.

The comedy of *The Europeans* blends gentle, urbane satire of the puritan temperament with a modulated evocation of the charms of innocence. The relaxed, mildly ironic tone lends an easy grace to the novel. The tone itself is a perfect vehicle—perhaps the principal reason for the excellence of the book. It is detached, yet genial, sympathetic yet neither serious nor sentimental, and it falls well short of either frivolity or cynicism. The narrative approach is old-fashioned, recalling Thackeray and Trollope rather than forecasting the later James. Throughout we hear the voice of the author gracefully and even ceremoniously telling his story and commenting on his characters. This voice is exceedingly tolerant, and yet it is witty at the expense of the characters; it gives a steady and barely perceptible control over our own judgment of the action, counseling us to refrain from both harsh judgments and suspicions that the story is merely trivial.

The experience which James renders in *The Europeans* is rather graver and less purely amusing than we generally expect in comedy, and yet not grave enough to be something else—such as tragedy, melodrama, or even romance. James deliberately

3. It seems probable that James intentionally made the New England scene considerably less urban and cosmopolitan than it actually was. In misrepresenting Boston of the 1840's, James aroused the civic loyalties of Thomas Wentworth Higginson, who reviewed *The Europeans* unfavorably in the *Literary World*, X (November 22, 1879), 383-84. The anachronisms are discussed by Cargill, pp. 62-63, 69.

mutes the moral issues that he lingers over in other novels. If the tone is slightly unsteady, the reason is James's reluctance to falsify certain deeper realities that the situation seems to bring forth. For example, Gertrude Wentworth occasionally over-reaches the simple role that James assigns her; she is hard-hearted and callous of others' feelings. This is a quality James often reveals in the American heroine,[4] but it is out of place in the translucent scheme of *The Europeans*. The novel softens and almost conceals the suggestion of unresolvable difficulties, but it does not omit them. The rigid structure and essential artificiality of classical comedy, the leisurely flow of the prose, and the unhurried lives of the characters make *The Europeans* a nearly perfect comic performance, but the novel remains something both more and less than comic. Even the neat resolution of the plots in the final half-dozen pages—in which four marriages are recorded, with Shakespearean finality and ceremony—does not disguise the special quality of the experience of the novel.

As in most comedy, James's principal technique is to represent his characters as undeviating simplifications. *The Europeans* is thus roughly an allegory, with each of the major characters representing a large aspect of the culture which has produced him. Yet a sense of complexity is achieved through James's characteristic technique of implying contrasts among characters and events. With the possible exception of Robert Acton, no single character is very complicated, but we can understand their significances only by perceiving how James has dramatically related each to each. For instance, Felix Young is an extremely simplified creation—in the mold of the gay young man of the well-made play—but to estimate his character we must consider his relation to the characters who frame him—not merely to his obvious foils, Mr. Brand and Mr. Wentworth, but also to Gertrude and to Eugenia. The structure follows from a

4. See R. P. Blackmur, "Introduction," *Washington Square* and *The Europeans* (New York, 1959), pp. 5-12.

revelation of complex inter-relationships among simple characters, all latent within the obvious and basic contrast between
Europe and America.

Superficially it would seem that the Europeans—Felix and
Eugenia—are to be admired, and the Americans—the Wentworths, the Actons, and Mr. Brand—are to be pitied. Freedom is
preferable to oppression, a positive view to a negative one, culture to barbarism, intelligence to irrationality, happiness to
gloom, and art to a distrust of art. Read solely in such terms,
the novel shows the gradual conversion of Gertrude and the final
resistance of Robert Acton to the European temperament, and as
a flat background to this central action, the utter rigidity of all
the other Americans. The mechanics of character selection and
the logical movement of the plot are obvious.

Yet it is a distortion of the experience of the book to suggest
where our sympathies should lie or to demonstrate which way of
life "wins." The Europeans have a larger role than to expose the
limitations of the Americans. Critics do not widely disagree in
their assessments of the New Englanders, but there are extreme
differences of opinion as to how Felix and his sister are to be
regarded. Felix is usually accepted as a thoroughly congenial
embodiment of European *joie de vivre*, but Eugenia has been
judged both a selfish schemer for wealth and position[5] and a
charming, graceful woman whose faults are essentially minor.[6]

5. Notably by Edward Sackville-West, "Introduction," *The Europeans*
(London, 1952), p. viii; Joseph McG. Bottkal, "Introduction," *The Aspern
Papers* and *The Europeans* (Norfolk, Conn., 1950), p. xix; and Osborn
Andreas, *Henry James and the Expanding Horizon* (Seattle, 1948), p. 45.

6. For example, by Rebecca West, *Henry James* (New York, 1916), p.
42. Richard Poirier identifies the viewpoint of the Baroness with that of
James in *The Comic Sense of Henry James* (New York, 1960), pp. 109,
and devotes most of his essay on the novel to a demonstration of the
admirableness of Eugenia. Peter Buitenhuis, "Comic Pastoral: Henry
James's *The Europeans*," *University of Toronto Quarterly*, XIII (January,
1962), 152-63, judges that James "meant to show [Eugenia] as not only
charming, when she wanted to be, but also as the vain, self-centered creature that she is . . ." (p. 157).

Certainly the title characters are the major figures in the novel. Everything that happens is an effect of their plotting; the Americans merely react to them. As the causes of the action, they create the structure of the novel. In the opening chapters their mere presence provides a means of contrasting two cultures, but afterwards everything develops from their various intrigues and sub-intrigues. We witness not merely a static contrasting of opposing national views, but the direct and conscious influence of the Europeans upon the Americans.

James's characterization of the two Europeans largely accounts for the structure as well as the tone of the novel. Eugenia and Felix are essentially different from most of the other Europeans in James's fiction. Their distinctiveness consists in the apparent lightness with which they are handled; they seem—at least to the tastes of critics who share some of the Wentworths' bias—to get off too lightly. Detached as they are from the vaguely malignant European scene, Felix and Eugenia are remote from the evil atmosphere that shrouds such European characters as the Bellegardes and Richard de Mauves. It is not just that the genial tone and the pastoral vision of things prohibit any strong suggestion of the sinister and the portentous. The European background of Felix and Eugenia is only faintly and indirectly conveyed, and then it is suggestive either of Graustarkian fable and comic opera (how else is the reader to regard Eugenia's stiuation as morganatic wife of Prince Adolph of Silberstadt-Schreckenstein?) or of fancifully picturesque travel posters and provincial misconceptions of the bohemian life (Felix, we are told, has strolled through Europe with a band of carefree musicians). When Gertrude first sees Felix, she glances upward from a volume of *The Arabian Nights*, and the vision she beholds is as miraculous as the story she has been reading. Gertrude is naïve, but the Europeans consistently behave in a manner in keeping with her fantasies. Also the Europeans are purged of ancestral evil. The connivances of Eugenia's remote brother-in-law are clearly not to be lingered upon; this is but a quaintness as extravagant and as charming as the childlike view of the Old World that fascinates Gertrude.

In one respect it is characteristic of James to represent Europe through such a pair as the good-natured Felix and the worldly Eugenia. In *The American*, for example, Valentin de Bellegarde has the same zest for life as Felix Young, while his brother and mother, like Eugenia, are much devoted to traditional manners. In *The American*, of course, the burden of manners is considerably heavier than in *The Europeans*, eventually oppressing even the frolicsome Valentin. Still the schematic arrangement of European characters in *The American* has much the same effect as in *The Europeans*.

Since Felix and Eugenia are removed from the hereditary guilt and rigid social apparatus that weigh upon the Bellegardes, they appear not only unusually free (more like Americans than Europeans) but also unusually simplified. Felix is the least credible character in the novel. He is childishly good-natured, single-mindedly bent on happiness, and thoroughly engaging and charming—a man with neither temper nor guile, seemingly incapable of thinking any but the most flattering of thoughts about anyone. Not only is he unrestricted by the demands of class that finally inhibit Valentin de Bellegarde, but he is free from the demands of any class or society, and yet at the same time highly civilized. He stands virtually alone in James as a man who has all of the benefits of worldliness but none of the faults.

With the Baroness, who likewise stands for a part of the generic European character, James has a more difficult artistic problem. For his intention seems to be to draw a thoroughly attractive kind of Madame Merle, and by extension to represent artfulness as an unequivocal good. But it is part of James's technique in sketching the Baroness to make her slightly ridiculous: she is so absurdly out of place in the world of the Wentworths that some of the amusement is at her expense—as in mock-heroic poetry the epic devices used to satirize must appear foolish in themselves.

What both Europeans embody is a highly refined form of opportunism, and they become involved with a group of Americans who embody the contrary quality of discipline. This opposition is the subject of *The Europeans*, the central idea that gives the novel its dramatic unity. The terms of this opposition are represented in their abstract essence in a dialogue between Gertrude and Felix. Felix remarks:

"You don't seem to me to get all the pleasure out of life that you might. You don't seem to me to enjoy. . . . You seem to me very well placed for enjoying. You have money and liberty and what is called in Europe a 'position.' But you take a painful view of life, as one may say."

. . . .

"I don't think it's what one does or one doesn't do that promotes enjoyment" [Felix continues]. "It is the general way of looking at life."

"They look at it as a discipline—that's what they do here [Gertrude replies]. "I have often been told that."

"Well, that's very good. But there is another way," added Felix, smiling: "to look at it as an opportunity" (pp. 103-5).[7]

The clash of "ways of looking at life" obviously accounts for the make-up of a number of the characters and for their roles in the drama. Thus, to Gertrude, Mr. Brand represents discipline and Felix represents opportunity. Robert Acton's sense of duty is concentrated in his devotion to his mother, and the Baroness personifies the life of self-gratification he is tentatively inclined to. But James's dramatic representation of the conflict of discipline and opportunity has a more pervasive role in the design of the book. For both opportunism and discipline are many-sided characteristics, particularly when they are regarded as cultural rather than merely personal attributes. The central characters in *The*

7. Page references are to *The Europeans* (Boston, 1879).

Europeans together manifest the complexities implicit in these abstract qualities, and the action which engages these characters tests the assumptions about life which impel them.

Felix and his sister express the various meanings latent in the principle of opportunism. In its simplest and most apparent form, their opportunism is a capacity for experiencing pleasure. Felix with his comic imagination finds everything delightful— even muddy roads. Though he may speak of the benefits of a high civilization, he is most often seen as a man fully responsive to the less obvious pleasures of life. His painter's eye is his dominant faculty, and life as he sees it is gaily colored and fundamentally amusing. The Baroness, on the other hand, converts raw experience into traditional forms. Felix delights in the harsh simplicity of the Wentworths' house—"it looks like a magnified Nüremberg toy" (p. 46), he remarks—but the Baroness elaborately decorates the neighboring cottage where she and Felix stay. The accumulated artifices of a traditional culture "make" life. Money, style, and tradition together transform the dreary into the pleasurable.

Both the responsiveness of Felix and the social art of the Baroness are to be held in high regard; each reflects "imagination," which the Wentworths sadly lack. The Europeans introduce the Americans to a way of seeing life and a way of refashioning life, and for doing so they are to be admired. But if their opportunism is a source of happiness and enrichment—for themselves and others—it is at the same time based on selfish motives.

Each is seeking economic gain from the New England relatives, Felix by painting their portraits and Eugenia by marrying one of them. If the Baroness is depressed and Felix is gay in the first chapter, their different moods should not conceal the similarity of their ambitions. Soon, however, their self-interest blends with a general benevolence. Even the Baroness feels a deep affection for her newly-met kin. The plot of the novel develops from the gentle aggressions of Felix and Eugenia. Each is quickly paired with a New Englander—Felix with Gertrude, the Baroness with Robert Acton. Though we never lose sight of the essential self-interest that governs the two foreigners as they intrigue for fortune and status, their separate operations are viewed sympathetically. Gertrude, after all, needs Felix, who will be the best of husbands for her; nor is there any suggestion of hypocrisy in his expressed love for her.[8] Similarly the Baroness' graces attract Acton, who would certainly profit from marriage to such a woman. Furthermore, if the Baroness is a schemer or adventuress, as some have claimed, she conducts herself with such delicacy that it is Acton, if anyone, who appears crass and self-centered.

The sub-intrigues which the Europeans concurrently undertake also show that their self-interest is in no way incompatible with good will. By the middle of the novel, Felix and Eugenia extend their operations. Felix, who alone sees the obvious affection between Charlotte and Mr. Brand, delicately suggests to Gertrude and to her former suitor that such a match would be a happy one. By directing Mr. Brand's attention to Charlotte, Felix of course eliminates a major obstacle to his own marriage to Gertrude. He additionally profits by asking the obliging Charlotte to plead his own case before her father.

The sub-intrigue engineered by the Baroness is equally a combination of disinterested benevolence and shrewd self-interest. Clifford Wentworth, recently suspended from Harvard for drinking, is a difficult problem for his father. As the scion of the family, he desperately requires reformation. The Baroness, "a woman of finely-mingled motive" (p. 173), undertakes to civilize Clifford, but at the same time she feels that Clifford may be kept in reserve as a potential husband should her relation with

8. Also, as F. W. Dupee remarks, Felix "actually rescues the family from possible disruption by this somewhat threatening daughter" (*Henry James* [New York, 1951], p. 102).

Acton come to nothing. "A prudent archer has always a second bowstring . . ." (p. 173), she tells herself.

Although the Baroness and Felix seem most suited to experience life in its fullness, they are also shielded from certain dimensions of reality because of their special talents and perceptions. Felix, who is called a child by his sister, has a spontaneity that is refreshing in the chilling atmosphere of New England, but those problems which cannot be viewed in a cheerful light he either flatly ignores or else brushes away with irrelevant jests. His good nature is indeed a tonic to the Wentworths—when they submit to it—but it depends upon a fundamental shallowness of vision. He can successfully disarm Mr. Wentworth and even Mr. Brand by refusing to recognize their distress, but in the significant closing scene with his sister he fails utterly to help her. After an exasperating meeting with Acton, during which she guesses that his reluctance to marry her will eventually lead to her rejection, she guardedly asks Felix to help her. But Felix, the only person capable of influencing Acton to propose, conveniently dodges the veiled message. He does nothing for his sister, choosing to evade a problem in which good humor might prove inadequate. And when he speaks with Eugenia following her defeat, he can contribute neither advice nor sympathy. In the end he is nearly as pathetic as Acton in his weak attempt to salvage a hopeless situation by incongruous jollity.[9]

In a different way, the Baroness is also shielded from certain kinds of experience by her devotion to forms. She is not so intolerant of depression as is Felix—and thus she can express a wider range of attitudes and emotions than he—but she is at a loss when feelings are expressed directly, unembellished by conventional graces. It is worth noting that the one person whom she cannot deal with at all is Lizzie Acton, whose "dangerous

9. Thus Felix is rather less than the "person of radical responsibility" he is called by F. R. Leavis, "The Novel as Dramatic Poem (III): 'The Europeans,'" *Scrutiny*, XV (Summer, 1948), 212.

energy" (p. 132) makes her a natural enemy to the Baroness. Clifford is merely gauche and ill-bred, but Lizzie, who finally "civilizes" Clifford while the Baroness fails, has an immediate sexual and emotional expression of herself that the Baroness partly envies and partly despises.

The Baroness' artfulness cannot compete with Lizzie's vitality, and to that extent it is a limitation. But her relation with Lizzie is counterweighted by her relation with Acton's mother, whose directness reveals social ineptness rather than refreshing honesty. Understandably, the Baroness is irritated by the dull tactlessness with which Mrs. Acton, whom she has met only once previously, announces that she is dying and requests Eugenia to remain in the community because "It would be so pleasant for Robert" (p. 233). In the exchange between the two women, art surely shows itself as superior to artlessness. In her ignorance of the rules of conversation, the old woman is unintentionally rude and offensive; the Baroness, through intelligence, self-control, and a respect for decorum, prevents the unpleasantness of the situation from coming to the surface. With the single exception of her relation to Lizzie (which is important, because Lizzie defeats her plans with Clifford), the Baroness' artificiality is an expansion, not a repression of herself. Her manner, her conversation, even her clothes and her furnishings fully express her. Robert Acton, on the other hand, most often uses his acquired finesse to conceal his deeper feelings—even from himself. His quasi-worldliness, like his conscience, protects him from reality.

The Baroness has mastered the art of knowing how to be looked at. For her, appearance not only takes on more importance than reality, appearance is reality. She feels it is preferable to carry one's self like a pretty woman than to be a pretty woman. Pathetically and ironically she is regarded by the New Englanders as hardly a person at all, rather a spectacle to be gawked at, or to be paraded before friends and neighbors like an exotic and unintelligible work of art. Eugenia is crudely rebuked by Acton, who acts as though manners and wit are in themselves sufficient bases of friendship, not requiring the further connection of marriage. Thus his relation to the Baroness remains that of an audience to a theatrical performer. Nor do the Wentworths ever acknowledge the Baroness' existence as a woman: "They were all standing round [Eugenia], as if they were expecting her to acquit herself of the exhibition of some peculiar faculty, some brilliant talent. Their attitude seemed to imply that she was a kind of conversational mountebank, attired, intellectually, in gauze and spangles" (p. 63).

The distinguishing qualities of both Felix and Eugenia point simultaneously to the special virtues and special limitations of both the Europeans and the Americans. Eugenia's artistic self-representation accounts for her own civilized grace, but it is also a measure of her failure to deal with life directly, particularly in its more vigorous aspects. Her grace exposes the severe deficiency of a Mrs. Acton, but it is the reason for her own inferiority to a Lizzie Acton. Correspondingly, Felix can experience a pleasure beyond the capacity of the Americans, but he cannot recognize the pain which they so exaggerate as an element of life.

But it must be said that there is very little of pain in the novel. Thus the Americans are exposed as quixotic in their fear of a nonexistent evil. Finally what oppresses them is a fear of the unconventional and a fear of pleasure. As representatives of these qualities, the Europeans are harmless. Their suggested faults—their plotting for self-gain, Felix' inability to acknowledge pain, the Baroness' inability to face raw experience—are in no way inimical to the Americans. The Europeans offer only the possibility of happiness to the entire group. If anyone suffers, it is the Baroness, though she is no less admirable than Felix. The reason is simply that Felix' bonhomie proves less difficult for the New World to endure than the Baroness' courtliness.

But Eugenia's failure is not the only unpleasantness in the book. James suggests grave realities underlying the experience of the novel, though the suggestion is too mild to distort the genial tone. Mainly the setting, the dialogue, and the witty narrative voice blend; the discordant notes remain beneath the surface, to be perceived, but not to offset the comic mood.

For instance, James casually develops a complicated symbolism of youth and age—a rhetorical and scenic set of paradoxes that strengthens the dramatic ironies involved in the conjunction of the two cultures. These ironies are simultaneously frivolous and substantive. New England, represented in the imagery both of youthful vitality and of death, is at once young and old. The book begins with a view of a dismal graveyard and ends with the death of Mrs. Acton. To the Baroness, "Gertrude seemed . . . almost funereal" (p. 54); and to Felix, "there was something almost cadaverous in his uncle's high-featured white face" (p. 52). But if these and other comments reflect something life-denying in these New Englanders, many others reflect their comic youthfulness. Just as Mr. Wentworth regards his eighty-year-old house as a "venerable mansion" (p. 47) and as James speaks of Boston as an "ancient city" (p. 1), so not even the puritan temperament can conceal the youthfulness of the American civilization. The New Englanders are untried and rather timid children. The Wentworth house is not really old, but very fresh; and America is "a comical country" (p. 8).

The Wentworth circle is both young and old—as young and old as the Golden Age. And in a different way, the same paradox applies to the Europeans. In the first chapter the Baroness tells Felix (whose surname is "Young"): "You will never be anything but a child, dear brother." "One would suppose that you, madam," answered Felix, laughing, "were a thousand years old." "I am—sometimes," said the Baroness (p. 21).

Felix' youth—a freedom from suppressions—and the Baroness' antiquity—an absorption in the manners of a very old civilization—help define their combined character. The two are not greatly different, for Felix' childishness differs only in degree from the Baroness' age; both exult in the promises of life. Age is wisdom for the Baroness, but only decay for the Wentworths; youth is gaiety for Felix, but only inexperience for the Wentworths.

The Europeans are both younger and older (happier and wiser) than the also young and old (innocent and decayed) Americans, specifically because they are opportunists. And—to compound the paradoxes—their opportunism is a characteristic of Americans rather than Europeans, especially as it is also associated with their freedom and their youth. James exploits the reputation of America as the land of opportunity (of course, in other of his works it is rather the land of opportunists, and Europe is the land of opportunity). If the notion of opportunity that motivates the Europeans is not exactly a standard American one, James nevertheless identifies the enterprises of the Europeans with the promises latent in America. At one point Felix thinks, "This was certainly the country of sunsets. There was something in these glorious deeps of fire that quickened his imagination; he always found images and promises in the western sky" (p. 217). Even Eugenia, who is considerably less absorbed in nature than Felix, responds to the promise symbolized by the primitive American scene. Walking through the streets of Boston, "She surrendered herself to a certain tranquil gayety. If she had come to seek her fortune, it seemed to her that her fortune would be easy to find. There was a promise of it in the gorgeous purity of the western sky. . ." (p. 19).

The suggestion that the Europeans are more archetypally American than the New Englanders is recurrent.[10] It establishes an additional relationship between the sets of characters and hence further refines the shape of the novel. In *The Europeans,*

10. See Poirier, pp. 139-40, for further evidences of this irony and for illuminating observations regarding it.

incidents, characters, and places become significant because they correspond to and yet contrast with other incidents, characters, and places. Thus the three prominent houses in the Wentworth neighborhood are each implicit criticisms of each other and of the kind of people who live in them: the Wentworths' is chaste and austere; the Baroness' is lavishly decorated; and Robert Acton's is an awkward compromise between the other two.[11] A less obvious pattern in the novel is formed by the repeated episodes in which lies are told or are commented on. The lie is a regular occasion for moral ambiguity in James; he nearly always employs the lie to differentiate the rigid moralist from the free spirit. To regard the telling of lies as per se heinous is to mark one's self as narrow and self-righteous. Indeed one of the clearest indications that Gertrude is imaginative is that she tells harmless fibs. A lie is partly responsible for the downfall of Eugenia, though to her (and to our) mind when she lies to Mrs. Acton in her son's presence she is only being courteous. In effect, the Baroness is regarded as a living lie; to the New Englanders she is performing a role rather than living a life. And Felix' flattering portraits of the Wentworth circle are at bottom lies. The New Englanders can regard forms of artfulness only in terms of ethics because they can express themselves only by a moralistic rhetoric. But the Europeans convert moral questions to aesthetic ones. Thus to Mr. Wentworth Clifford's alcoholism is a moral failing, while to Eugenia and Felix it represents a lapse in manners.

Gertrude Wentworth is the only New Englander who accepts the offerings of the Europeans. James represents her as a kind of potential Eugenia, with the same tastes and habits though in a cruder, less articulate form. They are the only characters who tell "lies," who respect appearances, and who are described as

11. See Edwin T. Bowden, *The Themes of Henry James* (New Haven, 1956), pp. 48-50, for a detailed analysis of the symbolic values of the three houses.

"restless" and "peculiar."[12] But the main effect of these resemblances is to throw their differences into relief. Thus Gertrude's mistaking the high cultivation of the Europeans for naturalness is evidence that she is at center merely rebellious. The novel implies that one is never so natural—in the sense of giving full expression to the imagination—as when he is endowed with the manners of a rich civilization; but such a perception is certainly beyond the capacity of Gertrude. Gertrude actually fails to respond to the civilizing influences of the Europeans; her main reason for wishing to be like them is to free herself from her "obligations" and "responsibilities"—such as attending church, marrying Mr. Brand, and telling the truth. She has not mastered the tact, the courtesy, and the geniality of Felix; she wants only his freedom. In her various self-assertions she is flippant and inconsiderate. Yet James does not present Gertrude in a harsh light; he simply reveals her as a rather ill-tempered and irritable girl who, in spite of her yearnings, has no real understanding of the life she has determined to lead.

But it is Eugenia rather than Gertrude who is excluded from the harmonious resolution of difficulties at the end. In the language of ancient comedy, Eugenia is what Northrop Frye calls the *pharmakos*—the rascal inimical to the well-being of society who is driven out in the comic resolution. Such an expulsion "appeals to the kind of relief we are expected to feel when we see Jonson's *Volpone* condemned to the galleys, Shylock stripped of his wealth, or Tartuffe taken off to prison." But the rejection of Eugenia pleases only if *The Europeans* is read as a total approbation of the New Englanders. As the novel stands, however, Eugenia's repudiation is somewhat like those "most terrible ironies known to art" such as "the rejection of Falstaff" and "certain scenes in Chaplin."[13]

12. Here I am summarizing Poirier, pp. 112-16, though, as I suggest subsequently, the differences between Gertrude and Eugenia are as striking as the parallels: the differences are striking precisely because of the parallels.

13. Frye, *Anatomy of Criticism*, p. 45.

In permitting the expulsion of Eugenia, James not only allows himself his only severe judgment of the New Englanders, but he gives a rather harsh turn to the otherwise genial tone of the novel. Eugenia dominates the final chapter, and if her dismissal does not nullify the gaiety of the multiple weddings it at least counterbalances the mood of joy with one of unpleasantness. Indeed the seasonal backdrop of the novel is attuned to Eugenia's spirits. Her early gloom is complemented by a late spring snowstorm, but the climate improves and summer arrives as Eugenia's mood lightens; but as Eugenia perceives that Acton will fail her, summer gives way to winter. "Les beaux jours sont passés" (p. 208), the Baroness says, contradicting her brother, and her words reflect both the climatic conditions and her own prospects. Eugenia is rejected not only by Acton, but by Clifford, by Lizzie, and by the Wentworths, and even by her brother, whose jollity in the end is an obvious limitation. Since the Baroness is an imaginative and resourceful woman, she resists mere pity, but there is a sense of loss and a mood of somberness in her departure.[14] We feel that the society which dismisses her is seriously deficient.

The artistic effect of Eugenia's failure is certainly not to tighten the structure of the novel. Rather the ending extends the small dimensions of the "sketch"—as James subtitled the novel—into a less restricted and conventional area. It would have been a simple matter for James to arrange the marriage of Acton and Eugenia (as he arranges the benign, yet unconvincing, acquiescence of Mr. Brand to Gertrude's marriage to Felix), but instead of granting his readers the fulfillment of their expectations, James forces them to revise their estimate of the entire affair. James seems unwilling to submit totally to the demands of comedy. He refuses to make the final sacrifice of his artistic

14. It is typical of James to decrease gradually the comic mood of his novels. *The American, The Spoils of Poynton, The Awkward Age,* and *The Ambassadors,* in particular, are novels in which the casualness and high-spiritedness of the opening chapters give way to tense seriousness.

freedom to the a priori requirements of an artificial form. Though he employs innumerable conventional comic techniques in *The Europeans*, he refuses to employ any for its own sake. Everything in the novel is carefully calculated to develop a central idea—the clash of a life based on responsibility with one based on opportunism—so that even the most mechanical of devices subserve an organic scheme. That there are many such devices may explain why James deprecated the novel. Never again was he to be so reliant upon such contrivances, and significantly *The Europeans* is the last novel of its type that James wrote.

VI · *THE PRINCESS CASAMASSIMA*

It is a common assumption that the main, perhaps the exclusive, theme of *The Princess Casamassima* is politics. The assumption is understandable for *The Princess* is James's only novel with a political subject. Furthermore the politics are of some obvious importance in themselves (unlike the remote parliamentary activities of Lord Warburton in *The Portrait of a Lady* and Nick Dormer in *The Tragic Muse*); the politics are also radical and insurrectionary. Perceptive recent essays on the novel by Lionel Trilling and Irving Howe have revived the debate on the question of James's achievement as a political novelist.[1] Mr. Howe's argument develops from the announced premise that the theme of *The Princess* is "the nature and power of social radicalism."[2] He finds James's handling of the subject "uncertain," and so

1. Irving Howe, "Henry James: The Political Vocation," *Politics and the Novel* (London, 1961), pp. 139-56; Lionel Trilling, "The Princess Casamassima," in *The Liberal Imagination* (New York, 1953), pp. 65-96.
   2. Howe, *Politics and the Novel*, p. 146.

disputes a sizable portion of Mr. Trilling's essay, in which historical evidence is cited to show that James accurately represented the English anarchists of the Victorian age. The issue is of ancillary importance in Mr. Trilling's essay, but to Mr. Howe it is apparently the only issue.

It would be rash to argue that *The Princess Casamassima* (in which several characters are anarchists) is no more a political novel than, say, *The Golden Bowl* (in which several characters are millionaires) is an economic novel. Still one suspects that such a category fails to define *The Princess*; it is not an irrelevance, but it is needlessly confining and slightly arbitrary. Mr. Howe implicitly prescribes that the political subject must either absorb or dominate everything else in the novel. If his formula properly applies to *The Princess*, his central argument is not to be dismissed: "that some motivating idea about the revolutionary movement, be it valid or not, was indispensable for bringing into full play the energies that lay waiting in the novel; and James the writer not only lacked such an idea, he did not really grasp the need for it."[3] The objection would seem to strike to the heart of the matter, but only if one judges *The Princess* to be a political novel. *The Princess* is "about" politics, but it is also about other things; and, as I shall try to argue, its theme is not political at all.

Following the lead of James's preface (and of certain letters and essays he wrote around the time of the publication of *The Princess*), we infer that he wanted to do something on the order of the social novels of the French naturalists and the English Victorians, especially the former.[4] Such an intention accounts for the often observed similarities between *The Princess* and the

3. *Ibid.*, p. 150.

4. For ample documentation see Oscar Cargill, *The Novels of Henry James* (New York, 1961), pp. 165-66; Lyall H. Powers, "Henry James and Zola's *Roman expérimental*," *University of Toronto Quarterly*, XXX (October, 1960), 16-30; and Leon Edel, *Henry James: The Middle Years* (Philadelphia, 1962), pp. 104-6, 181.

other two novels of the same period, *The Bostonians* and *The Tragic Muse*. In these three novels James most nearly matches Balzac, Zola, Dickens, and Thackeray in his representation of a dense, sprawling "world." James, it would appear, sought a kind of reconciliation between the scope, solidity, and variousness of these French and English authors and the craftsmanship of such precisionists as Daudet, Flaubert, and Maupassant. His overriding structural problem was to do justice to the vastness and multiplicity of his subject without modifying his regular passion for tightness and coherence. The lesson that Balzac taught James is an ideal fusion of magnitude and penetration—"Quantity and intensity are at once and together his sign; the truth being that his energy did not press hard in some places only to press lightly in others. . . ."[5] However, Balzac's achievement is diminished because his enormous appetite for facts prevents his novels from achieving unity.[6] The English Victorians offer magnitude, but for intensity substitute only the pallid appeal of "charm" and appear indifferent to the value of unity.[7] Zola's intensity is diminished by the author's narrowing scientific ideas.[8] But before considering James's techniques for achieving intensity and coherence in *The Princess*, it will be well to discuss the magnitude or "quantity" of that novel.

The preface makes clear that the subject of *The Princess* is London, a city overwhelming in its variety, immensity, and seeming impenetrability. James's habit of walking the London streets "provokes, all round, a mystic solicitation, the urgent appeal, on the part of everything, to be interpreted and, so far as may be, reproduced" (*P*, p. 59). The novel justifies the statement of

5. Henry James, *The Question of Our Speech; The Lesson of Balzac: Two Lectures* (Boston and New York, 1905), pp. 177-78.

6. See Henry James, "Honoré de Balzac," in *Notes on Novelists* (London, 1914), p. 115.

7. See *P*, pp. 49, 63, 84.

8. See Henry James, "The Art of Fiction," in *Partial Portraits* (New York, 1888), p. 408.

intention in the preface. London is a constant and forceful presence throughout the book, represented both as the sum total of its multitudinous details and as a massive absorbent unity. The sense of London is realized less in passages of description than in action, dialogue, and streams of consciousness. The force of the city is felt in everything that engages its occupants. Some characters bear the indelible stamp of the city—notably Hyacinth ("a product of the London streets and the London air" [V, 79]), Millicent ("a daughter of London" [V, 61]), Pinnie, Mr. Vetch, and Captain Sholto.

It is also significant that Hyacinth does not dominate the novel, as James's centers of consciousness commonly do. To be sure, it is his "passion of intelligence" (*P*, p. 69) that brings the other characters into focus; but, as the preface implies, he is as much a vehicle for revealing them as they are for revealing him. There are lapses in consistency of point of view in *The Portrait of a Lady* and other James novels that employ the central consciousness, but in none are the lapses so frequent and so undisguised as in *The Princess*. In the preface to *The Tragic Muse* James says that *The Princess* makes no claim to consistency of point of view. It rather employs the technique of "multiplication of *aspects*"—a requirement for "so frankly panoramic and processional" (*P*, p. 90) a novel. *The Princess* is not a portrait of its major character but of his city. London is more than a setting, more even than a Zolaesque environment; it is a Balzacian society, and thus a kind of character in its own right.

Towards the end of the novel, during one of his countless walks through the darkened London streets, Hyacinth senses—as he has often sensed before—the overwhelming reality of London: "The great city . . . lay round him . . . like an immeasurable breathing monster" (VI, 266). This conception of the city is supported by nearly everything in the novel. For it is as an organic force that the presence of London directs and organizes James's work.[9]

Most of the characters view the city quite otherwise—as a static, compartmentalized organization of individuals, each locked in a particular economic, occupational, or social class. A commonplace metaphor of social heights and social depths runs through many of the conversations. According to this view of the society, the rich are up, the poor are down, and stirrings of "underground" movements point to "the ground's heaving under our feet" (V, 220). Both anarchists and conservatives look upon social change as some future cataclysm. However, an irony that broods thoughout the novel, from the first chapter on, is that revolution is an actual present process, engaged in by all the characters, and not the distant apocalypse that everyone either hopes for or dreads. In James's London nearly everyone is in motion, both horizontally and vertically. The horizontal movement is the general drifting away from national, cultural, and social ties. Hyacinth is the offspring of a marriage that is not only socially mixed, but also nationally mixed, his father being English and his mother French. The Poupins are French exiles, Schinkel and Hoffendahl are German, the Muniments are from a family of miners from the north of England, Madame Grandoni is a German whose husband is Italian, and Captain Sholto is a rootless sybarite who returns to his English home from a Monte Carlo casino or an African safari only to pursue

9. Thus the descriptive passages are not static, isolated set pieces. Change and process are stressed in the London scenes. Also the settings are made dramatic—as active impressions in the minds of the characters. The following passage is representative: "In the vulgar districts the smaller shops and open-air industries were doubly active, and big clumsy torches flared and smoked over hand-carts and costermongers' barrows drawn up in the gutters. Hyacinth had roamed through the great city since he was an urchin, but his imagination had never ceased to be stirred by the preparations for Sunday that went on in the evening among the toilers and spinners, his brothers and sisters, and he lost himself in all the quickened crowding and pushing and staring at lighted windows and chaffering at the stalls of fishmongers and hucksters (V, 81-82).

the Princess. Of course, the Princess, the American wife of an Italian prince, is the major illustration of the general denational-ized condition. James thus gives us a London that is a polyglot world of aliens, exiles, and adventurers. The odd and fluid internationalism is even illuminated by the title of the novel, which gives an old world Italian name to a story about modern London.

The international types of *The Princess*, unlike those of *The Portrait of a Lady* and *The Golden Bowl*, are deracinated; they are not so much shaped by a foreign culture as they are culture-less. So the forefront of the novel dramatizes their various verti-cal movements—that is, their efforts to find an identity within different social classes. They demonstrate not only envy but also instability in their pursuits of their opposites. The novel is full of occasions in which someone sets out to discover, possess, or be absorbed into an alien class. The titled women, the Princess and Lady Aurora, court lower-class revolutionaries; Millicent aban-dons her Lomax Place origins to make a situation for herself in the fringe world of high fashion; the progress of the "disin-herited" (*P*, p. 71) Hyacinth is tentative, yet complex and instructive: he gains a drab security through his job as book-binder, and from there is tempted by the contradictory appeals of upper-class aesthetics and lower-class politics. Pinnie and Rosie achieve a vicarious gentility through the friendship of Lady Aurora; and Muniment, the political radical, is really seek-ing a commonplace bourgeois security.[10]

Characteristically James suggests countless parallels between apparent opposites: the Prince and Hyacinth secretly observe the Princess betraying them; proletariat Rosie receives her callers in a manner as grand as that of the Princess; a stroll with the Princess reminds Hyacinth of a stroll with Millicent; Muniment,

10. An oddity in James's portrait of London society is the near absence of the bourgeoisie, a class represented solely by Crookenden, Hyacinth's employer. James's scheme, which calls for the interaction of the upper and lower classes, requires the virtual elimination of the middle class.

like Sholto, introduces Hyacinth to a new life. This practice is a familiar one in James; it is the technique of multiple reference that he admired in Balzac's novels, wherein "The relations of parts to each other are at moments multiplied almost to madness. . . ."[11] In *The Princess* the purpose of the ironic parallels is not simply to achieve intensity, but to define the quality of human existence in London. It is a society in which class distinctions are of little account; more accurately, no one gains any security from social rank and everyone imitates—intentionally or otherwise—those of his opposite class. Everyone acts in much the same way. The most prominent details of the novel—details of character, situation, and incident—all reveal a society in flux.

But these are the given facts, the external evidences of what life is in the "immeasurable breathing monster" of London. In appropriating such a vision of the modern city as the controlling subject of his novel, James found the usual problem of unity and coherence to be especially difficult. The general problem was again one of finding an action to illuminate the subject, of discovering the "logic" of the given relationships, of economizing and yet leaving room for the development of the germ. The special problem was one of giving formal control (economy and symmetry) to a subject whose essence was enormity and fluidity. A remark in his notebooks, more typical of Dickens than of James, is a confession of uncertainty:

It is absolutely necessary that at this point I should make the future evolution of *The Princess Casamassima* more clear to myself. I have never yet become engaged in a novel in which, after I had begun to write and send off my MS., the details had remained so vague. . . . The subject of the *Princess* is magnificent, and if I can only give up my mind to it properly—generously and trustfully—the form will shape itself as successfully as the idea deserves. I have plunged in rather blindly, and got a good many characters on my hands;

11. *The Question of Our Speech; The Lesson of Balzac: Two Lectures,* p. 85.

but these will fall into their places if I keep cool and think it out
(*N*, p. 68).

Though one suspects that James's hopes were imperfectly
realized, he did succeed in giving the central action a rounded
shape. The plot has a typically Jamesian structure. As in *The
Portrait of a Lady*, the first half is centered on the hero's initiation into a society and the second half exposes the insufficiency of
that society; the first half creates the illusions, the second half
demolishes them. *The Princess Casamassima* differs from the
pattern only in that Hyacinth's enchantment and subsequent
disenchantment are not with one but with (apparently) two
societies. Yet there is a sense of simultaneity in his being introduced by the Princess to the world of aesthetic elegance and by
Muniment to the world of political revolution; there is also a
sense of simultaneity in his betrayals by both sides. The effect is
that of a single society, but one that is most complex, even
contradictory. The effect is heightened when the Princess becomes Muniment's lover; then the distinct acts of betrayal
merge in a tacit conspiracy.

But it is questionable whether James succeeds completely
in unifying all the sprawling diffuse materials. Probably the
fault lies in the major strategy. Clearly this strategy is to use
Hyacinth Robinson not simply as a means of bringing together
many characters and social viewpoints, but as a character whose
private crisis is intended to crystallize the themes of the book.
Hyacinth's crisis, originating in his dual identity as aristocrat and
working man, operates as a paradigm of the London world, a
shapeless, fluid world in which everyone is in motion. It may be
that James's predilection for symmetrical coherence proves inap-
propriate for *The Princess*. To represent the quality of life in a
society in upheaval James places great symbolic weight upon
the opposite social stations of Hyacinth's parents. James's scheme
requires that the bastard son of a French prostitute and an
English nobleman be drawn in equal measure to a pity for the

suffering poor and a reverence for aristocratic culture. His personal life follows the same pattern, as he is alternately fond of an elegant Princess and a Cockney working girl. On this contrivance James insistently builds the novel. The very rigidity of the design seems especially out of place in a novel whose subject is social flexibility. The effect is not to recover order from disorder; it is to impose order on disorder. Actually the dualities that so disturb Hyacinth cut out too much of the experience in the novel. The quality of London life is pictured in images of density and obscurity and dramatized by social interpenetration. It resists James's dichotomous formula.

As I have tried to show, James's controlling vision of London is of a city anything but formless, but its form is not the stratified class structure that most of the characters assume it to be. Its form is organic, not mechanical: not only is it marked by a self-generated fluidity, but its members are all expressions of the whole. However, James seems to require for his novel a more emphatic kind of unity and coherence. Thus he severely patterns Hyacinth's social initiation and requires his hero to view his experience as a set of balanced alternatives. True, all this is sadly ironic: for example—as I later elaborate—Millicent turns out to be not very different from the Princess. James yet exploits Hyacinth's misconceptions to his own literary advantages, constructing his novel in accordance with his hero's false judgments. The resultant symmetry is not much more forced than in some other James novels, but it is quite obtrusive here. By contrast, the tidy parallels that govern the form of *What Maisie Knew* seem suitable expressions of a social world that has reduced marriage to a barren ritual; the frivolous tone of the society and the satiric tone of the novel are underscored by the artificiality of the plot structure. However the symmetrical form of *The Princess Casamassima* rather clashes with the steady emphasis given to the massive impenetrability of the social scene the novel seems intended to represent.

One of James's intentions is to equate revolution and betrayal, and Hyacinth's tragic situation is his principal means of doing so. Finally the treachery is directed not against the social system, but against Hyacinth. Not merely the plots of the anarchists, but the various aggressions of the Princess, Millicent, Lady Aurora, and Sholto have as their most immediate and extreme result the betrayal of Hyacinth's friendship. Though Hyacinth finally chooses suicide over the alternatives of betrayal of the revolution or betrayal of the aristocracy, he is not entirely guiltless of infidelity himself. At least he looks upon his visit to the Princess' country house as a kind of betrayal of Pinnie, who falls ill during his absence. The conservatives, the Prince Casamassima and Mr. Vetch, abhor social transformation and hold fast to their original loyalties. In every scene in which she appears, Madame Grandoni has something to say about the need for fidelity: such as "... I'm not false" (VI, 10) and "... I've always been faithful to [the Princess]" (VI, 77). Her dilemma, like Hyacinth's, amounts to a conflict of loyalties; finally her sense of obligation to the Prince overcomes her commitment to the Princess, whom she deserts. The final hundred pages of the novel dramatize Hyacinth's growing estrangement from his friends. In a succession of valedictory meetings with Millicent, Poupin, Vetch, and the Princess, he discovers the unwillingness or inability of each to save him. Four times he receives a Judas-like kiss as he is sent away to face his crisis alone.

The flaw in this final turn of the novel is that the public theme and the private theme do not quite coalesce. Before the novel is two-thirds complete, it is perfectly clear to Hyacinth that political insurrection necessitates a betrayal of art and culture; or, as Hyacinth interprets the situation, assassination of the duke would amount to a *"repetition"* (VI, 419) of the murder of his aristocratic father. The combination of Hyacinth's delicate sensibilities and his tour of the aesthetic capitals of Europe makes his dilemma complete; the aristocratic side of his consciousness not only makes him responsive to art, but also compels him to honor his pledge to Hoffendahl. Thus the general moral terms of the crisis are firmly established well before the end of the novel. James must hold them in abeyance throughout the final chapters that are given over to Hyacinth's private betrayals. The effect is not so much to extend the implications of the conflict between aesthetics and reform, but rather to make the social subject much less pervasive than it had been before. In effect the novel changes directions in its final movement. The great "political" issue that has troubled Hyacinth and engaged nearly everyone is certainly redefined and perhaps even transcended. The social question counts far less than the question of whether Hyacinth's few friends will offer him the loyalty and compassion that he is shown to require. Revolution implies infidelity all through the novel, but toward the end the scope is narrowed; the dramatic context is Hyacinth's private circle and not "the great grey Babylon" (*P*, p. 59) of London. True, James continues to place his characters against detailed London settings, ever evoking the sense of the city, but this alone fails to compensate for the structural flaw: Hyacinth's tragic dilemma has been too soon formed.

As several critics have observed, part of James's difficulty with Hyacinth lies in the protagonist's extreme passivity—a hypersensitivity that withholds him from aggression and renders him defenseless against the intrusions of those less thoughtful and selfless than he. The description, of course, fits most of James's protagonists; the unusual and troublesome element in Hyacinth's moral fineness is the attempt James makes to associate it with an upper-class refinement, though the logic of the novel requires this.[12] It may also be objected that Hyacinth's mind is too full of vast political and social questions; he is too poetically respon-

12. F. W. Dupee complains that "Of all [James's] important characters Hyacinth perhaps suffers most from being so stuffed with the [Jamesian] chivalry . . . it is a kind of gentility that Hyacinth assumes . . ." (*Henry James* [New York, 1951], p. 157).

sive to the world around him. His own insignificant role does not justify, much less require, such an intense moral and aesthetic involvement in human history. He is bound to appear a bit priggish, perhaps quixotic, as he broods over the relative merits of traditional civilization and violent reform.

The problem is not so much one of characterization as of technique, as a consideration of Hyacinth's major function in the novel may demonstrate. James gives us an important clue in the preface as to what Hyacinth's intended role is. Hyacinth's response to the London world is much the same as James's; both roam the streets, both are on the outside looking in—albeit James looks in at the poor and Hyacinth at the rich. But the important point is that James's "notes . . . on the much-mixed world of my hero's both overt and covert consciousness . . . were exactly my gathered impressions and stirred perceptions, the deposit in my working imagination of all my visual and all my constructive sense of London" (*P*, p. 76). Hyacinth becomes a kind of Tiresias, whose "sense of London" is as complex and inclusive as the author's; it is a sense of the city, not just of his own place in the city.

It is no surprise for James in the preface to liken the comprehensive intelligence of Hyacinth to those of Maisie and Vanderbank, but it may seem a bit extravagant for him to compare it to those of Hamlet and Lear. Maisie and Vanderbank comprehend a very small social relationship; Hamlet and Lear comprehend the world. Hyacinth's consciousness is presumably of "all the swarming facts" (*P*, p. 60) of the London world. James devotes a large portion of the preface to countering the foreseen objection that such an expansive intelligence is too burdensome for the insignificant Hyacinth to bear. "I recognise . . . and in planning 'The Princess Casamassima' felt it highly important to recognise, the danger of filling too full any supposed and above all any obviously limited vessel of consciousness" (*P*, p. 63). James goes on to insist that even the most enlightened consciousness should experience some "bewilderment" (*P*, p. 64), but he then spends several pages defending the author's right to endow his protagonist with a "full consciousness" (*P*, p. 68). But there is no contradiction. Hyacinth's judgments are often wrong, based on illusion;[13] his vision is yet complex and inclusive, particularly in the manner in which he sees relations of persons to each other and to the London setting. The bewildered consciousness may also be a full one. As an "ardent observer of the 'London world'" (*P*, p. 71), Hyacinth is necessarily more seer than actor; and though there is a painful appropriateness to such scenes as that in which he stands with the Prince in the darkness outside Madeira Crescent to watch the Princess admit Muniment to her house, we feel that Hyacinth is less a victim than a spectator of his own tragedy.

No doubt James wishes us to regard Hyacinth as both agent and spectator, as one whose "passion of intelligence" (*P*, p. 69) fuses his own crisis with the whole London scene. The novel itself affords ample evidence that such is James's plan, but there is the added suggestiveness of his comments on Émile Zola. On the occasion of Zola's death James wrote a most laudatory appraisal of the naturalist's work, considerably more admiring than the earlier review of *Nana* and comment in "The Art of Fiction." Yet James made a single reservation, one which he was to repeat in "The Lesson of Balzac": "It is not of course that multiplication and accumulation, the extraordinary pair of legs on which he walks, are easily or directly consistent with his projecting himself morally; this immense diffusion, with its appropriation of everything it meets, affects us on the contrary as perpetually delaying access to what we may call the private world, the world of the individual."[14] Later in the essay James rephrases his objection—that Zola failed with "subjects of the

13. See Sister Jane Marie Luecke, "*The Princess Casamassima:* Hyacinth's Fallible Consciousness," *Modern Philology*, LX (May, 1963), 274-80.

14. "Émile Zola," in *Notes on Novelists*, p. 57.

private and intimate order," though he gained "great distinction" with the "promiscuous and collective."[15]

Though written more than a decade after *The Princess*, the essay on Zola is an indirect comment on the basic plan of that novel. It seems clear that James's effort in *The Princess* is not simply to match Zola's bulk, solidity, and accumulation of detail, but to effect some fusion of this "totally *represented* world" with "the private world"[16]—in other words, to create a private consciousness that is also a public consciousness, so that the two become one. To an extent the fusion is gained simply by a reduction of Zola's (or Balzac's) scale: excessive facts, relevant to the texture of society but not to the moral and emotional lives of the characters, are ruled out. More positively, all the persons whose lives touch Hyacinth's are made to lead public lives.[17] Economically, politically, or culturally, they speak for some part of London society; the intelligent Hyacinth clearly sees them as such, just as he sees them as part of the buildings, streets, and general density of the city. Of course, his own insignificance— like his self-consciousness, his seriousness, his naïve gentility— also has a representative value. So the question of James's achievement with Hyacinth comes down to the issue raised in the preface: is James's sense of London credibly transferred to Hyacinth, and is the restricted mind of Hyacinth capable of possessing such a complete awareness? The imperfections that I have suggested may well be implicit in the scheme of the novel, since Hyacinth is required not just to possess a consciousness of London, but ever to be organizing the materials of that consciousness—to be, in fact, both actor and artist. In any case, the

15. *Ibid.*, p. 64.
16. *Ibid.*, pp. 56-57.
17. James found the method effectively used in Turgenieff's *Helene:* "[The secondary characters] thoroughly animate the little world that surrounds the central couple; and if we wonder how it is that from half a dozen figures we get such a sense of the world's presence and complexity, we perceive the great sagacity of the choice of types" ("Ivan Turgenieff," in *French Poets and Novelists* [London, 1919], p. 228).

aesthetic requirements that James makes of his protagonist add up to his most penetrating critique of the naturalist novel. Hyacinth is the absorbent moral intelligence who gives unity and significance to "the thick undergrowth"[18] of Balzac and Zola.

Hyacinth is not James's only means of unifying his picture of a complex society. For it is surely not accidental that there are many recurrent elements in the novel. At first it will be best simply to mention the more prominent recurrences—an easy matter, for they are rather obvious ones—and then to assess their significance—a more difficult matter, for James requires that the details speak for themselves. The attentive reader will probably note the following: the artistic and quasi-artistic activities of many of the characters, their theatricalism, the allusions to Dickens—explicit and implicit—and other nineteenth-century novelists, the many occasions in which a small light surrounded by darkness fixes the scene and the emphasis on light and darkness in general, the pastoral scenes standing in sharp contrast to the dominant urban drabness. None of these recurrences has the moral importance of the common elements in Hyacinth's relations with the other characters: that is, his having so many surrogate parents (Pinnie, the Poupins, Vetch, the Princess, Muniment), each of whom betrays or fails him. But those recurrences which have little to do with plot have much to do with defining the structure of the novel, and therefore with defining the structure of London society.

The first impression we receive from the artistic interests of the major characters is that they are a way of showing these characters' shifting from one class to another. Bookbinding, Hyacinth's occupation, is appropriately both an art and a trade—"the most elegant of the mechanical arts" (V, 102). The same is true, at least to the vulgar mind, of Pinnie's profession as dressmaker, for she conceives herself as a genteel artist specializing in "Modes et Robes" (V, 34). Vetch is a failed gentleman reduced

18. "Honoré de Balzac," in Notes on Novelists, p. 109.

to fiddling in a music hall. Even Millicent regards her job as modeling in a pretentious dress shop as an artistic or dramatic performance. In her last scene we recognize her modeling to be a ritual prostitution, but to Millicent it is an entrance into the sublimity of the upper classes. Hyacinth once attends a "musical party" at his employer's house (*"chez les bourgeois"*), and James uses the occasion to satirize middle-class pretensions to art: "He made the acquaintance of half a dozen Miss Crookendens, an acquaintance which consisted in his standing in a corner behind several broad-backed old ladies and watching the rotation, at the piano and the harp, of three or four of his employer's thick-fingered daughters. 'You know it's a tremendously musical house,' said one of the old ladies to another (she called it '' 'ouse'). . ." (VI, 256). The Prince delights in playing the piano. Unlike the commercialized and vulgarized art of Hyacinth, Pinnie, Vetch, Millicent, and Crookenden's daughters, the Princess' art is entirely aristocratic. Her fondness for music makes her appear somewhat false in her adoption of the conspirators. She even gains a power over the poor by playing her piano before them; the aristocratic technique works as well with the lowly. She is really as pretentious in aping plebian ways as is Millicent in aping aristocratic ways. Art always stands in some relation to class, and the relation is ambiguous. When the lower classes are vulgar, the reason is not an inherent grossness, but a pretended (or, in the case of Vetch, compromised) delicacy. The fact that Hyacinth is the only real artist undercuts most of the assumptions about art and class held by Millicent, Pinnie, and Hyacinth himself. Aside from the Princess' performances at the piano, the only other evidences of art are the buildings, paintings, and statuary of a remote (and non-English) past.

The occasions of Hyacinth's growing enthusiasm for aristocratic art and manners seem oddly unreal. At least such is the effect of the various scenes in which he is initiated into high culture. Not only is the Princess herself very theatrical, but we first see her, as does Hyacinth, during the performance of a melo-drama called *The Pearl of Paraguay*. It is difficult to ascertain whether this scene, which is very fully rendered, is used to estab-lish the seeming unreality or the actual unreality of the Princess —probably something of both. Furthermore, the scene is an initiation for the Princess as well: to her Hyacinth's class is as remote and unapproachable as that of the Princess is to Hyacinth. When Hyacinth joins the Princess in her box, the play on the stage and his own "drama" in the box become one: "so pleasant was it to be enthroned with fine ladies in a dusky, spacious receptacle which framed the bright picture of the stage and made one's own situation seem a play within the play" (V, 208). Not only does the Princess appear theatrical to others—she is often thought to be "playing with life" (V, 177)—but "the grey immensity of the people" (V, 216) appears the same to her. Millicent discovers "something jaunty and romantic, almost theatrical, in [Hyacinth's] whole little person" (V, 79). Some of the other characters are much given to playing roles, to acting out fantastic idealizations of themselves. Poupin easily slips into a stereotyped revolutionary passion regardless of the occasion; with his "declamatory, reclamatory, proclamatory" (V, 105) outbursts and his archaic incendiary slogans, he always acts the part of a man of '48. Lady Aurora, of course, is ludicrously theatrical: impressing Hyacinth as "a personage in a comedy" (V, 123) and her admirers as "one of the saints of old come to life again out of a legend" (V, 137). But, in the end, after her dreams of marrying Paul Muniment have come to nothing, she reverts to her former role as grand lady. Appropriately the transformation is marked by a radical change in her clothing. For, in contrast to the Princess, who comes to adopt "a very dull gown" suggesting a "thrifty housewife" (VI, 185), Lady Aurora, in her final appearance, greets Hyacinth wearing, for the first time, the clothing appropriate to her class: a "faintly-rustling dress," "a languid plume that flushed into little pink tips," "a pair of white gloves" (VI, 352).

The Princess Casamassima places a great emphasis on the clothes—actually the costumes—of its characters; rather the characters themselves place such an emphasis. Pinnie makes dresses, Millicent models them, Hyacinth covers books. Much is made of the uniforms of the workers—Vetch's tuxedo, Hyacinth's overalls, and Millicent's gowns. Muniment's marks of identity are his large working-man's shoes and the chemical stains on his fingers. The Princess takes to imitating Lady Aurora's unfashionable style of dress. Characters are so defined by the appearances they assume that Hyacinth even wonders whether in such a society one may have a private identity: "His own character? He was to cover that up as carefully as possible; he was to go through life in a mask, in a borrowed mantle; he was to be every day and every hour an actor" (V, 86).

These instances of compulsive theatricalism should be seen in a larger context. Nearly all of James's novels have something of a fairy-tale quality, but few to such a degree as *The Princess Casamassima*—with its elaborate mystification about the orphan's parentage, its succession of god-parent figures, and its exposure of the lowly hero to varieties of the fabulous. James draws our attention to the resemblances between his story and the fiction of make-believe. Lionel Trilling is surely right in locating *The Princess* in the tradition of novels dealing with "the Young Man from the Provinces," which "has its roots both in legend and in the very heart of modern actuality."[19] There is a good deal to suggest that both the legendary and the actual origins of the tradition attract James. One even suspects that James derives an ironic effect from the stereotypes he appropriates. Let us consider the ways in which he relates the story of Hyacinth Robinson to the most patently conventional and least "naturalistic" components of the Victorian novel. The borrowings from

19. "The Princess Casamassima," in *The Liberal Imagination*, p. 69.

Dickens are of importance here. Several critics have noticed the Dickensian qualities of Mrs. Bowerbank and the Millgate prison scene; Mr. Trilling mentions the similarities between Rosie Muniment and Jennie Wren of *Our Mutual Friend*; and F. R. Leavis sees traces of *Little Dorrit* in *The Princess*.[20] James's London, like Dickens', is a tangible atmosphere of smoke, grit, and gloom, so intense and so pervasive as to be a moral atmosphere. Also some parts of *The Princess* approach a Dickens-like sentimentality—notably the occasions of Pinnie's and Mr. Vetch's pure benevolence to Hyacinth and the chapters dealing with Pinnie's death.

James's London is not Dickens' London, as Hyacinth is not David Copperfield. But like some others in the novel, Hyacinth has the habit of seeing himself and those he meets as fictional characters. It is a habit that James encourages through such passages as the visit to the prison and the death of Pinnie. Our sense of the presence of other literary works is increased by the numerous references to titles, characters, and authors of nineteenth-century novels. In part James wishes simply to "place" his characters in a specific time and place (usually he is unspecific about such matters); he also shows how literary-minded some of his characters are. Twice an incidental figure reminds Hyacinth of Mr. Micawber (VI, 176; VI, 261). Captain Sholto's "romantic chambers" bring "certain of Bulwer's novels" (V, 267) to his mind. The pouring of a glass of wine at Medley, (the Princess' country house) reminds him "of some lines of Keats in the 'Ode to a Nightingale'" (VI, 5). The Princess strikes Hyacinth "as a sudden incarnation of the heroine of M. Feuillet's novel. . ." (VI, 16). The entire stay at Medley leads Hyacinth to "perceive that, like some famous novel, he was thrilling. . ."

20. W. H. Tilley, *The Background of* The Princess Casamassima, University of Florida Monographs (Gainesville, 1960), pp. 2-3; S. Gorley Putt, "A Henry James Jubilee, I," *Cornhill*, No. 969 (Winter, 1946), 189; Lionel Trilling, "The Princess Casamassima," p. 92; F. R. Leavis, *The Great Tradition* (New York, 1950), p. 172.

(VI, 56). Even when the Princess moves to humbler quarters, she still inhabits a fictional world for Hyacinth, for the room in Madeira Crescent "evoked the idea of the *vie de province* he had read about in French fiction" (VI, 269). The Princess also has a fondness for literary comparisons, as when she likens Lady Aurora's solitude in her Belgrave Square home to "something in some English novel" (VI, 198) or finds the prospect of Hyacinth's assassinating someone "like some silly humbug in a novel" (VI, 274).

When to these details are added the frequent mentions of literary works (most of them books Hyacinth is binding or reading), one realizes that James has done more than show that Hyacinth and the Princess like to read. The effect is complicated. If the Princess and Hyacinth are disposed to melodramatize their experiences, there is a great deal of the melodramatic in them, especially in the opening visit to Millbank prison, the discovery that Hyacinth's mother murdered his father, the assassination plot, and Hyacinth's suicide. But the first three of these events originate in past action, the assassination never takes place (and is itself a plot conceived by men captivated by a melodramatic view of history), and the effect of Hyacinth's suicide, which is not dramatized, is anything but melodramatic. In sum then, the nature of their experience does not quite justify the melodramatic points of view taken by the major characters.

This cast of mind is at odds with the realities of society. As James everywhere makes clear, London society is an organic whole, a complex fusion wherein the rigidities of class have broken down. The theatrical point of view assumes a settled, traditional order in which the act of moving from one class to another is judged a unique and spectacular expansion of self. Hyacinth applies fictional criteria to the upper world, as does the Princess to the lower world. So it is something of a disillusion to each when their putative opposites turn out to be not very exceptional: Hyacinth fails the Princess because he is a gentleman, and the Princess fails Hyacinth because she falls well short of the aristocratic ideal, selling herself to Muniment in order to be intimate with the poor in much the same way as Millicent sells herself to Sholto in order to be intimate with the rich.

A theme to be found in *The Bostonians* and *The Tragic Muse*, as well as in *The Princess Casamassima*, is the destructiveness of abstract thinking. Many of the characters of these novels commit themselves to some formal ideology (much more consciously than the characters in the international fiction who possess an allegiance to a national culture). In *The Bostonians* the conflict is simply between the public life and the private life, or between ideas and existence. The question to be resolved is whether Verena Tarrant will allow a formal conception of womanhood to destroy her life as a woman. The matter is more complicated in *The Tragic Muse*, a novel just as full of speeches, theories, and public postures. In both novels the heroine is extremely lacking in self-consciousness. Though Verena must be jolted into an acceptance of herself as an intuitive, unreflective person, Miriam Rooth comes early to such a recognition. She has neither self-doubts nor even self-awareness, whereas the men in her life are torn apart by conflicting notions of convention, duty, ambition, and love. No one in *The Princess* is very much like Miriam Rooth, whose liberation from ideas is complete. Yet Hyacinth eventually comes to see the folly of ideas: he pleads to Millicent, "Let us live in the world of irreflective contemplation—let us live in the present hour" (VI, 333). Of course, the very formulation of such a wish precludes its fulfillment. Unlike Miriam, he cannot be an artist, and unlike Verena he cannot marry. He is denied his art (that of bookbinder and possibly of author) and his marriage (to Millicent) by the all-pervasiveness of theatrically pursued formal attitudes. Conspiracy proves to be betrayal not because the ideas behind it are radical, but because all ideas are anti-human. Hyacinth's relationships—to the Poupins, the parent figures; to Muniment, the friend; and to the Princess and Millicent, the potential lovers—collapse beneath the pressure of loyalties to abstractions.

The moral lesson is an old and simple one—that a person is of more consequence than "the people." Hyacinth's tragedy is far more significant than the sufferings of the masses. Of Hoffendahl, the remote formulator of the revolutionary ideals and plots, James writes that "Humanity, in his scheme, was classified and subdivided with a truly German thoroughness. . ." (VI, 55). Muniment, an equally detached revolutionary, is spoken of as "moving ever in a dry statistical and scientific air" (VI, 137) when he discusses political matters. The Princess, to be sure, is a woman of considerable passion, but it is all committed to an idea—"the idea of a tremendous risk and an unregarded sacrifice" (VI, 405).

The characters most intractable in their formal beliefs are significantly the Prince Casamassima, the ultimate conservative, and Schinkel, the revolutionist whose commitment to political terrorism is totally impersonal. "It's none of [Muniment's] business any more than ours," Schinkel tells the Poupins just before giving Hyacinth his letter of assignment; "it's none of any one's business" (VI, 372). The Prince too denies personal responsibility for his actions. To him social injustice is divinely ordained; to Schinkel, violence—including the sacrifice of Hyacinth—is a historical necessity. There is a deep irony in this implied resemblance of one who obeys the will of the Pope to one who obeys the will of Hoffendahl. Differences between ideas are less consequential than the impersonal nature of all ideas. The ideas that suffuse *The Princess* have to do with the pre-eminent importance and absoluteness of social and economic class distinctions. Since the holders of these ideas are themselves *déclassé*, their categorical judgments always seem hollow. So it is most fitting that James should stress the theatricalism and bookishness of their conceptions of themselves and each other. Though everyone accepts illusion for reality, only Hyacinth pays for the mistake. He realizes too late not just that "the sacred cause" (VI, 144) of revolution masks the "ulcer of envy" (VI, 158) of revolutionists, but that every expression of "values" is empty.[21]

The imagery of *The Princess Casamassima* is so consistent and emphatic that the pictorial content of the novel seems nearly as significant as the dramatic content. The recurrent image is that of a spot of light surrounded by limitless darkness. The darkness is often that of the London night, as when Lady Aurora looks "away into the thickening dust, at the smutty housetops, the blurred emanation of lamplight above the streets" (V, 250) or when Hyacinth rides in the cab to the meeting with Hoffendahl: "The cab jogged along murky miles, and by the time it stopped our young man had wholly lost, in the drizzling gloom, a sense of their whereabouts" (V, 363). The darkness of the city also intrudes into confined interiors, like "the landing at the top of the stairs in Audley Court [which] was always dark" (VI, 159), the "dark tortuous greasy passage communicating with the outer world" (V, 357) in the Sun and Moon Café, and the "dismal *chiaroscuro*" (VI, 90) of Lomax Place. In the beginning Hyacinth associates the pervasive darkness with his own obscurity and poverty. Thus he reaches out to whatever figures or places of light present themselves, especially to the "bright" (VI, 76) and "dazzl[ing]" (VI, 40) Princess Casamassima (who is, of course, Christina Light). To Hyacinth her eyes suggest "that profuse mingled light which seemed to belong to some everlasting summer. . ." (VI, 14). The Princess' various residences with their golden chairs and bright saloons reflect her radiance. Millicent strikes Hyacinth as "the most brilliant figure [Lomax]

21. The exception is, of course, the value of loyalty (to people, not ideas)—evidenced positively in Hyacinth's final dilemma and Madame Grandoni's adherence to the Princess and negatively in the multiple betrayals. But the essence of loyalty is self-sacrifice, whereas the lofty articulations of the Princess, Muniment, Poupin, Lady Aurora, and others are ways of glorifying quite selfish interests.

place had ever contained" (V, 59) and she is usually represented as "bloom[ing]" or "shining" (V, 61). Lady Aurora is explicitly, if absurdly, a bearer of light. The aptness of her name is not lost on Rosie Muniment: "Isn't it right she should be called the dawn when she brings light where she goes" (V, 126)?

James achieves obvious atmospheric effects from his patterns of light and darkness, but the significance is that the light is illusory and the darkness real. Thus the first appearance of the Princess is more of a promise than a realization of brilliance: she "was partly overshadowed by the curtain of the box, drawn forward with the intention of shielding her from the observation of the house; she had still the air of youth, and the simplest way to express the instant effect upon Hyacinth of her fair face of welcome is to say that she dazzled him" (V, 205-6). In terms of the rhetoric of images operative throughout the novel, this first sentence describing the Princess contains in essence the entire history of her future relations with Hyacinth: the brilliance, far from overcoming the shadow, is to remain an obscured vision of a radiance that will eventually be withdrawn altogether. The same is true of the other lights that attract Hyacinth: that of the pointedly named Sun and Moon Café, wherein the anarchists gather; that of Lady Aurora, whose presumed saintliness turns out to be tainted. The feeble lights of candles and gas lamps that burn in the dingy rooms of Mr. Vetch, the Poupins, and the Muniments express futility from the start.[22] The European capi-

22. James ingeniously manages several abrupt transitions through manipulation of light imagery. Book Third concludes with Hyacinth's staring "into the turbid flame of the candle" in Mr. Vetch's room, visualizing "the most brilliant scenes" (VI, 116) of Paris. Book Fourth begins with the sentence: "The Boulevard was all alive, brilliant with illuminations . . . the dazzle of shops and cafés . . . the flamboyant porches of theatres and the flashing lamps of carriages. . . " (VI, 119). The antithesis of dark and light underscores the radical difference between the last scene of the first volume and the first scene of the second volume. The former concludes with the cab ride through the murky London streets to the meeting with Hoffendahl, and the latter begins with the brilliant morning at Medley.

tals visited by Hyacinth are brilliant, but distant and unattainable.

As I have suggested, Hyacinth is not so much the victim of an unresolvable dilemma as he is the victim of the persons in whom he has trusted and who finally fail him. Toward the end the prevailing figurative pattern of light and darkness loses its aesthetic and economic connotations and in Hyacinth's mind stands rather simply for what is far more real to him: the need for human comfort and the agony of abandonment. So it is that, after receiving his commission, Hyacinth seeks, if not positive relief, at least some intimacy with his "friends": "The evenings were bitter to him now and he feared them in advance. The darkness had become a haunted element; it had visions for him that passed even before his closed eyes—sharp doubts and fears and suspicions, suggestions of evil, revelations of pain. He wanted company to light up his gloom, and this had driven him back to Millicent. . ." (VI, 347). It turns out, of course, that neither Millicent nor anyone lights up his gloom.

Even more ironic is the light which appears in the last few pages of the novel, the "small glow proceeding from the chink" (VI, 429) beneath Hyacinth's door that reveals to the Princess and Schinkel that Hyacinth is dead. This light is the dimmest of all: "that of a single candle on the mantel; it was so poor that for a moment she made out nothing definite. Before that moment was over, however, her eyes had attached themselves to the small bed. There was something on it—something black, something ambiguous, something outstretched" (VI, 430). If nothing else, these stark sentences make it clear that the recurrent images of light and dark refer neither to the rich and the poor (as the Princess and Lady Aurora would have it), nor to the beautiful and the ugly (as Hyacinth once would have it), but to love and desolation. The failure of light is the failure of love.

The point has been made that with few exceptions James's London is a place of crowds, grime, fog, and a nearly palpable darkness. But the exceptions are significant. On four occasions, at fairly regular intervals, Hyacinth escapes from the urban murkiness and congestion into what can accurately be called a pastoral experience. In Chapter Eleven Hyacinth strolls with Millicent in Hyde Park; the time is summer. In Chapters Twenty-Two through Twenty-Six he spends a few days with the Princess at Medley; the time is spring. In Chapter Thirty-Five Hyacinth and Muniment have a Sunday outing at Greenwich; the time is the "warm bright September" (VI, 203) of the following year; in Chapter Forty-One Hyacinth takes another walk with Millicent through Hyde Park; the time is spring. Each of these scenes stands in sharp contrast to the usual urban drabness and also to the usual unpleasant weather. Of course the bare details of the pastoral chapters, showing the changes of the seasons, allow James to indicate the passage of time. More important, the first two outdoor scenes are occasions of illusion for Hyacinth; he is never happier with Millicent and the Princess. The final two scenes are the occasions of his desertion by Muniment and Millicent. The Medley scene is the only picturesque one, as it is removed from London. The park in Greenwich is "charming" but "shabby" (VI, 209); it also affords a view of the London water front. Hyacinth thinks of his final stroll with Millicent through Hyde Park as a "small cheap pastoral" (VI, 340), but it is sufficiently bucolic for Millicent: " 'Well, there's nothing so pretty as nature,' Millicent observed at a venture, surveying the smutty sheep who find pasturage in the fields that extend from Knightsbridge to the Bayswater Road" (VI, 332). But even the shabby London pastorals provoke Hyacinth to dreams of release—in the beginning from his anonymity and in the end from his irreconcilable duties.[23] Since they are the only

23. A similar (though not ironic) pattern controls *The Bostonians*: the dingy enclosed urban scenes show Verena Tarrant in oppression and the pastoral scenes show her being offered freedom by Ransom. The pattern is more symmetrical than in *The Princess*, for each of Verena's three lec-

occasions of sunlight in the novel, the pastoral scenes support the prevailing imagery of ineffectual light, as they lead not to "rest" and "protection" (VI, 340), but to betrayal. Here too the light fades and the darkness prevails.

The various recurrences of images, scenes, and motifs are of obvious structural importance, but they have less to do with unifying the many strains of the novel than the full consciousness of Hyacinth. Therefore, if *The Princess Casamassima* is looked upon as an experiment in the French naturalist or the English social novel—or both—it can hardly be concluded that James has sacrificed unity to multiplicity. If anything, James has sacrificed multiplicity to unity, especially in his tactic of making Hyacinth's involvement with London follow so schematic a pattern, though he otherwise represents a London resistant to such imposed designs. Though his accomplishment is not flawless, James's rich dramatization of the relations of his protagonist to his crowded and diversified London environment is a literary achievement very nearly unique.

---

tures is juxtaposed with an outdoors meeting with Ransom—in the Harvard Yard, in Central Park, and on Cape Cod.

VII · *WHAT MAISIE KNEW*

It is a little difficult to speak of such a thing as "the form" of *What Maisie Knew* or, indeed, of that of any of the novels of James's "middle period." In any case, my own approach to the structure of *Maisie* has been from three rather distinct directions. What I hope ties together the diverse strands of the present chapter is the conviction that *What Maisie Knew* is demonstrably a unified novel. I have chosen to consider the book from the points of view of three separate and overlapping compositional techniques. All of these have at least been mentioned by other critics, but, to my knowledge, none has been analyzed for its contribution to the organic structure. The methods are, first, James's borrowing of the three-act organization of the drama; second, the severe parallelism of the plot; and, third, the ambiguous quality of Maisie's intelligence. The subsequent discussion follows this order.

In the course of writing his preliminary notes for *What*

Maisie Knew, James digressed briefly from his consideration of the details of scene development and character placement to celebrate the general method he was following: "Ah, this *divine* conception of one's little masses and periods in the scenic light— as rounded ACTS; this patient, pious nobly 'vindictive' [(James's note) 'vindicating'] application of the scenic philosophy and method—I feel as if it still (above *all*, YET) had a great deal to give me, and might carry me as far as I dream" (*N*, p. 258). We need belabor neither the details of James's practical experience in the theater, nor the manner in which he carried over dramatic techniques into fiction.[1] More to the immediate point is the structural tension resulting from the union of the novel form, with its inherent developmental pressure, and the dramatic form, with its rigid, pre-established dimensions.

The notebook commentary on *The Spoils of Poynton*, *What Maisie Knew*, and *The Awkward Age* demonstrates that James relies upon dramatic technique not simply to insure intensity, objectivity, and economy,[2] but to organize what he calls his "clear order and expressed sequence" (*N*, p. 208); that is, he conceives of these short novels not merely as successions of distinct, spare, coherent scenes, but rather as unified wholes totally organized according to the dramatic principle, structurally determined by "the scenic philosophy." In the novels of the 1896-1901 period, James customarily began with the notion that chapters should correspond with dramatic acts and that these chapters should be about the same in number as the acts in a play. *What Maisie Knew* was planned as a ten-thousand-word tale, and *The Spoils*

1. The subject has been thoroughly covered elsewhere. See especially Leon Edel, *The Complete Plays of Henry James* (Philadelphia, 1949), pp. 59-66; and Elizabeth L. Forbes, "Dramatic Lustrum: A Study of the Effect of James's Theatrical Experience on His Later Novels," *New England Quarterly*, XI (March, 1938), 108-20.

2. Intensity, objectivity, and economy are the "dramatic" qualities stressed by Joseph Wiesenfarth, F. S. C., in his study of the novels of the 1896-1901 period, *Henry James and the Dramatic Analogy* (New York, 1963).

of Poynton was designed to run from fifteen to twenty thousand words. James says that he has "no better example" than *The Awkward Age* of those works "projected as small things [which] had finally to be provided for as comparative monsters" (*P*, p. 98). *The Awkward Age* turned out to be the longest of the dramatic novels, and, since "The beauty of the conception was in [the] approximation of the respective divisions of my form to the successive Acts of a Play . . ." (*P*, p. 110), the novel finally bears a resemblance to a ten-act play. From the first extended notebook comment on *The Spoils of Poynton*, it is evident that James looked to the drama to supply a model for the total form of that novel: "What is wanting is a full roundness for the action—the completeness of the drama-quality. . . . I seem to see the thing in three chapters, like 3 little acts. . ." (*N*, p. 198). Subsequent comments on *The Spoils* show James making repeated concessions to the demands of the material to consume more space. What is most revealing, however, is James's refusal to sacrifice the original three-act scheme (as he seems willing to do in *The Awkward Age*). The chapters swell freely, far exceeding the original three. The completed chapters possess scenic integrity, but they cease to correspond with acts. Yet the act arrangement is still meaningful. From the notebooks and from the novel, we detect James's effort to subdivide his work so as to have three denouements, each indicating a climax to what has taken place and—in the case of the first two of the divisions—producing the conditions which further stimulate the action. The climax of "Act I" is the engagement of Owen and Mona;[3] the climax of "Act II" is Mrs. Gereth's despoliation of Poynton; and the climax of "Act III" is her return of the treasures and

3. In the original plan, the first section "terminates with the son's marriage to one—the dreaded one—of the Brigstocks" (*N*, p. 198). But after writing the first few chapters, James rejected the idea, on the grounds that "the center of gravity of the piece, which is that Owen marries Mona, is in danger of being thrust much too far forward, out of its place" (*N*, p. 208).

the consequent marriage of Owen and Mona. The novel deviates from the original plan only in that the acts expand into clusters of chapters.[4] But, far from violating the plan, the developments considerably enrich it.

What produces the unforeseen length and complexity is the involvement of Fleda Vetch in the affairs of the Gereths. As James's insight into his chosen subject deepened, Fleda's role became increasingly more important to him. Finally it is Fleda's response to the controversy over the spoils that gives the novel its major interest. But Fleda's importance in no way counteracts the emphasis supplied by the three-act structure, since her own developing moral crisis takes its form from the actions of others— especially from those actions that determine the crises of each of the three acts. To be specific, in the first act, not only does Owen engage himself to Mona, but Fleda hopelessly commits herself to the embroiled situation by acknowledging her loyalty to both Owen and his mother. Here she falls into the false position that occasions all her later troubles. Fleda's second principal decision is to tell a lie to Mrs. Gereth—to conceal from her Owen's report that Mona will not marry him unless the spoils are returned. Fleda's lie constitutes her own moral and psychological "climax" in the second part, following immediately upon the more overt climax of that act, Mrs. Gereth's plunder of the spoils. Likewise, in the final section, after the return of the spoils, Fleda succumbs to Mrs. Gereth's pleas (and her own suppressed desire) and pursues Owen, only to learn of his marriage. In sum, it is not just the external situation that under- goes three distinct movements, but also Fleda's response to that situation.[5] Thereby the three-act structure, as it yields to the

4. That the third "act" turned out longer than the first two combined shows only that it was susceptible to much more "development" than the others. In *What Maisie Knew*, the second of the three "acts" is dispro- portionately long.

5. In suggesting that Fleda's personal story falls into three phases—that of her commitment to both the Gereths, that of her lie to Mrs. Gereth,

developmental pressure, represents the total design of the novel, not simply its plot. And in the end it has nothing to do with the most superficial aspect of the novel's form—the individual chapters that were initially designed to be complete acts.

As James completed the final chapters of *The Spoils of Poynton*, the plan for *What Maisie Knew* took form in his notebooks. Although James does not explicitly propose that it conform to the organization of a three-act play, the finished novel gives evidence of such a scheme. The first of these "acts," including Chapters One through Seven, ends with the remarriage of Maisie's parents—Beale to Miss Overmore, and Ida to Sir Claude. The long middle section of the novel, extending from Chapter Eight through Twenty-One, concentrates on the developing relation between Sir Claude and Mrs. Beale and concludes with the total abandonment of Maisie by her original parents. Finally, Chapters Twenty-Two through Thirty-One, all set in Boulogne, lead up to Sir Claude's proposal to Maisie that she reject Mrs. Wix and culminate with Maisie's counterproposal that Sir Claude reject Mrs. Beale.

Maisie is the constant element, always in the middle but surrounded by different groupings of characters. At first the tension between Beale and Ida contains Maisie. Then the surrounding milieu grows more complex as not only Mrs. Beale and Sir Claude but a succession of Ida's and Beale's lovers cluster about her. Ida and Beale battle both each other and their new mates, who, in turn, are drawn toward each other. In the third act, Ida and Beale, along with their retinues of lovers, have been displaced by Mrs. Beale and Sir Claude. The cast of characters has been reduced, and Maisie has ceased to move about from one home to another; to this extent the action and the cast of Act III are more restricted than those of Act I, as both are more restricted

---

and that of her pursuit of Owen—I do not imply any precise interpretation of her character. The pattern suggested here seems adaptable to the analyses both of those who admire Fleda and find her consistent and of those who disparage her and find her inconsistent.

than those of Act II. The design is also given emphasis by Mrs. Wix's resumption in Act III of the major role she assumed in Act I, in contrast to her absence in Act II.

The most significant progression in Act III is that of Maisie herself, as, for the first time, she becomes a moral participant in the drama. In the first two sections, she is mostly acted upon. In the first, as the "bone of contention" (*N*, p. 127) between her parents, she is a bearer of insults who is at the start possessively guarded by each and subsequently abandoned by each to the other. In the second section, she provides a bare legitimacy for the affair between Sir Claude and Mrs. Beale. Maisie takes pride in her role in the formation of this union ("I've brought you and her together" [XI, 64], she tells Sir Claude), and it is an accomplishment that she never forgets. But Maisie's "role" in bringing together Sir Claude and Mrs. Beale is only slightly more active and volitional than her role as victim and center of the Beale-Ida feud. This dubious service to her stepparents is a transition from the total passivity of her original condition to the active control that she exerts only in the final pages, when she announces her terms to Sir Claude. Furthermore, Maisie's first intervention follows the moral law of the adults; the second intervention accords to her own moral law, discommoding rather than assisting Sir Claude and Mrs. Beale. In the final act, Maisie is agent rather than spectator, herself a figure in the pattern of relationships that heretofore surrounded her but did not include her. She, Mrs. Wix, Mrs. Beale, and Sir Claude create the climactic tension, and Maisie and Sir Claude are the ones who struggle to resolve it.

Hence it can be seen that, as in *The Spoils of Poynton*, the three-act structure of *What Maisie Knew* directs the inward progression of the central intelligence as well as the outward progression of the plot. *Maisie* has a more evident symmetry, a more straightforward "march of . . . action" (*P*, p. 308) than *The Spoils*. The three major changes in the relationships among the characters are more prominent and more radically disruptive; and the reflecting character's growth of moral awareness, though ambiguous and difficult to define, is more obvious than in the earlier novel. Maisie's final position is both different from her earlier ones and a logical outgrowth from them. Fleda's development follows a less certain course. In both novels, however, the a priori structure—that of the three-act play—proves most elastic and resilient, capable of an organic growth that directs and yet bends to the complexities inherent in the subject, not the least of which is the moral life of the reflector. Though we may be more conscious of the admirable economy and directness of the individual scenic chapters than of the over-all structure of the novels (for the construction of the chapters is explicit, and the three-act arrangement of the whole is not very emphatic), it is nevertheless demonstrable that the structure of the drama corresponds with the total organization of these novels.

Two years after the publication of *What Maisie Knew*, James commented in his notebooks (in reference to a suggestion that he again try his hand at a play) on his continuing enthusiasm for the drama. He referred to the drama as "the divine little difficult, artistic, ingenious, architectural FORM that makes old pulses throb and old tears rise again" (*N*, p. 268). James's next notebook entry, made five days later, shows that in his mind the architectural form of the drama was interchangeable with that of "some strong short novel" (*N*, p. 269). "How, through all hesitations and conflicts and worries," he wrote, "*the* thing, the desire to get back only to the *big* (scenic, constructive 'architectural' effects) seizes me and carries me off my feet. . ." (*N*, p. 269). The comment hints, as do some passages in the prefaces, that James sometimes thought of the structural devices in the drama as more pronounced (thus "bigger") than those usually found in the novel; these were the effects that James wished to carry over into his own novels. When we try to determine how these "constructive 'architectural' effects" are in fact achieved in fiction, we find in addition to the imitations of dramatic scenes and acts the regular Jamesian method of extremely sharp contrasts and balances.

More precisely, in the dramatic novels James depends upon a system of bipolarity. Most often the poles are two distinct settings or clusters of characters, frequently identified with houses.[6] This use of houses is central to *The Spoils of Poynton*, in which the grotesque Waterbath and the sublime Poynton embody the two standards of taste that are opposed throughout the novel. The tactic is somewhat less prominent in *What Maisie Knew*. Here there is little emphasis given to the physical structures themselves; rather it is given to the separate domestic and matrimonial establishments of Beale and Ida. These locations do not contrast, as do the houses in *The Spoils*, so much as balance each other in their brutality and grossness.

As in the case of Fleda, a double awareness is forced upon Maisie—an awareness of the house she happens to be in and also of the other house, just as much a threat. Fleda is preoccupied with Owen and Mona (Waterbath) when she is with Mrs. Gereth (Poynton) and preoccupied with Mrs. Gereth when she is with Owen. Most often in the dramatic novels, the paired characters or groups are themselves little interested in the outsider: they are indifferent (as are the alleged sets of lovers in *The Sacred Fount*), self-absorbed (as are Captain Everard and Lady Bradeen in "In the Cage") exploitive (as are Mona Brigstock and Mrs. Gereth), or else they are all of these (as are Beale and Ida).

In these novels of the nineties, James reduces the scale and alters the emphasis of his earlier (and later) international contrasts. True, there is a sense in which Maisie is caught between Ida and Beale, and Fleda between Waterbath and Poynton, in

6. James's practice of using houses to characterize their inhabitants has been discussed by Edwin T. Bowden, *The Themes of Henry James: A System of Visual Observation* (New Haven, 1956), pp. 34, 40-42, 48-52, 61, 67, 80, 83, 92-93, 100.

much the same way as Isabel Archer is caught between Gardencourt and Osmond's house in Rome, Hyacinth Robinson between Lomax Place and Medley, or Strether between Woollett and Paris. But in the more spacious novels of the early and late periods, James seldom restricts himself to two fields of operation. For example, Isabel's house in Albany comes to symbolize a degree of freedom (albeit aesthetically impoverished) to be found neither in Gardencourt nor in Rome. Furthermore a number of the characters, representing varieties of moral possibilities, are not shown to belong to certain houses. Even in *The Golden Bowl*, in which the Prince's Portland Place and Mr. Verver's Eaton Square are as insistently opposed as the houses in *The Spoils of Poynton*, the bipolarity is not very prominent. Not only are there other morally relevant settings, especially Fawns, but the dense symbolic texture of the novel precludes the dominance of the contrasting houses.

In those novels of the "middle period" in which the system is emphatic, there is a much stronger sense of restrictiveness, of oppressive confinement for the central character than in novels of other periods. Perhaps more significantly, the protagonists of earlier and later fiction are morally or psychologically committed to one of the alternative modes of experience, perhaps eventually to change allegiance, as Strether does, but not forced to maintain a delicate balance in the midst of two camps. Maisie and Fleda really belong nowhere. When they are not rejected by one or both of the "houses" that have some claim on them, it is they who reject the houses. The dramatic form, with its enforced economy and "architecture," is doubtless both cause and effect of James's reduction of the scale of operations of his characters and of his identification of the moral possibilities open to them with alternating settings.

The Other House plainly demonstrates James's fondness for the technique of the double setting, both in its title and in its system of character arrangement. Part of the weakness of *The*

Other House is attributable to the mechanical procedure whereby the scene shifts from Bounds, the home of Tony Bream, to Eastmead, that of his neighbor, Mrs. Beever. As a transformed play-scenario,[7] *The Other House* betrays the author's heavy-handed effort to move his characters on and off the stage. "The other house" (that is, whatever house happens *not* to be the immediate setting) is little more than the off-stage home for the characters when their presence is not required. The device of the two neighboring houses has little to do with the moral configurations formed by the characters: that opposition, for example, of the "good heroine," Jean Martle, and the "bad heroine," Rose Armiger.[8]

But the method comes to life elsewhere. When it succeeds, the reader shares the viewpoint of the victim in the middle, that of the figure who stands apart from both of the houses and whose life is yet inexorably determined by them. (The only one remotely filling this role in *The Other House* is the murdered infant, hardly a character at all, though having a pale kinship to the child victims of the other dramatic novels). It is interesting that the character of Fleda Vetch was a late addition to the plans for the novel that she finally dominates. Both in the notebooks and the preface to *The Spoils of Poynton*, James states that the germinal idea is that of a woman of refined taste competing with a woman of vulgar taste for the precious things. Fleda, who at first is conceived as little more than a contrast to Mona Brigstock,

7. For a history of the various forms of the work, see Leon Edel, "Introduction," *The Other House* (London, 1948), pp. x-xii, xviii-xx.

8. This is not to deny that the two houses form a moral contrast. As Mr. Bowden points out, Mrs. Beever's "house represents stability and peace and natural order, taking much of its tranquility from the contrast offered by the showy and splendid 'other house'" (p. 80). However, this contrast is not very vital to the subject. More than anything, it seems an attempt to disguise the mechanical rigidities of the scheme.

It is to the point that the title *The Other House* was selected only when James's suggestion, *The Promise*, was rejected by the publisher. See Edel, "Introduction," p. xiii.

an appendage of Mrs. Gereth, gradually takes on more importance, until finally "the progress and march of my tale became and remained that of her understanding" (*P*, p. 128). Like Maisie's, Fleda's "progress" is one from baffled passivity to relative comprehension and fitful action. She becomes the intelligent reflector of the "not directly articulate" (*P*, p. 127) spoils and of those who compete for them. Fleda, as the character who most nearly comprehends "the real center" (*P*, p. 126), the spoils of Poynton, is, to that extent, identified with the object of competition. She approaches Maisie's position, which is to be both the occasion of the conflict and the fullest understanding of it. Also like Maisie, Fleda is herself homeless, anchorless between two dramatic bases.

Because she is intelligent, the houses are of more than aesthetic consequence to her. In fact, the dower house, Ricks, communicates more of human significance to her than either the museum-like Poynton or the garish Waterbath. In Ricks Fleda recognizes a kind of moral beauty well beyond the vision of both Mrs. Gereth and Mona Brigstock:

> It was all, none the less, not as bad as Fleda had feared; it was faded and melancholy, whereas there had been a danger it would be contradictious and positive, cheerful and loud. The place was crowded with objects of which the aggregation somehow made a thinness and the futility a grace; things that told her they had been gathered as slowly and as lovingly as the garden flowers of the other house. She too, for a home, could have lived with them: they made her fond of the old maiden-aunt; they made her even wonder if it didn't work more for happiness not to have tasted, as she herself had done, of knowledge. . . . The more she looked about the surer she felt of the character of the maiden-aunt, the sense of whose dim presence urged her to pacification. . . . The poor lady had passed shyly, yet with some bruises, through life; had been sensitive and ignorant and exquisite: that too was a sort of origin, a sort of atmosphere for relics and rarities, though different from the sorts most prized at Poynton (X, 54-55).

Here then is a kind of dialectic of houses. Ricks, embodying the virtue of quiet suffering, stands as an alternative to the blatant aggressiveness of the mistresses of both Waterbath and Poynton.[9] The value of Ricks is the only one finally available to Fleda—the value of intelligent and morally responsible renunciation.

The use of juxtaposed houses is rather different in *What Maisie Knew*. What is readily apparent in the later novel is the way James varies and multiplies the scheme of doubleness. The pattern is established in the introductory chapter, much of which details the grotesqueries of Beale and Ida. After some attention to the disproportion of Ida's form, James turns to Beale, to "the eternal glitter of the teeth that his long moustache had been trained not to hide" (XI, 8). The two parents continue to echo one another, first in insulting each other through Maisie, then in preventing Maisie's going to the other, then in preventing Maisie's returning from the other, then in remarrying, then in carrying on continuous sexual liaisons, then in lying, then in deserting Maisie entirely. The parallels are so precise that each tries to bribe Maisie and then reclaims the money. A chapter representing an aspect of one's vileness is followed by a chapter representing the same aspect of the other's vileness. Ida and Beale are in near perfect balance, equally contemptible, equally contemptuous. There is some irony in the fact that these two who loathe each other are virtual duplicates, but James's real interest lies elsewhere: their hatred creates the conditions of Maisie's life, the extraordinarily "adult" situation which her unassisted intelligence tries to comprehend.

The initial pair, Ida and Beale, expands to two pairs, Ida-Sir Claude and Beale-Mrs. Beale. Other pairs compose at a bewilder-

9. One must disagree with Oscar Cargill's exclusively aesthetic critique of the houses: "Is not James saying that the furnishings of both Poynton and Ricks have especial merit because they were chosen specifically for Poynton and Ricks, and that, as separate pieces these furnishings are not absolutely precious" (*The Novels of Henry James* [New York, 1961], p. 230)?

ing rate and the original partners are realigned. Like those other perplexed and imaginative outsiders in James's fiction of the nineties—such as the governess in "The Turn of the Screw," the narrator of *The Sacred Fount*, and the telegraphist in "In the Cage"—Maisie tries to understand and even direct the lives of those who surround her. Maisie is one of those Jamesian intelligences confined in "a world of whiffs and glimpses," whose passion is not for her own life but for "her theories and interpretations" (XI, 386) of others' lives. Unlike some other tales in which the central consciousness thrives on inference and speculation, *What Maisie Knew* presents no epistemological difficulties. Maisie and the reader alike know quite well who is linked with whom in the adult world, although Maisie's interpretation of these evident facts is less than perfect. Maisie's prime mode of existence is nonetheless intellectual: she is the one who knows and the one whom the adults would shield from knowledge. Her confined and neglected state requires even that she "know" rather than live her own life. Her "sharpened sense of spectatorship was the child's main support . . . a sort of compensation for the doom of a peculiar passivity. It gave her often an odd air of being present at her history in as separate a manner as if she could only get at experience by flattening her nose against a pane of glass" (XI, 107). Maisie might well agree with the slightly more self-determining young girl in "In the Cage": "All I get out of it is the harmless pleasure of knowing" (XI, 447).

In most of the dramatic novels, the intellectual curiosity of the observer-outsider creates certain ethical problems. The most straightforward instance of this ambiguous tie between the level of intellect and the level of ethics is *The Sacred Fount*. Whatever the theme of this odd novel may be, it cannot be overlooked that the narrator's intense and detached curiosity about the relations among the various country-house guests originates, in part at least, in a chilling intellectual pride. He does not scrutinize in order to judge—as do the governess in "The Turn of the

Screw" and Laura Wing in "A London Life"—but to be happy in the fact of knowing. The telegraphist's fondness for discovering patterns in the cavortings of her fashionable customers represents a retreat from reality and responsibility. The ethical problem raised by Maisie's passion for knowing is quite different. It is interesting that most of the critics of the novel have concluded either that Maisie in the end acquires "a moral sense" (to use Mrs. Wix's phrase) or that she never rises above the selfish expediency of the adults.[10] In any case, what perturbs Mrs. Wix is what interests the reader. Does Maisie possess or acquire an idea of right and wrong, or is her enthusiasm for knowing simply indulged in for its own sake and finally put to the use of a selfish opportunism?

According to the preface, Maisie's quality of mind is the central subject of the novel: the "very principle of Maisie's appeal" is "that vivacity of intelligence by which she does vibrate in the infected air. . ." (*P*, p. 149). What then is the connection, if any, between the attention given to Maisie's intelligence—to the way she knows as well as to what she knows—and the bizarre symmetry of the plot, and to what extent does the geometrical design of the adult world bear on the question of her own moral character? The various contrasts, parallels, and balancings no doubt transform the otherwise tedious folly of the real and quasi-parents into comic ceremony, just as they create interesting and ironic structural patterns—what James calls "constructive 'architectural' effects" (*N*, p. 269). But if this

10. To document this point fully, it would almost be necessary to cite the entire bibliography of criticism of the novel. Two writers who have recently taken opposing stands are James W. Gargano, *"What Maisie Knew:* the Evolution of a 'Moral Sense,' " *Nineteenth-Century Fiction,* XVI (June, 1961), 33-46, who argues that Maisie retains her innocence and develops a moral superiority to the adults; and John C. McCloskey, "What Maisie Knows: A Study of Childhood and Adolescence," *American Literature,* XXXVI (January, 1965), 485-513, who is in direct disagreement. I shall suggest that the dichotomy assumed by these and other critics—that Maisie must be either moral or expedient—is false.

geometrical form is to be judged organic it must have some relevance to the "light vessel of consciousness" (*P*, p. 143) that is the center of the novel. The remark in the preface that the ironic theme of the novel is "the close connexion of bliss and bale" (*P*, p. 143), that is, of innocence and corruption, in no way accounts for the symmetry of the external action, though it invites us to seek the "connexion" between this action and its reflector. To discover the relation we must pay closer attention to the unique quality of Maisie's intelligence.

Maisie is such an "extraordinary 'ironic center'" (*P*, p. 147) because she is an observer of a sexual entanglement who is ignorant of the meaning of sex, a child with no conception of the properieties of adult relationships and therefore unable to recognize the improprieties. Her language and her criteria come solely from the environment created by the adults. Because she possesses not only "an innocence so saturated with knowledge" (XI, 173) but a knowledge so saturated with innocence, she comes to know things as objective facts, not as moral evidence. Her innocence is most manifest in her freedom from the hypocrisy, selfishness, greed, and lust of her parents and stepparents; the principal limitation of her knowledge is her ignorance of these.

She is thus a literalist. Early in the story, "She was at the age for which all stories are true and all conceptions are stories. The actual was the absolute, the present alone was vivid" (XI, 14). Yet Maisie develops a sense of "rightness"; she acquires a notion of the way things should be. Her moral sense is by no means Mrs. Wix's doctrinaire list of commonplaces, but an improvised and inductively apprehended set of standards. To trace the growth of this conception is to trace the expansion of Maisie's consciousness.

Even in the beginning, when Maisie is at the age of six, her thoughts are rather complex. We learn not simply that she is most often baffled by life ("Everything had something behind it:

life was like a long, long corridor with rows of closed doors"
[XI, 33-34]), but that she has quite consciously developed a
strategy for dealing with adult demands—simply to pretend
ignorance. But she seeks more than simple self-preservation,
though this interest is always important to her. She has also
established certain standards of preference. At first these standards are exclusively aesthetic and indeed they remain largely
aesthetic throughout the novel. She judges people on the basis of
their table manners, the fashionableness of their clothing, their
beauty or handsomeness. She compares the adults to the "perfect" ladies and gentlemen in the storybooks read to her by Mrs.
Wix. The aesthetic standards are principally those of Mayfair
society, with the difference that for Maisie they are absolute, not
to be altered by fluctuations of passion. In the scene in which
Beale snatches Maisie away from his wife and takes her to the
home of the American "countess," "the brown lady," the reader's
attention is drawn to Beale's callous egotism, but Maisie's mind
is full, not of moral judgments, but of aesthetic sensations: of
the "loveliness" of the ornate rooms, of the poise of her father,
and, above all, of the hideousness of the "countess." "Oh no, she
wanted to go nowhere with *her*, for her presence had already, in
a few seconds, dissipated the happy impression of the room and
put an end to the pleasure briefly taken in Beale's command of
such elegance. There was no command of elegance in his having
exposed her to the approach of the short fat wheedling whiskered
person in whom she had now to recognise the only figure wholly
without attraction involved in any of the intimate connexions
her immediate circle had witnessed the growth of" (XI, 194).

Circumstances make it clear to Maisie that there are some
matters more important than aesthetic ones—for the reason that
they more acutely affect her own welfare. But it is with a mild
shock that she arrives at such recognitions: for example, that Mrs.
Wix is "good" in spite of her ugliness. To Maisie Mrs. Wix "was
lower in the scale of 'form' than Miss Overmore" (XI, 41); "She

had struck her at first, just after Miss Overmore, as terrible; but something in her voice at the end of an hour touched the little girl in a spot that had never even yet been reached. . . . What Maisie felt was that she had been, with passion and anguish, a mother, and that this was something Miss Overmore was not, something (strangely, confusingly) that mamma was even less" (XI, 23-24). In appearance Mrs. Wix remains "a figure mainly to laugh at" (XI, 25); yet she is "soothingly safe" and gives "a sense of a support" (XI, 26-27). What James stresses in the chapter introducing Mrs. Wix is that she is a paradox to Maisie; she upsets the child's theory that only those who are beautiful can be right and good. This is not to say that from this point Maisie abandons her aesthetic criteria. Though she is forced from time to time to admit exceptions to her rule (a rule, incidentally, given great support by Mrs. Wix's romantic convictions that only the beautiful are true), her thoughts turn habitually to the beauty or ugliness of everyone she knows and meets.

One sign of this aesthetic preoccupation is Maisie's developing awareness of symmetry. What may well be (to James) a child's natural disposition to seek order is heightened in Maisie by the curious patterns formed by her elders' lives. She possesses "the positive certitude . . . that the natural way for a child to have her parents was separate and successive, like her mutton and her pudding or her bath and her nap" (XI, 17). The arrangement that we judge to be perverse and bizarre is to Maisie natural and orderly. The judgment that she shall spend six months at the home of each parent is to Maisie properly logical; beyond this, it accounts to some extent for her notions of the symmetry that should govern the forming of relationships. Her sense of proportion is plainly more developed than her sense of "morality": "She was now old enough to understand how disproportionate a stay she had already made with her father . . ." (XI, 37), but not old enough, presumably, to understand why. The feeling for neat patterns is further encouraged by the emphasis placed by her elders on superficial form, on adhering to the letter of the law of respectability. But to Maisie alone are appearances reality, and quite early in her childhood she becomes even more adept than her various parents in devising "proper" forms of relationships. It is this habit of mind that creates the comedy and the irony of the following exchange:

[Maisie] remarked to Miss Overmore that if she [Miss Overmore] should go to her mother perhaps the gentleman [Sir Claude] might become her tutor.

"The gentleman?" The proposition was complicated enough to make Miss Overmore stare.

"The one who's with mamma. Mightn't that make it right—as right as your being my governess makes it for you to be with papa?"

Miss Overmore considered; she coloured a little; then she embraced her ingenious friend. "You're too sweet! I'm a *real* governess."

"And couldn't he be a real tutor?" (XI, 40).

Maisie speaks not simply from innocence and naïveté, but from a desire to impose her own idea of "right," or symmetrical, arrangements. Her system makes no allowances for those conventions which prescribe certain rules for spouses and others for lovers, and require that relations between men and women take different forms from relations between those of the same sex. But Maisie's system has a logic of its own, a logic that James shows to be a natural one for a child in her circumstances to acquire. That it is more insistently symmetrical than those of her elders points not primarily to Maisie's naïveté, but to the elders' hypocrisy, as a conversation between Maisie and Sir Claude evidences: "'You see, my dear [says Sir Claude], if I shall be able to go to you at your father's it yet isn't at all the same thing for Mrs. Beale to come to you here.' Maisie gave a thoughtful assent to this proposition, though conscious she could scarcely herself say just where the difference would lie" (XI, 84).

One of Maisie's basic judgments about the adult world is that though the actors are always changing places, the same pattern prevails. Maisie necessarily looks at things from her own fixed perspective, that of one who is always tenuously attached to a pair of adults. The identities of the adults continually change, but the arrangement is constant. Maisie thus conceives of her state as that of permanence amid process. It is this notion that guides her thoughts as Sir Claude suggests to her that Mrs. Wix be "squared" (that is, gotten rid of): she thinks "that though she had been happy indeed between Sir Claude and Mrs. Wix she should evidently be happier still between Sir Claude and Mrs. Beale" (XI, 132).

In Maisie's system the inviolable principle of social existence is that people belong in pairs, so that the pair including Beale should balance with the one including Ida. Her analysis of Beale's affair with the American "countess" develops from this principle: "Papa's Captain—yes—was the Countess" (XI, 193). Once she comprehends the elementary social pattern, Maisie takes an interest in grouping the adults herself. She does so from a vague sense that she helps people by bringing them together and also from what James calls "a passion that precedes knowledge" (*P*, p. 149)—a passion for putting things into what she conceives to be their right places.

Beyond this, Maisie responds to her condition out of a spirit of the game. She has the child's unquestioning acceptance of the arbitrary yet systematic rules of play. Maisie repeatedly draws analogies between the behavior of the adults and the conduct of players in a game, even more so than she likens them to characters in Mrs. Wix's storybooks. In the beginning she translates her father's counsel to Miss Overmore to "save" Maisie (from Ida's influence) into the language of the playground: "Maisie's ignorance of what she was to be saved from didn't diminish the pleasure of the thought that Miss Overmore was saving her. It seemed to make them cling together as in some wild game of

'going round' " (XI, 18). She interprets the news of Ida's engagement to Sir Claude as "a game like another" (XI, 47). As the
situation grows more complicated—after the two marriages
begin to disintegrate and new hostilities and new affections are
established—the adult world is intelligible to Maisie only as a
complicated game whose rules she does not quite understand: "If
it had become now, for that matter, a question of sides, there was
at least a certain amount of evidence as to where they all
were. . . . It sounded . . . very much like puss-in-the-corner, and
she could only wonder if the distribution of parties would lead
to a rushing to and fro and a changing of places" (XI, 94-95).

There are several reasons for the balanced placement of characters in the novel. We know that the ironic situation which first
interested James in the subject was that of "a child [who] was
divided by its parents in consequence of their being divorced"
(*N*, p. 126). The germ emphasizes balance. We have already
noted the various compositional advantages created by the
parallels. But there is also the fact that because her elders arrange
themselves symmetrically, Maisie comes to regard symmetry as a
norm. Furthermore, Maisie, both through her "forlornness" (*P*,
p. 143) and through her active interference, "makes . . . an
extraordinary link between a succession of people" (*N*, p. 235). It
is true that Maisie's role in "bringing together" Sir Claude and
Mrs. Beale is an accidental accomplishment. But according to
the preface, Maisie grows more interesting as she grows more
active: "instead of simply submitting to the inherited tie and the
imposed complication, of suffering from them, our little wonder-
working agent would create, without design, quite fresh elements of this order—contribute, that is, to the formation of a
fresh tie, from which it would then (and for all the world as if
through a small demonic foresight) proceed to derive great
profit" (*P*, p. 142). Mrs. Beale and Sir Claude exaggerate
Maisie's role in uniting them so as to use the child as a pretext for
their meetings. But to Maisie it is a true achievement. More-

over, it gives her a precedent for her unambiguous manipulations of the adults in the final chapters.

By that time it has become apparent to Maisie that people belong in pairs and that trios are particularly awkward groupings. She revises her earlier notion that there is "a kind of natural divergence between lovers and little girls" (XI, 204). For she assumes that she, as well as Mrs. Beale and rather more so than Mrs. Wix, qualifies as Sir Claude's "lover";[11] she "knows" that only one of the women can leave with him for Paris. Maisie therefore rejects Sir Claude's bid that she join him and Mrs. Beale—not because she has acquired "a moral sense" (she is quite agreeable to abandoning Mrs. Wix), nor even because she wants exclusive possession of Sir Claude, but because her whole experience has led her to conclude that she can be only the loser as the third party in a relationship. She wants to be in, not "between," a pair. In the end she prefers to pair herself with Mrs. Wix.[12]

I do not mean to suggest that Maisie's aesthetic sense alone accounts for what she knows and how she judges. Clearly she likes people to like her, she abhors discord and craves peace, and she feels that relations should be permanent. These attitudes

11. That is, in Maisie's sense of "lover." The argument that she gains a sexual awareness of herself and tries to seduce Sir Claude—proposed by Harris W. Wilson, "What *Did* Maisie Know?" *College English*, XVII (February, 1956), 279-82—places considerable strain upon the text.

12. Though he errs in assuming that Maisie's self-interest is incompatible with the growth in her of a moral sense, Mr. McCloskey correctly analyzes the way her mind works: "When Mrs. Beale explains that she has 'squared' her husband, Maisie's father, Maisie remarks: 'I know how. By letting him do what he wants to on condition that he lets you also do it.' This is a measure of Maisie's empiric observation, her faculty of drawing inferences, and her awareness of the mores of her peculiar world. It is an equation, as many of the other situations, symmetrically conceived, are equations; the ultimatum at the end is also a sort of equation, disjunctively conceived as an either-or dilemma. The nice balance of things, the disturbing imbalance, and the restoration of balance again are notable features of the situations involving the characters whose actions constitute the stuff of Maisie's education" (p. 495).

spring from her nature (her "freshness" [*P*, p. 146]), for they are in no way a product of her environment. But most of Maisie's judgments are rooted in an idea of form. These formal judgments represent a kind of improvised morality, perhaps all that one in Maisie's circumstances can be expected to achieve. But we should not belittle her intellectual accomplishment, her creation of a conscience. Maisie's morality of aesthetic propriety is the only kind possible in a world given over to expediency and selfishness and expressing itself in a language of subterfuge, bestiality, and deadly gamesmanship.

Especially in the novels and tales of the nineties, James is absorbed in the question of how conscience may develop and thrive in a moral chaos. The moral sense is either shaped or tested by the given conditions—unless it be some set of official formulae like those which give comfort to Mrs. Wix. In *The Spoils of Poynton*, the situation is slightly different, for Fleda imposes on her circumstances an archaic conception of honor that strikes Mrs. Gereth (and sometimes the reader) as an irrelevance in that scene of callous struggle for things and people. But Maisie, somewhat more so than those other youthful protagonists who are most like her—Morgan Moreen, the telegraphist, Nanda Brookenham—must scratch about for a moral code in an environment that recognizes none at all. What these child heroes have in common is an ultimate preference for permanence and sincerity over the self-serving frivolities of the adults. Finally Maisie's recognition that Sir Claude is a liar and a weakling and that a life with him and Mrs. Beale would be very brief, coupled with her impression that people belong in pairs, adds up for Maisie to what is "right." It may be argued that honesty and permanence are in themselves closely related to aesthetic values, strengthening rather than diluting Maisie's acquired sense that order is what counts the most. Undeniably in the end Maisie wants to be part of a relationship that is ordered and permanent and honest. Her achievement consists in her struggle to extract from the base materials of her life the substance of a durable moral code.

Finally, therefore, an organic connection does exist between the arbitrary plot and the spontaneous central intelligence. The foolish symmetry that grows out of the lusts and betrayals of Maisie's many parents hints of a moral standard that only Maisie comprehends. She alone comprehends it because she alone desires to find it.

The procedure of this chapter has been to begin with form and to end with character. I have sought to demonstrate how the preconceived form achieves its relevance and vitality as the novel undergoes its major "development"—the exhibition of Maisie's growth of mind. The severe dimensions of the three-act play yield to the requirements of Maisie's young intelligence, though it is the three-staged plot that creates the conditions to which her intelligence responds. The same rule applies to the other important aspect of the novel's outward coherence—the symmetrical character arrangements. The balanced groupings are Maisie's world as well as the novel's design. Accordingly, Maisie's interpretations and responses make the diagrammatic character formations essential to the novel, not merely fanciful decorations. The original scenario, a mechanical design, is contained in, not concealed by, the completed novel. It has been less altered than transcended, for the intelligence and psychology of Maisie are allowed only to dominate the form, not to exist apart from it.

VIII · *THE WINGS OF THE DOVE*

Even before the publication of F. O. Matthiessen's *Henry James: The Major Phase*, critics commonly bracketed together *The Ambassadors, The Wings of the Dove,* and *The Golden Bowl.* Though there is some notable disagreement as to whether these novels represent James at the height of his creative powers, it is seldom questioned that they share basic resemblances in style, form, and subject matter. Of late some important studies have emphasized the relations between the three novels and the shorter works of the late nineties, but even here the novels are judged major, a separate achievement, the end towards which the earlier fiction logically leads. Quentin Anderson and R. P. Blackmur are in the minority in their claims for a rigid thematic unity that fuses the works into a *de facto* trilogy, but most of James's other recent critics, such as Professors Crews, Wegelin, and Cargill, give some weight to the correspondences among the three novels, even though they discuss each as self-contained.[1]

1. F. O. Matthiessen, *Henry James: The Major Phase* (New York,

Unfortunately the practice of grouping the books together (or, as in the case of Blackmur, of tracing a thematic progression from *The Ambassadors* to *The Golden Bowl*) has tended to blur some important formal differences among the three novels. I refer primarily to the narrative techniques. For not only are the techniques used in the three novels quite radically different, but the basic schemes represent the fulfillments of three major methods which James had experimented with and refined over the course of several decades.

The Ambassadors confines the reader to the presence, mind, and purview of a single observer. As James states in the preface, the novel is Strether's "process of vision" (*P*, p. 308). The technique is employed in *The Ambassadors* with an especial thoroughness, delicacy, and richness; but the method is James's most common one—that, for example, of *Roderick Hudson*, *The American*, *The Spoils of Poynton*, and *What Maisie Knew*. Strether is a synthesis of both the type of the passive observer (such as Rowland Mallet) and the type of the active observer (such as Christopher Newman). And it goes without saying that James is nowhere more successful than in *The Ambassadors* in consistently maintaining the point of view of his reflector.

The Golden Bowl makes use of a narrative form that is less common in James than that of *The Ambassadors*, but a form with which he had experimented from quite an early date. This is the method of paralleling halves. To be sure, there is no other novel or story in which the precise technique of *The Golden Bowl* is used—the scheme requires that the first half be located in the mind of one character and the second half in the mind of

---

1963); R. P. Blackmur, "The Loose and Baggy Monsters of Henry James," *Accent*, XI (Summer, 1951), 129-46; Quentin Anderson, *The American Henry James* (New Brunswick, N.J., 1957); Frederick C. Crews, *The Tragedy of Manners: Moral Drama in the Later Novels of Henry James* (New Haven, 1957); Christof Wegelin, *The Image of Europe in Henry James* (Dallas, 1958); Oscar Cargill, *The Novels of Henry James* (New York, 1961).

another—but, as I have mentioned, both "Daisy Miller" and "An International Episode" are *nouvelles* in which the principle of organization is that of balanced halves. In both cases James locates a figure in one setting in the first half of the work, and in a contrasting setting in the second half. Presumably James saw reason to abandon the method during the middle of his career. No doubt the dependence of the form on some geographical movement rendered it impracticable for the exclusively English novels. More important, the form probably proved difficult for James to accommodate with his increasing preoccupation with inner states and his declining interest in manners. "Daisy Miller" and "An International Episode" are both semi-satirical treatments of manners, stories in which contrast is essential and ironic discords between character and setting produce the major effects. The next chapter deals with the evolution of that simple form to the complex structure of *The Golden Bowl*. Here I wish only to note that this novel represents a fusion of the paralleling technique and the reflector technique.[2]

My immediate concern, *The Wings of the Dove*, is structurally the most difficult of all James's novels. The difficulty arises because the chosen narrative form provides no pre-established system of organization. The "law of successive Aspects"[3] imposes no restraints. James had employed the method of shifting perspectives before, most prominently in *The Tragic Muse* and with less variation in *The Portrait of a Lady*, *The Bostonians*, and *The Princess Casamassima*. In *The Awkward Age* the situation is revealed also through multiple aspects, but the extreme dramatic objectivity of that novel gives it a unique status in James's canon. In each of these novels there is a rather obvious principle determining each change in perspective. In *The Portrait of a Lady* and *The Princess Casamassima*—to take

2. As I shall point out, the structure of *The Wings of the Dove* is somewhat dependent on the technique of balanced halves.

3. Notes to *The Ivory Tower*, ed. Percy Lubbock (London, 1917), p. 268.

the simplest cases first—the shifts are simply shifts away from the controlling reflector. These are novels in which James has no choice but from time to time to violate the authority of the central consciousness. So when James temporarily abandons the mind of Isabel to represent a conversation between Osmond and Madame Merle, it is with a sense of disturbing the unity. Such deviations are entirely absent in *The Ambassadors*, and so slight as to be unobtrusive in *The Spoils of Poynton* and *What Maisie Knew*. As we have seen earlier, in *The Princess Casamassima* James seeks a kind of fusion between the representation of the growth of the mind of Hyacinth Robinson and the representation of his social milieu: thus the deviations from Hyacinth's perspective are judged necessary to convey the bulk and variety of the dense London world.

The Tragic Muse adheres to a different principle, for this is by no means a novel *essentially* governed by a single character's vision, one in which the deviations from that point of view are manifestly exceptions to the rule. In *The Tragic Muse*, multiplicity of aspect is the rule. But the multiplicity is most systematic. The novel is simply the fusion of two arbitrarily connected stories, those of Nick Dormer and Peter Sherringham, and the agent of the fusion—"the *link* between the two other cases" (*P*, p. 89)—is the third principal character, Miriam Rooth. The subject of the novel, the relation between the public life and the aesthetic life, guarantees a loose thematic unity and, furthermore, justifies and accounts for each of the shifts in perspective—back and forth from Peter to Nick. James's problem is only one of distributing the parts equally and of preserving their mutual relevance: he must prevent either Nick's or Peter's becoming a "*usurping* consciousness" (*P*, p. 90) and, at the same time, guard against the reader's sensing that the various stories alternate rather than merge. To James the "interest" consists in "keeping Nick Dormer's story his and yet making it also and all effectively in a large part Peter Sherringham's, of keeping

Sherringham's his and yet making it in its high degree his kins-man's, too. . ." (*P*, pp. 88-89).

Questions of controlling consciousnesses have no bearing at all on the design of *The Awkward Age*. In that intensely objective novel, each of the ten books "lights" a different aspect of the general social situation, often concentrating on a single character's relevance to the whole,[4] but the dominance of dialogue, together with the restrictedness of Mrs. Brookenham's circle, insures an overriding unity as it diminishes the separateness and independence of the individual chapters.

One of the purposes of the present study is to trace James's development as a novelist in terms of his constant effort to balance his contrary inclinations toward constraint and freedom. In most of the works discussed in earlier chapters, the constraints are literary modes and conventions. More compelling, if less aesthetically interesting, prohibitions that James often had to adjust to his personal artistic requirements were those imposed by magazine editors. We find James in his notebooks repeatedly trying to reconcile the "explosive principle in one's material" (*P*, p. 278) with promises made to editors. Also he undertakes to modify the effect of mechanical arrangement as he organizes his novels for serial publication. As we have noticed, James found certain advantages in these external and arbitrary restrictions; they directed his efforts to gain economy, to seek an action, to effect roundness and balance. Ideally he preferred a total free-dom—not a freedom from all restrictions, but a freedom to impose those of his own making. It is in the preface to *The Wings of the Dove* that James comments on this question. Since his efforts to publish *The Wings* serially had failed, James for the first time possessed the kind of ideal freedom his note-books show him to have constantly sought.

4. For an analysis of the structure of *The Awkward Age*, see Eben Bass, "Dramatic Scene and *The Awkward Age*," *PMLA*, LXXIX (March, 1964), 148-57.

Perhaps it is more important that at this advanced stage in his career, James no longer worked within the confines of established literary genres and sub-genres. Unlike most of the other works that I have discussed, *The Wings of the Dove* (and, for that matter, *The Ambassadors* and *The Golden Bowl*) is neither a refashioning nor a transcendence of a conventional model. James has gone beyond that very long phase in his career when he required the external controls (which is to say, stimuli) afforded by such forms as the comedy of manners, the well-made play, and the naturalistic novel, not to mention those forms largely of his own invention, like the anecdote and the story based on the contrast of international types. As we have seen, in *The Wings* James also chooses to forego the luxury of confining himself to a single character's point of view and the exacting control which such a method necessitates. James interprets this freedom from both artificial and self-imposed restrictions as an authorization to discover and employ whatever compositional "law" is latent in the subject. According to the preface, it is a unique opportunity. James writes that "conditions of publication" (and presumably other external conditions) "often operate as a tax on ingenuity—that ingenuity of the expert craftsman which likes to be taxed very much to the same tune to which a well-bred horse likes to be saddled. The best and finest ingenuities, nevertheless, with all respect to that truth, are apt to be, not one's compromises, but one's fullest conformities, and I well remember, in the case before us, the pleasure of feeling my divisions, my proportions and general rhythm, rest all on permanent rather than in any degree on momentary proprieties" (*P*, pp. 295-96).

The "law of successive Aspects" is the most implicitly free of all James's characteristic forms. On the face of it, it seems no law at all. The book with shifting centers offers no predetermined pattern for the novelist to follow. It is, after all, an easier matter to devise the basic structure of a novel like *The*

Ambassadors than that of one like *The Wings of the Dove*. James's decisions regarding the transference of point of view and the composition of distinct "blocks" of material must follow solely from his intelligent apprehension of the demands of the novel, not from any (comparatively) simple conception of unity or consistency. Nor are the "successive aspects" of *The Wings* dictated by the kind of formulae apparent in the other novels that employ broadly the same method.

To search out the structural principle of *The Wings of the Dove* it is first necessary to describe the outer shape of the novel, the form in its most superficial aspect. The flaws which James acknowledges in the preface are on this order of measurable form: not the organic relation of part to part but the appearance of the shell. First there is a flaw in symmetry. *The Wings of the Dove* "happens to offer perhaps the most striking example I may cite . . . of my regular failure to keep the appointed halves of my whole equal" (*P*, p. 302). In other words, like *The Tragic Muse* it has a "misplaced middle": the preparation is excessive, requiring a too severe foreshortening of the denouement. The flaw is then double-sided, for not only does the resolution begin too late (presumably the "middle" should be both the physical center of the book and the point at which the basic representation of the characters and their situations ends and the resolution of the conflict begins), but the second half is necessarily "deformed" (*P*, p. 302). James might also have cited other (though contingent) areas in which his valued principles of propriety, proportion, and roundness are sacrificed. An important instance of exterior shapelessness is the general irrelevance of the chapter and book divisions. Books First, Second, and Third (as James designates them) each possess two chapters, each of which centers on a specific happening. Each book is controlled by the consciousness of a single character; each concludes with insistent finality. To be specific:

Book	Chapter	Length	Center	Event
First	I	24 pp.	Kate	conversation with father
	II	20 pp.	Kate	conversation with sister (conclusion: decision to live with Aunt Maud)
Second	I	28 pp.	Densher	conversation with Kate
	II	25 pp.	Densher	conversation with Aunt Maud (conclusion: engagement to Kate and departure for America)
Third	I	24 pp.	Susan	observation of Milly on mountain
	II	15 pp.	Susan	conversation with Milly (conclusion: decision to go directly to England)

The extreme regularity (of the kind that is consistent throughout *The Ambassadors*) begins to weaken in Book Fourth. Here there are three instead of two chapters, and the point of view shifts internally from Susan to Milly. But it is in Book Fifth and thereafter that the ten-book structure disintegrates into an entirely superficial scheme: one that neither controls the material nor conveys its inward order, but merely indicates certain scene divisions. In the fifth book there are seven chapters, and though most of these are briefer than those in the earlier books, the fifth book as a whole is twice the length of the first book. Furthermore, James disregards the earlier rule that chapter correspond with scene: the first four chapters of Book Sixth represent a single dinner party at Lancaster Gate. Book Seventh is split between two chapters set in London and two set in Venice— in spite of the fact that major geographical changes signalize book divisions in other places: Milly's departure from Switzerland and Densher's arrival in London from Venice. James buries the movement of Milly and her retinue (from London to Venice) in the midst of Book Seventh. This is a case in which the organizing principle is that of point of view (Book Seventh is located in the joint consciousness of Milly and Susan), necessitating the abandonment of a principle of division used elsewhere—that of physical setting.[5]

5. In the preface, James makes it clear that the book and chapter divi-

I mention such mechanical details only because, for James, they constitute a failure in proportion and consistency. Of course, the reader with less severe geometrical standards may well disregard them. But such a reader may be less inclined to set aside James's other reservation about the form of the novel—that the second half is too extremely foreshortened. The indirect representation of Milly Theale in the eighth and ninth books has been often lamented. It is compellingly argued that Milly's last meeting with Densher and her feelings just before her death are entirely too significant to be represented in any but the most direct fashion. The omission has been defended by certain critics on artistic grounds,[6] and by James on the grounds of "good taste," the "charm" of the difficult way, and, of course, economy (*P*, pp. 289, 306, 302). It is the last of these justifications that interests us here. James, so the preface states, has left himself space enough only for the most essential scenes, so that the persistent pressures of economy are even more than usually compelling. In omitting the final meeting between Densher and Milly, James judges that the gain in intensity and economy more than compensates for the loss in immediacy. He resolves the difficulty by conveying the effect of that meeting through Densher's report to Kate. He renders two scenes in one.

Quite often in *The Wings of the Dove* important conversations are discussed or recollected rather than actually presented: for example, Susan's talk with Sir Luke Strett, Lord Mark's

sions are arbitrary and superficial; the organic compositional units are the "blocks" of material encompassing (usually) several books (*P*, p. 296).

6. F. O. Matthiessen writes that the indirect method "succeeds extraordinarily in making us feel as though Milly has been wrapped around and isolated by sinister forces" (*Henry James: The Major Phase*, p. 57). Laurence Bedwell Holland, *The Expense of Vision: Essays on the Craft of Henry James* (Princeton, 1964), devotes a large portion of his discussion of *The Wings of the Dove* to an elaboration of Matthiessen's remark. He argues persuasively that "the form is made to be analogous to the action which the novel is about" (p. 320); that is, "in failing to do justice to Milly, the novel betrays her" (p. 321).

revelation to Milly, the meeting of Kate and Densher after his return from America. *The Wings* exceeds all James's novels in the frequency of events which are reflected upon rather than dramatized. *The Ambassadors*, by contrast, is a much more fully rendered novel, full of occasions that are both directly represented and retrospectively analyzed. We are given not only a full dramatic rendering of the first meeting of Sarah Pocock and Madame de Vionnet, but in addition extended reconsiderations of that meeting by Strether and Maria Gostrey, Strether and Madame de Vionnet, and Strether and Sarah. It may well be that in *The Wings* James must exert more than the desired "minimum of strain" to achieve a "maximum of intensity" (*P*, p. 56). Otherwise it is easy to appreciate the benefits James gains by squeezing two incidents into one. By withholding our knowledge of Densher's final meeting with Milly until he reports to Kate, James requires that the reader learn what happened just as Kate does, thus heightening the dramatic and revelatory content of the scene. In the preface to *What Maisie Knew*, James alludes to this method of gaining intensity. He speaks of the "associational magic" (*P*, p. 147) produced by his refusal to allow us to see the adults without Maisie in their presence. Accordingly, in the scene we have been discussing in *The Wings of the Dove*, we are made to apprehend at once Milly's suffering and Kate's brutality.

Looked at from another angle, it is not the extreme compression of the second half which seems to weaken the novel. Rather it is James's strategy of placing his strong emphasis on the consciousness of Merton Densher. For—what is seldom observed—it is not only Milly who is remote from the reader's apprehension, but also Kate. Milly, after all, acts as the central consciousness in parts of the seventh book, but Kate's mind is closed to us throughout all the final nine books. Since we see Kate only through the thoughts of Densher and Milly, the process of her transformation from a woman governed by ideas of loyalty to one who sends her fiancé to make love to another woman remains something of a mystery. The transformation is convincing, because the groundwork of her character and situation has been well established in the first two books. Yet we witness the transformation entirely from the outside, just as we witness Milly's spiritual metamorphosis entirely from the outside.

I have dwelt at some length upon these disproportions (which are not characteristic of James) and ellipses (which carry to an extreme his common practice) of *The Wings of the Dove* not because they describe the basic design of the novel, but because they may lead us to it. The outer disorder refracts an inner order; it is the price James pays for a deeper, integral consistency and coherence.

To seek the principle of organization—the law governing the "divisions," "proportions," and "general rhythm" (*P*, p. 296) of the book—we should also study the affirmative as well as the negative statements in the preface, the reasons given to justify (in part) the deficiencies. James writes that the "idea" of the novel "is that of a young person conscious of a great capacity for life, but early stricken and doomed, condemned to die under short respite, while also enamoured of the world. . ." (*P*, p. 288). But he soon makes it clear that the book is not a "portrait," a novel of character. It is a novel in which "relations" are the center. For Milly is but half of the subject, and what James variously calls those drawn into her whirlpool, those constituting the other side of her coin, and those forming the circumference of her center (*P*, pp. 291-94) are implicit in the germ. Densher, Kate, and the other characters come to be equated with "life," "the world," and finally "doom."

Not only do these others "make up together, for [Milly], contributively, her sum of experience," but the reverse is also true: they "inherit . . . from their connexion with her strange difficulties and still stranger opportunities . . ."; "their participation . . . becomes their drama too. . ." (*P*, p. 291). It is an important detail, one that bears on James's revision of his old theory of "relations." Earlier James had regarded character relations (or "connexions") as means rather than ends. In *The Portrait of a Lady*, the prime example of the original method, the relations between Isabel and the other characters exist to reveal Isabel. Essentially everyone is subordinate to her, functioning as *ficelle* or confidant. Also James valued relations, especially complex ethical relations, as the raw materials of intelligence: the stuff of experience that only the superior mind can comprehend. In his later work these familiar uses of relations are by no means abandoned. Susan Stringham is both a confidante and a "reflexion" of Milly. Milly's own significance is measured by her "consciousness of all relations" (*P*, p. 289). Yet in *The Wings* (as in most of the late novels, probably beginning with *The Tragic Muse*), relations among characters actually constitute the subject. *The Wings of the Dove* (like *The Golden Bowl*) is a pure instance of the novel of relations. In *The Ambassadors*, on the other hand, the focus on complex relations is slightly at odds with the concentration on the mind of a single character. The novel of relations logically requires the technique of multiple points of view; the technique not only supports the subject, it is the subject.

Such is the reasoning behind James's recognition that the "compositional key" (*P*, p. 294) of the novel is the technique of alternating points of view. He is rather vague in describing the details of the method: ". . . I must trust myself to know when to proceed from the one [consciousness] and when from the other" (*P*, p. 294). Though he devotes some pages of the preface to explaining the logic of the alternations in the first half of the book, he fails to deal with the more difficult questions raised by his choice of reflectors in the second half. James acknowledges and apologizes for this reticence (*P*, p. 306).

It is of the first importance to surmise the principles underlying the "establishing of [the] successive centres" (*P*, p. 296).

James speaks of Kate's acting as reflector in the first two books—what he calls the first "block." But he adds that in Book Second, "her mind is not . . . rigorously, the one reflector" (*P*, p. 299). When Densher's consciousness assumes control, he and Kate are spoken of as together forming a "community of vision" (*P*, p. 300). The "community of vision" composed of Milly and Susan makes up the second of James's "blocks"—Book Third. The scheme becomes less traceable thereafter. According to the preface, Book Fourth initiates (or perhaps constitutes) a third "block": Milly's vision still prevails, but since the occasion is the confrontation of the two groups or "communities" separately represented earlier, James regards Book Fourth as a new unit. Unfortunately the discourse on the strategy of "arranged alternation" (*P*, p. 301) does not explain why Merton Densher's consciousness virtually dominates the second half of the novel. Of the final five books, Densher's point of view directs all but Book Seventh, which is governed by the "community of vision" of Milly and Susan.[7]

The procedure can be defended as a mechanical expediency. Densher, with his mind so full of both Kate and Milly, functions as an economical means of representing both women, but we should be reluctant to attribute such a bold tactic (either solely or mainly) to an overriding compulsion to be brief. So too we should question whether the technique called "*fusion* of consciousness" (*P*, p. 299), a concept nowhere else mentioned in the prefaces, is but a makeshift excuse for abandoning a fixed center.

7. James seems to err in the preface when he writes that Kate Croy "is turned on largely at Venice, where the appearances . . . are treated almost wholly through her vision of them and Densher's. . . . It is in Kate's consciousness that at the stage in question the drama is brought to a head. . . . Milly's situation ceases at a given moment to be 'renderable' in terms closer than those supplied by Kate's intelligence, or, in a richer degree, by Densher's, or, for one fond hour, by poor Mrs. Stringham's. . ." (*P*, p. 301). This is clearly not true. Though we get very close to Kate in her conversations with Densher, her consciousness is closed to us after the first book.

Generally James berates himself for deviating from his chosen central consciousness. Two other matters stressed in the preface also beg to be given more significance than James claims for them: the use of indirection and the "play of the portentous" (*P*, p. 305). James praises his indirect method, but in such a way that the approach seems merely idiosyncratic, of an order of preference not to be reached by analysis: indirection simply satisfies "the author's instinct everywhere" (*P*, p. 306) and provides a way of handling Milly's sickness and death with "good taste" (*P*, p. 289). Of the portentous chapters, those which prefigure or prepare the scene for later ones, James says only that ". . . I like . . . the 'portentous' look . . ." (*P*, p. 303), that ". . . I cherish [the portentous] so as a 'value' and am accordingly for ever setting [it] in motion" (*P*, p. 305). More helpfully, he adds that both methods give "carrying power" or interconnectedness to the otherwise distinct "solid *blocks* of wrought material" (*P*, p. 296). But the principle of dynamic unity alone fails to account for our sense of the relevance of these techniques to the theme and substance of the novel. To read *The Wings of the Dove* is always to be aware of the extent to which the future is implicit in the present, or—to put it differently—the present is implicit in the past. The quality of life in the novel is portentous. So too with the various communities of vision: one exists insofar as he possesses or is possessed by the thoughts and will of another. Likewise the "alternations of vision" and the extreme reliance upon indirection make vividly dramatic the plot of deceit and the theme of concealment. These methods are so vital to the character of the book that it seems inadequate to limit our discussion to their technical functions.[8]

Following the lead of the preface, most critics of *The Wings of the Dove* have discussed the relation between Kate and Milly as fundamentally a dramatic one: it is a relation between

---

8. It is, of course, routine for James to reduce literary and philosophical questions to the level of mechanical execution.

victimizer and victim, with the two exchanging roles at the very end of the book. Actually the relation between the two women represents a refinement of the regular Jamesian tactic of balancing and opposing characters. Since, as the preface states, Milly and Kate are the centers of the two communities of consciousness which alternate throughout the novel, they are mutual reflectors. The technique necessitates that they be contrasted and paralleled. Often in the past James had been content to let his contrasts remain static—fixed structural guidelines rather than dynamically interacting centers. But the relation between Kate and Milly is of a different order from those of Mary Garland and Christina Light, Millicent and the Princess, Jean Martle and Rose Armiger, and Nanda and Little Aggie (to limit ourselves to varieties of the "good heroine"—"bad heroine" antithesis).

Still such a contrast is important in *The Wings of the Dove*. The contrast is addedly emphatic because the two women share some basic resemblances. The similarities between Milly and Kate, though not always spelled out, are prominent, so as to restrict the distance that is bridged when we shift from one block to another. The opening three books present the two heroines as they successively decide to make their aggressions on life. These early sections have as their climaxes two important decisions: that of Kate to "surrender" to Aunt Maud and that of Milly to cut short her idle tour of the continent to seek out the human community of London. It is with a sense of burned bridges and of intense urgency that these decisions are made: Kate's formal pledge of engagement to Densher, following her submission to Maud, and Milly's determined utterance, "Risk everything" (XIX, 140), following her symbolic observation of the kingdoms of the world. The chosen destiny of each is Lancaster Gate, and there is a unifying irony in their mistaking the ponderous vulgarity of Aunt Maud's world for a place of magnificence (Kate) and a place in which life is lived at a pitch of intensity (Milly). Conversely, neither woman is blind to the brutality of upper-middle-class London. For Kate the decision to turn herself over to Aunt Maud is made with reluctance; for Milly, whose isolation is so extreme that she readily identifies Aunt Maud's society with "life," the decision is made in desperation. For Kate, Maud's wealth must somehow compensate for the sacrifice of her "narrow little family feeling" (XIX, 71) and somehow be reconciled with her love for Densher. For Milly, Maud's society must compensate for a condemnation "to die under short respite" (*P*, p. 288).

The parallels may be extended. Though Kate is poor and hence extremely confined by circumstances beyond her control and Milly is immensely rich and hence free to do what she pleases, both women have "a great capacity for life" and both are "doomed" (*P*, p. 288). They have similar origins and are in some undefined manner predestined to re-experience the disasters of their parents.[9] Both love Merton Densher and both conceal their affection. In the beginning Milly and Kate are alike chaperoned and honored. The women who "shepherd" and celebrate them (who are themselves old friends, and whose tacit competition through their charges gives further stress to the parallel between Kate and Milly) are both distorting reflections of the younger women, simplifications and exaggerations of their dominant infirmities. Maud's savage vulgarity exposes the tarnished underside of Kate's passion for magnificence. Susan too seeks to invest her young friend with glamor but succeeds only in debasing her. Milly's spokesman lends only a journalistic and sentimental cheapening of Milly's fragility, inward beauty, and romantic adventurousness.

To a large extent *The Wings of the Dove* is the story of two young women affronting their separate destinies. In the beginning their efforts are distinct, but James soon contrives to bind their lives. It is this interaction that forms the basic plot. The

9. I have discussed this elsewhere. See *The Imagination of Disaster: Evil in the Fiction of Henry James* (Lincoln, Nebraska, 1961), p. 130.

plot charts the gradual formation of Kate's intrigue against Milly and concurrently of Milly's gradual apprehension of it. The developing relation between Kate and Milly is further represented through the reiteration of the dove image—Kate's creation. The figure of the dove regularly reflects upon both Kate and Milly; as a description of Milly it defines her relation to Kate, in the beginning as her victim and in the end as her conqueror.[10] There is no need to rehearse the details of the plot, for the most casual reading makes it clear that everything follows from the interaction of the two women, even though in most of the second half their effects on each other are indistinct, since Densher stands between them, not however as a positive and separate force, but as a conductor of the energies emitted by Kate and Milly.

Intertwined as their lives are, the two young women are shown at certain times to be independent, not merely acting upon or reacting to one another. Quite obviously in the first three books, in which the two are apart from and ignorant of each other, James not only prepares the ground for the eventual encounter but places considerable weight on the symbolic and ceremonial gestures of decision made by both Kate and Milly. Milly's view from the mountain peak is as momentously important in her life as is Kate's formal pledge to Densher in hers. But the parallels extend further. Critics have sometimes judged the two occasions when Milly is identified with works of art to be the major climaxes of her life. The first of these takes place when Milly recognizes the resemblance between herself and the woman in Lord Mark's Bronzino painting. The portrait is of "a very great personage—only unaccompanied by a joy. And she was dead, dead, dead" (XIX, 221). Without attempting a close analysis of the scene, we may yet agree that here James offers some pictorial and symbolic summation of Milly's entire predica-

10. Matthiessen provides a full discussion of the figure; see *Henry James: The Major Phase*, pp. 68-72.

ment: especially her fear, eventually to be realized, that her full beauty and triumph can be gained only in death.[11] The scene has its companion in Book Eighth, in which her long-delayed descent to the "great saloon" (XX, 203) of her rented Venetian palace is explicitly likened (by James as well as by Susan) to one of Paolo Veronese's great ceremonial tableaux.[12] Like the literal Bronzino, the imagined Veronese painting statically represents Milly's complete history: she is in the position of Christ in the center of the picture, with her conspirators grouped around her.[13] She is doomed, yet magnificent, a victim consenting to be a victim and transcending her appointed role. It is the last we see of Milly; yet it manifests all that will happen to her: her coming to full knowledge of the plot against her, her sublime gesture of forgiveness, her death. The Veronese scene fulfills the prophecy of the Bronzino scene, and both are latent in the Alpine scene.

We can also cite certain ritualistic incidents which compress Kate's entire history. Like Milly's, Kate's drama begins in a determination to conquer and ends in submission. In the same chapter in which Milly "comes down"—that is, "surrenders" herself to the will of others—Kate surrenders to Densher by promising to come to his rooms.[14] What relates the scene to Kate's earlier promise of engagement is not only the similarities of content, but the ceremonious formality of both events. In Book

11. See Holland, *The Expense of Vision*, pp. 303-4.

12. The preface makes it clear that James thought of Milly's "festal evening" in Venice as the "mate" of "her introduction to Mrs. Lowder's circle" (*P*, pp. 301, 300).

13. See Holland, *The Expense of Vision*, pp. 305-13, for a detailed and exceptionally perceptive account of the relevance of the Veronese painting to the scene.

14. "Surrender" is but one of the figures applied at various crucial times to both Kate and Milly, as well as to Densher. Each of the major figures "comes down" from figurative and literal "heights" into the social "abyss." See R. W. B. Lewis, "The Vision of Grace: James's 'The Wings of the Dove,'" *Modern Fiction Studies*, III (Spring, 1957), 36-37; and *The Imagination of Disaster*, pp. 134-39.

Second Kate says to Densher "with extraordinary beauty: 'I engage myself to you forever.' The beauty was in everything, and he could have separated nothing—couldn't have thought of her face as distinct from the whole joy. Yet her face had a new light. 'And I pledge you—I call God to witness!—every spark of my faith; I give you every drop of my life'" (XIX, 95).

It is principally the regal cadences and the stately phrasing of the pledge that elevate the scene to a nearly unique level of importance. The only occasion to match it is its companion piece. Reluctantly, but with comparable ceremony, Kate agrees to come to Densher's rooms. The scene ends with the exchange:

"On your honour"?

"On my honour."

"You'll come"?

"I'll come" (XX, 231).

Kate's second pledge is (to her) a grim fulfillment of her first pledge, though a logical development from it. The first is to compensate Densher for the complicity required of him in the "game" with Aunt Maud; the second is to compensate him for the more heinous deception required of him in Kate's "design" with Milly. The exploitation of Milly, after all, is a more profitable and more feasible scheme than the exploitation of Aunt Maud. In both her promises to Densher, Kate strives to salve his demands for passion without relinquishing her own demands for a fortune. Finally this is not only immoral (so that the pledge of "honour," virtually parodying her initial defense of family honor, is nearly blasphemous), but quite unworkable.

Coming between these separate ceremonious occasions in the lives of Milly and Kate which are the high points of the beginning and the end of the novel is the long inert middle, given over largely to the details of equivocation and intrigue, and concentrated on the sad perplexity of Milly and Densher. It is clear, I think, that the contrast between Milly and Kate (or, as some would have it, between an ideal of spiritual love and an ideal of practical intellect) is the central theme of the novel, and that the mind of Merton Densher is the theater in which this contrast becomes a dramatic conflict and in which the conflict is resolved. To say this much is to capsulize the novel rather than to describe the character of life rendered from page to page. By the rendered character of life, I mean the moral culture that is the environment of the novel. This culture is sorely inadequate (failing, as it does, the moral nobility of the persons who suffer from it though they share in creating it). Our sense of life is principally our sense of the hollow, mannered gestures of a decadent upper-middle class. Such an atmosphere dominates the long tedious stretches of the novel beginning with the first formal dinner party given for Milly at Lancaster Gate and ending with the party she herself gives at Palazzo Leporelli. These are the scenes in which very little is stated directly and everything means something else, in which simple acts bespeak complex motives. In *The Ambassadors*, by contrast, manners ennoble and intensify human relations. They insure dignity and restraint; more important, as an accumulation of traditional verbal gestures and allusions, manners extend the possibilities of communication. However in *The Wings of the Dove* the frozen code of manners institutionalized by Aunt Maud's society only inhibits and dilutes human intercourse. It not only debases language; it provides approved formulae for the telling of lies. The basic action, Kate's plot, comes to epitomize the conspiratorial quality of Aunt Maud's England.

Technique and theme are thus one. The portentous, the reflective, and the indirect rule everything. Those critics who lament the novel's failure in immediacy, concreteness, and realism are really of one mind with Milly Theale and Merton Densher. Certainly one of the things that Milly means by "life" is the participation in an honest and simple relationship. For her there is "no decent substitute for a felt intensity' (XX, 157-58). The discrepancy between appearance and reality strikes Milly as the hard central fact of English society. If such a condition makes Lord Mark sinister to her, it makes Kate Croy remote and unapproachable. Milly feels that Kate's withholding of her knowledge of Densher wrecks the possibility of their becoming friends: "She became conscious of being here on the edge of a great darkness. She should never know how Kate truly felt about anything such a one as Milly Theale should give her to feel. Kate would never—and not from ill will nor from duplicity, but from a sort of failure of common terms—reduce it to such a one's comprehension or put it within her convenience" (XIX, 190-91). If the failure is remediable at all, Milly reasons, it can only be by convincing Kate of her own good faith. Thus she takes the first occasion to try to establish a confidence. She will divulge her own "secret," her illness, which is analogous to Kate's secret, her friendship with Densher. But Milly's gesture of asking Kate to accompany her to the physician's office—which is to expose her vulnerability—fails to reduce the distance between them; Kate continues to conceal her knowledge of Densher.

From the beginning to the end of the novel, Merton Densher "wanted to keep [Kate] where their communications would be straight and easy and their intercourse independent" (XX, 19). But, like Milly, he is frustrated. His frustration is not simply of sexual passion, but of his sense that appearances and reality should correspond. Just as Milly must accept the conditions that Kate has imposed on their relation—that it be an apparent friendship, but an actual remoteness—so Densher must accept the conditions that Kate has imposed on his relation with her—that it be an apparent hostility, but an actual passion. Densher regards Kate's duplicity less a private ethical failing than an expression of the English social style. Dishonesty is simply consonant with gentility: "perfect manners" preclude the "operation of real affinities" (XIX, 295, 301). The second volume exposes the diabolical capacity of what Densher calls "The mere aesthetic instinct of mankind" (XX, 299), but our regular reaction to this instinct and to the manners which manifest it is a sense that the more basic instinct for honesty and reality has been frustrated.

This tension between the desire for authenticity and the dependence on subterfuge sets the course of the plot: the intrigues of everyone against Milly and Milly's own counterstrategies of deception. This same tension creates the essential rhythmic movement from chapter to chapter. Often this movement is made up of two scenes, the first "portentous" and the second recollective, with the central "event"—the encounter between characters that is planned and then reflected upon—either sketched very lightly or omitted entirely. To take a single example, such a movement underlies the action of the final two chapters in the sixth book and the first chapter in the seventh book. In the first of these scenes—at one of Aunt Maud's dinner parties—Kate urges Densher to "console" and "make up to" Milly (XX, 52, 56). In the next scene Densher obeys her wish by calling on Milly at her hotel and taking her for a ride in a carriage. But only the prologue of the encounter is represented. There is little conversation between Milly and Densher, but instead some extensive introspection by Densher. The final third of the chapter is devoted to another "portending" meeting between Densher and Kate, who enters the sitting room while Milly has gone to dress. Kate repeats her earlier instructions ("You must simply be kind to her" [XX, 95]) and leaves before Milly returns. At this point the chapter ends; we see nothing of the actual carriage ride toward which everything has seemed to point. The next chapter is occupied mainly with Susie's recollection of another "event" that has earlier been planned in some detail but left undramatized—her meeting with Sir Luke Strett. In the same chapter, Milly makes a glancing allusion to her ride with Densher. With a sense both of what Sir Luke has divulged to Susie and of what Densher has withheld from herself, Milly directs the conversation to its grim conclusion:

"What do you think, now that you've seen him, of Mr. Densher?" [Milly asked.]

It was not till after consideration, with her eyes fixed on her friend's, that Susie produced her answer. "I think he's very handsome."

Milly remained smiling at her, though putting on a little the manner of a teacher with a pupil. "Well, that will do for the first time. I *have* done," she went on, "what I wanted."

"Then that's all *we* want. You see there are plenty of things."

Milly shook her head for the "plenty." "The best is not to know— that includes them all. I don't—I don't know. Nothing about anything—except that you're *with* me" (XX, 104-5).

There is an appropriateness in the omission of the carriage scene. To Milly the long exchange with Densher has been obviously unsatisfactory, a failure rather than an achievement of "affinity." Since Milly recollects the scene as a void, there is a sense in which its real substance has been dramatized by the fact of its being unrepresented.

James's usual narrative procedure has much in common with the structural pattern that Francis Fergusson discovers in the agon of the Greek tragedy: the progression from "purpose" (the preparation for conflict), through "passion" (the conflict between antagonists), to "perception" (the understanding of what has happened).[15] Normally in James the pattern is matched by the alternation of pictorial and scenic chapters, with the pictorial containing reflections both on what has happened and on what is about to happen and the scenic dramatizing the event itself. However, in *The Wings of the Dove* the rhythm is so abbreviated that the central encounter, the "passion," is omitted, so that we jump almost without pause from "purpose," equivalent to plotting, to "perception," the victim's realization that communication has failed.

The most striking instance in the novel of such a sequence is

15. *The Idea of a Theater* (Princeton, 1949), p. 18.

that section in which the final meeting between Densher and Milly is elaborately prepared (in "portentous" talks between Densher and Susie, and Densher and Sir Luke) and elaborately recounted and evaluated (by Densher and Kate), but dramatized not at all. The exclusion may seem less perverse when we realize that the method here accords to the compositional logic of the book as a whole.[16] This logic requires that characters successfully communicate only with those sharing a "community of vision" with them, that the juxtaposed centers interfuse but do not merge.[17] In practice this means that Densher can be direct only with Kate, and Milly only with Susan. Until the final pages Densher and Milly are kept apart. In her groping for some closer community with both Kate and Densher, Milly, at least twice, uses intermediaries. Once she pours out her agonies to the dense Lord Mark, whose obtuseness paradoxically makes him "figure . . . to her for the moment as the one safe sympathiser. It would have made her worse to talk to others, but she wasn't afraid with him of how he might wince and look pale" (XX, 151). Again in the ninth book, when Susan asks Densher to lie to Milly about his engagement to Kate, Densher looks upon

16. We are granted a single extended conversation between Milly and Densher. But the substance of this exchange in the eighth book is Densher's reluctance to show Milly his rooms, out of his sense that her presence there would defile his recent intimacy with Kate. The meeting is wholly frustrated by his troubled allegiance to Kate; yet it is no more strained than any of their conversations. Doubtless James reasoned that it would be redundant to represent in full all these encounters. Thus the scene in Book Eighth is a paradigm of all their meetings, stressing Milly's aggressiveness and Densher's tortured loyalty to Kate. To say this, however, is not to suggest that there are no positive structural benefits gained by the omission of all their encounters but this one.

17. It is in this respect that the unique terminology of the preface is most significant: that is, the references to "the associated consciousness of my two prime young persons," "a practical *fusion* of consciousness," "a represented community of vision" (*P*, pp. 299, 300), etc. These phrases, far from being exclusively technical terms, bear on the major movement of the novel—the transition of Densher from sharing a union of consciousness with Kate to his sharing one with Milly.

Susan not only as an intermediary between himself and Milly, but also as a spokesman for Milly. With Susan, Densher can get far closer to the truth of his position with Milly than he can with Milly herself. So in Densher's conversation with Susan, as in Milly's conversation with Lord Mark, at least there is the illusion of intimacy. But the actual contacts between Densher and Milly are barren, principally because they are so calculated and unspontaneous. They lead not to mutual understanding, but to solitary meditation. So it is fitting that the contents of Milly's deathbed letter to Densher are never divulged, never indeed known. The letter, it is true, is a communication founded on knowledge, requiring no subterfuge. But it is wholly consistent that Kate, who has regularly prevented intimacy, should burn the unopened letter. It is also in accord with the logic of the novel that the final contact between Densher and Milly is a silent harmony between the living and the dead.

The direct progression from preparation to recollection establishes the rhythm that rules most of the chapters, but the pattern is from time to time punctuated by episodes of another kind, those which tend to represent the total situation as a static symbolic picture or to concentrate on someone's isolated reflections on his irreducible moral condition. Of the former, we have already noted those scenes which pictorialize Milly's state: the Alpine, Bronzino, and Veronese scenes. There are some others, less prominent but of the same type, such as Susan's extended comparison of the relation between Kate and Milly to that between figures in a Maeterlinck play. These sections, which would seem to owe much to Hawthorne (to the scaffold scenes in *The Scarlet Letter* and the pageant scenes of *The Marble Faun*) and to James's interest in the plastic arts, are either actual occurrences assuming the condition of metaphor or metaphors extended and vivified as miniature dramas; the distinction between the two methods seems not very important. There are also the scenes like the famous chapter in *The Portrait of a Lady* in which

Isabel sits alone before the fire and allows the full misery of her situation to penetrate her consciousness. The most memorable instance of such introspection in *The Wings of the Dove* is the scene in which Milly sits alone in Regent's Park. Following her visit to her physician, she directly faces the fact of her imminent death and of the universal condition of mortality: "Here doubtless were hundreds of others just in the same box. Their box, their great common anxiety, what was it, in this grim breathing-space, but the practical question of life" (XIX, 250)? Nearly as prominent are those occasions in the middle of the second volume when Densher takes his solitary walks through Venice, anguished by his passivity and failure of will. Some of the tableau scenes pictorialize a social relation (like the Veronese episode) and others pictorialize a purely personal situation (like the Alpine episode), but the introspective occasions focus on characters in their separateness. Taken together, both types of scenes intermittently retard the basic rhythmic movement from the portentous to the recollective. They are scenes that have little to do with the immediate dramatic context. Rather they compress the totality of the experience of the novel into symbolic pictures or mental dramas.

Thus far I have discussed certain recurring and unchanging structural elements which tend to make *The Wings of the Dove* approximate what James calls a "picture": the parallels between Milly and Kate, the theme and technique of indirection, the underlying rhythm, the scenes that synthetically depict the whole. There is another technique that shows James's effort to imply that the full story is latent in the beginnings. Commonly events in the early stages of a character's history forecast what is to happen to him. For example, the devastating revelation which Milly receives from Lord Mark in Book Ninth is prefigured in Book Fourth by her recognition of Kate's secret relation with Densher. The early discovery of Kate's knowledge of Densher is followed by the Bronzino scene, emblematic of Milly's ultimate beauty's emerging only through her death; the graver discovery of Kate's engagement to Densher in the second half is followed by her actual death and the fulfillment of the promise of her spiritual magnificence. Correspondingly, Densher's position in the second half is a tragic extension of his position in the first half. In Book Second, after Kate has pledged herself to him, Densher acquiesces in her wish that the job of "working" Aunt Maud be left to her. He is mildly annoyed by his own willingness to let Kate do the requisite lying, but in the end he submits, accepting her explanation that "men *don't* know. They know in such matters [of social politics] almost nothing but what women show them" (XIX, 99). This scene in Book Second looks directly ahead to Book Sixth, when Densher once more reluctantly acquiesces to Kate's idea, this time to the revised plan that Milly rather than Maud be "worked." In the later instance, Densher is required to be more active—"to make up to a sick girl" (XX, 56)—but it is essentially the same role that he performs. In sum there are a number of private crises common to both halves of the novel, so much so that the second half may be regarded not so much as a change in the original situation as a duplication of it, but a duplication in which the end results are grave and irreversible.

This is not to suggest that there are no important progressions or developments. The plot of course develops, charting the collapses of the immense expectations of Densher and Kate on the one hand, and of those of Milly on the other. The plot is grimly logical; the outcome is predicated by the basic situation.[18] Because of its inevitability, the progression of the plot requires less analysis than the progression from one center of consciousness to another. It is this system of progression (assuming for

18. The preface emphasizes this fatalism. James not only stresses the "portentous" and "prefigurative" aspects of the construction, but also the inevitability of the plot: Milly "couldn't but fall somehow into some abysmal trap—this being, dramatically speaking, what such a situation most naturally implied and imposed" (*P*, p. 293).

the moment that there is a system) that accounts for the working of the method of "arranged alternation." What stands behind James's decision to concentrate on Kate's consciousness in the first two books, on Milly's in the next three, and on Densher's in four of the final five?[19] Though less than severe, an order is yet apparent. The novel has three movements—Kate's segment, Milly's segment, and Densher's segment. In essence, we observe each of these three main figures (either directly or through the mind of one sharing his "community of vision") confronted with like problems and, to an extent, following the same course. Milly's crisis is a shadowy mirroring of Kate's crisis, and Densher's bears resemblances to those of both the women. Here then is another, perhaps the major, way in which the "portentous" aspect controls the design of the novel.

In the beginning Kate tries to respond to the cruel conditions imposed on her by her father and her aunt. The pressures of these two on Kate set the pattern for other, equally harsh, pressures that Kate is to bring upon Milly and Densher. We observe the parallels between certain events in the first volume and certain events in the second volume. In the first chapter Lionel Croy virtually forces Kate to abandon her considerable family loyalties to seek out the more lucrative opportunities afforded by a life as Aunt Maud's ward. In the beginning of the second volume, Kate in effect changes places with her father, and Merton Densher adopts Kate's earlier role. Here Kate states the terms of Densher's dilemma: that he set aside and even betray his affection for her and pretend fondness for Milly. Lionel Croy repudiates his paternity when he evicts his daughter because he hopes for eventual wealth; Kate repudiates her

19. I disregard here both the use of Densher as reflector in the second book and of Susan as one in the third book and in parts of the fourth and seventh. As the preface states, in these sections the reflectors are less important than the persons they reflect. Densher's *mind* does not assume prominence until the sixth book, and Susan is always either *confidante* or mirror (albeit distorting) of Milly.

engagement by evicting her fiancé also because she hopes for eventual wealth. In the final chapter we come full circle. Densher's proposition to Kate—that she take either the love or the money—recreates her original dilemma. Although in this final instance it is integrity rather than callous opportunism that directs Densher's formulation of the alternatives, the echoing of the first chapter is resonant. The envelope effect produced by the correspondences between beginning and ending gives to the book the symmetry and roundness that James regularly requires; but the cyclic design is also dramatically relevant. It reminds us that Kate's position has not changed. Because of her reaction to the proposals of her father and her aunt, she finds herself at the end where she was at the beginning.

One reaches the same conclusion by examining the ways in which one conspiracy evolves into another—until, in the end, it is Kate, the original victim of the *de facto* Lionel Croy–Maud Lowder conspiracy, who is once again the victim, this time of the *de facto* Merton Densher–Milly Theale conspiracy. Kate's conspiracy with Densher (and tacitly with Maud, Susan, and Sir Luke) against Milly is her response to the threat against her. Milly's response to Kate's aggression—the response of forgiveness—creates the conditions that bring about Densher's forcefulness in the final pages. The envelope form of the novel, emphasizing the proximity of the very first and the very last chapters, modifies the otherwise dominant effect of immense rearrangements in the central triangular relationship. Milly has died, Densher has at last acted, and Kate acknowledges that "We shall never be again as we were" (XX, 405); all has changed except Kate's status. For at the end she is very much where she was at the start—no longer living at Lancaster Gate but back in the company of her father and her sister, once more refusing Densher's terms of marriage because they require her to forego the chances for a fortune.

Perhaps even more significant is the force exerted by the

absent Milly in both the first chapters and the last. As James writes in the preface, Milly's appearance is virtually predicted by the initial perplexity of Kate and Densher: "They are laying a trap for the great innocence to come. If I like, as I have confessed, the 'portentous' look, I was perhaps never to set so high a value on it as for all this prompt provision of forces unwittingly waiting to close round my eager heroine. . ." (*P*, p. 303).[20] In the end Milly is also absent—a "ghost" of the past rather than a "great innocence to come." The basic rhythm that we have noticed drawing together different segments of the book also draws the entire novel together. It would not be a distortion to summarize the novel as a progression from an anticipation of Milly Theale to a recollection of her.

The portentous also rules the development of the novel from its location in Kate's consciousness, to its location in Milly's, and finally to its location in Densher's. As Ian Watt has pointed out, the novel's opening words, "She waited, Kate Croy . . ." (XIX, 3) "prefigure [Kate's] role throughout the novel—to wait."[21] The opening scene, which begins with an observation of Kate waiting for her father, places Kate in a position of total dependency. She hesitates to choose between her father and Lancaster Gate. By the second book, she has made her choice, having submitted to the pressures of her father, her sister, and her aunt. Thereafter Kate's patience, simply her ability to wait, does not waver, as she withdraws from Densher and contrives her plot against Milly. I emphasize this because Kate is not the only one who is introduced as "waiting." Susan judges Milly to be "al-

20. Of course, the reader has no way of forecasting the appearance of a character of whose existence he is ignorant, even though the first two books are certainly ominous. But this is to assume only a single reading, and it is a truism that at least two readings are required if the full structural coherence of James's late novels is to be perceived. James's definition of the novel as "picture" in itself greatly minimizes the importance of the narrative line.

21. "The First Paragraph of *The Ambassadors*: An Explication," *Essays in Criticism*, X (July, 1960), 270.

most tragically impatient" (XIX, 115). Milly renounces waiting to "risk everything." In the second book, Densher is described as one plagued by "leisure," "with nothing at all to do," whose actions are "wanting in point" (XIX, 47). This characteristic aimlessness and passivity is of no moral consequence until the sixth book, when he becomes the central consciousness. Then, even though he tells himself that "waiting was the game of dupes" (XIX, 8), he consents to wait.

In succession we observe Kate, whose instituted diplomacy of waiting amounts to a moral code; Milly, who revolts against a lifetime of waiting; and Densher, who reluctantly accedes to Kate's strategy of waiting. The novel is about procrastination, just as it is about prevarication; and in both respects it is Kate who sets the pace for the others to follow. There develops a pervasive disparity between the efforts of Densher and Milly to grasp moments of intimacy and intensity and the contrary pressures that enforce inactivity and tedium. Milly's aggressiveness has seldom been noted by critics, probably because it is so often thwarted. In the beginning Milly pushes ahead of the conventional schedule of European tourists, arriving at Switzerland out of season; then she rushes on to England. She presses her intimacy with Kate, invites Densher to ride in a carriage with her, and in Venice even invites herself to his rooms. She is never more aggressive than when she makes her will; finally she succeeds in overwhelming Densher with her love. Densher's passion for Kate impels him in much the same way. He grasps moments of intimacy with Kate—a few minutes before Maud comes down for tea or before Maud and Susan leave the shop on the Piazza San Marco; finally he settles for the seized pleasure of his conquest of Kate in his rooms. The need of Milly and Kate to live in the present is regularly frustrated, so that the day-to-day life of each is wasted away in inactivity and solitude. While Milly remains alone in her palazzo, Densher aimlessly paces the Venetian streets. Kate, in London, waits, dictating that these others must also wait.

A distinct pattern governs the periodic removals of each of the three principals from the scene. I have commented on the fact that Milly's absences from the beginning and the end of the novel are in large measure responsible for the envelope effect of the total form. It is equally significant that Kate and Densher are at times separated. Like that of Mrs. Newsome in *The Ambassadors,* their power is a constant force when they are physically remote. Densher's felt presence is registered by Milly. She first sees in Kate "the clear shadow of some probably eminent male interest" (XIX, 173). When she deduces that Kate must know Densher, she concludes that he must be the "male interest." Finally, through Kate's changed manner, she detects Densher's return from America: "[Kate] hovered there as with conscious eyes and some added advantage. Then indeed, with small delay, her friend sufficiently saw. The conscious eyes, the added advantage were but those she had now always at command—those proper to the person Milly knew as known to Merton Densher. . . . It seemed to pass between them in fine without a word that he was in London. . ." (XIX, 272-73). In the second volume the tables are turned. In Book Ninth (which has the same position in the second volume as does Book Fourth in the first), Kate has departed from Venice and Densher remains responsive to her will. He still shares with her "a community of vision." The parallel extends into Book Tenth, when Densher's altered manner reflects the enormity of Milly's effect upon him. "Her memory's your love," (XX, 405), Kate shrewdly guesses. Kate "reads" the presence of Milly in Densher in a way that recalls Milly's earlier sensing of the presence of Densher in Kate.

The revolution which converts Densher from an allegiance to Kate to an allegiance to Milly is not completed until the final lines of the novel. But this process begins early in the second volume. The reader recognizes the growth of a bond between

Densher and Milly well before Densher does. For the course that
Densher follows is much the same as Milly's. Kate drives the
point home to Densher:

[Densher] just brooded. "She takes things from you exactly as I
take them?"

"Exactly as you take them."

"She's just such another victim?"

"Just such another. You're a pair."

"Then if anything happens," said Densher, "we can console
each other?" (XX, 63).

Densher's "surrender" to Kate, his reluctant submission to her
will, recalls not just Kate's surrender to Aunt Maud, but, more
proximately, Milly's surrender to Kate—her unhappy acceptance
of the role of "dove" that Kate has assigned to her. To Milly
this identity that has been forced upon her is that of one who
had "so little time to live that the road must always be spared
her" (XIX, 285).

In sum, Densher grows closer to Milly not simply as "another
victim" of Kate, but as one required to give over the control of
his life to others, as one whose suffering springs not mainly from
revulsion against the dominant brutality, but against the frustration of a need for honesty and directness, as one whose "patience"
is sorely inadequate in a scene of waste, delay, and deception.
Inadvertently and unknowingly, Densher undergoes a trial that
has him torn between Kate and Milly. It seems unnecessary to
chart the steps in his conversion;[22] it is necessary only to remark
that it is because of his inward conflict that Densher is the
central consciousness in most of the second volume. He is, of
course, most alert to the needs and the attitudes of the two
women whose contrary requirements make up the substance of
his mind. Milly and Kate are by no means "absent" during the

22. The best account of Densher's turnabout is that of Dorothea Krook,
The Ordeal of Consciousness in Henry James (Cambridge, England,
1962), pp. 221-31.

long passages devoted to Densher's introspections. His consciousness is rather "like a set and lighted scene, to hold the play" (*P*, p. 16), as James describes the mind of Rowland Mallet of *Roderick Hudson*.

James from the start has concentrated on the consciousness of whichever character is the major victim.[23] In the beginning Kate is the weak one, the pawn manipulated by Aunt Maud, Lionel Croy, and Marian Condrip. Milly's consciousness, when we are absorbed in it, is just as full of her sense "that she was still in a current, determined, through her indifference, timidity, bravery, generosity—she scarce could say which—by others; that not she but the current acted, and that somebody else always was the keeper of the lock or the dam" (XIX, 274). In the end it is Densher's turn to be the victim, at first of Kate's social skill and ultimately of Milly's "stupendous" (XX, 403) generosity, and elsewhere of the various urgings of Aunt Maud, Susan Stringham, and Sir Luke Strett.

Our focus then is consistently on the character who passively suffers. Though most of James's novels are records of defeat and victimization, only in *The Wings of the Dove* is the technique of "multiple aspects" so finely adjusted to this habitual concentration. This accord between subject and method is at least partly responsible for the failures in proportion that James laments in the preface. *The Wings of the Dove* represents James's most extreme departure from the high standards of external symmetry that he generally imposed on himself. On the other hand, the novel represents his most extreme indulgence in the constant temptation to allow the material to develop

23. Leo Bersani, "The Narrator as Center in 'The Wings of the Dove,'" *Modern Fiction Studies*, VI (Summer, 1960), p. 135, writes that "James's main reflectors in the novel are different images of the passive but highly responsive self trying to find its way in a maze of demands being made on it by the external social world." Though, I think, inadequate to support the allegorical interpretation, the remarks on the passivity of each of the reflectors is just.

freely.[24] It has been my attempt to demonstrate that this novel is anything but formless, though its form has very little to do with its outer shell.

24. Of course, James's efforts to restrict development are obvious. But, as the preface states, the restrictions largely apply to the relations among the minor characters. The rivalry between Aunt Maud and Susan, for example, though of some prominence in the beginning, is lost sight of after Maud leaves Venice. James manages a considerable economy (at the cost of some awkwardness), but he falters in external symmetry.

IX · CONCLUSION:

THE GOLDEN BOWL

The preface to *The Golden Bowl*, the final one in the New York Edition, is in part a ceremonious leave-taking, the artist's valedictory tribute to his craft and the work of his lifetime. It impresses James that nearly all the tales, *nouvelles*, and novels that he has reread and revised for the edition demonstrate a total unity, a fine consistency and continuity. More precisely, the process of revision reveals to James "the whole growth of [his] taste," indeed the growth of his "active sense of life" (*P*, p. 340). The "accumulated 'good stuff'" (*P*, p. 341) of decades, which has been all but forgotten, retains its appeal; it has an intimate bearing on his present aesthetic standards and ideals—so much so that he can say of the task of revision that "the whole thing was a *living* affair" (*P*, p. 342).

Similarly, when the reader looks backwards from the vantage point of *The Golden Bowl* to the earlier fiction, he is made vividly aware that James was a writer who refashioned and transformed the themes and techniques of earlier works, not one who discarded the old for the new. Certainly this is true of the structures and structural motifs of his earlier efforts. *The Golden Bowl* is a palimpsest—a great and delicately unified novel in its own right, but also a repository of many of the older forms and experiments. We may rightly follow James's own precedent of using this novel as a basis for a summing-up. No other work provides a more convenient or more appropriate means for bringing together a number of ideas advanced in the present study.

The Golden Bowl is the ultimate demonstration of James's passion for "intensity" and "relations." Here the concepts are absolutely inseparable; the intensity of the work consists in its total absorption in the multiple relations among five people. At one point these various sets of relations are enumerated by the Assinghams, who see them as so many "cases":

"There's Maggie's and the Prince's, and there's the Prince's and Charlotte's," [said Fanny].

"Oh yes; and then," the Colonel scoffed, "there's Charlotte's and the Prince's."

"There's Maggie's and Charlotte's," she went on—"and there's also Maggie's and mine. I think too that there's Charlotte's and mine" (XXIII, 75).

Though imposing, even the Assinghams' tabulation of "cases" is incomplete. These relations, not simply in their basic form, but in all their nuances and transformations, guarantee that the novel will be intensely wrought.[1] "Intensity," like "relations," is both technique and subject matter. So too the paired concepts are indivisible, two aspects of the same thing.

To establish and maintain these complex relations, James depends considerably on some of the methods that we have discussed in earlier chapters. To begin with relatively minor matters, there is the kind of play on the ambiguity of youth and age that supports the structure of *The Europeans*. Maggie

1. See Stephen Spender, *The Destructive Element* (Philadelphia, 1953), pp. 87-98.

and Adam Verver (like the Wentworths) are often described as childlike—in their moral naïveté—while their spouses (like the Baroness Münster and Felix Young) are old—in worldly knowledge—beyond their years. Fanny's judgment, "It's Mr. Verver who's really young—it's Charlotte who's really old" (XXIII, 393), points up the paradoxical relation between the husband and the wife, giving it definition and "composition." To see one character fully is to see the others fully. James again shows his indebtedness to Balzac by multiplying the ways in which characters are compared, contrasted, and paired, in which one throws light on another, in which the appearance of one is the reality of another.

Another familiar method for gaining this kind of balance (so as to insure that the intensity will be coherent, not simply complicated) is to represent character as a composite of the private self and acquired national traits: that is, the method of "Madame de Mauves" and other early international novels and tales. It will be remembered that in "Madame de Mauves" all the major characters experience some tension between what their cultures impose upon them and what they discover to be their private needs. Longmore and the Baron de Mauves come to recognize and finally acknowledge some unfamiliar passion within themselves, while Euphemia resists a corresponding pressure within herself. A more complex version of this situation is to be found in *The Golden Bowl*. In each of the four principals, especially in the Prince and Maggie, James shows a like tension between the public self and the private self. "There are two parts of me," the Prince recognizes: "One is made up of the history, the doings, the marriages, the crimes, the follies, the boundless *bêtises* of other people. . . . But there's another part, very much smaller doubtless, which, such as it is, represents my single self, the unknown, unimportant . . . personal quality" (XXIII, 9). Maggie, less explicitly, is just as burdened by her national heritage of innocence. This suggested parity between the Prince and the

Princess not only contributes to balance, but also indicates an inevitable difficulty in the marriage which will have to be repaired. This division between one's national mold and his private self is virtually the entirety of the "logic" in "Madame de Mauves," whereas it is but contributive in *The Golden Bowl*—but it contributes to the same end, that of insuring coherence and intensity.

We notice too the borrowings from the drama: the balancings and regroupings of the small cast,[2] the concentrated scenes, the expansion of the structure of drama into something akin to a six-act play, with each of the acts luxuriantly developed. Furthermore James extends upon that technique of *What Maisie Knew* which most insures the inseparability of plot and character: Maisie's talent for bringing people together anticipates the skills of Fanny, who unites Maggie and the Prince, and of Maggie, who does the same for Charlotte and Adam. One is also reminded of *Maisie* when Maggie recognizes that her problem can be solved only by severing Charlotte from her marriage. Her silent tactic at the end is like Maisie's less subtle repudiation of Mrs. Beale. Another method reclaimed from the dramatic period is the identification of characters with their houses and the contrasting of these houses. Like the houses in *The Spoils of Poynton*, Portland Place and Eaton Square become emblematic of those who stay in them. The first comes to represent the worldliness of the Prince and Charlotte, the second the quiet domesticity of Adam and Maggie.

These methods which dominate earlier works become subordinate in *The Golden Bowl*. Nevertheless one of the principal methods in that novel is also a reconstitution of an earlier form: the careful division of the book into two balanced parts. As in some earlier works, the matching halves suggest that we are to regard the novel more as a "picture" than as a progressive action.

2. See John Bayley, *The Characters of Love* (New York, 1960), pp. 207-11.

In other words, the two halves have a geometrical as well as a chronological relation: the second reflects the first quite as much as the first reflects the second. As in those earlier and simpler illustrations of the method, we are invited to consider Volume II a deepening rather than an extension of Volume I. The "handsome wholeness of effect" (*P*, p. 329) that James seeks requires that a minimal emphasis be placed on the fact that the Prince's mind is exhibited *before* the Princess's. What is emphasized (in the preface) is that the two illuminate each other: "It is the Prince who opens the door to half our light upon Maggie, just as it is she who opens it to half our light upon himself. . ." (*P*, p. 330). In the second volume, "we see the same persons and things again but as Maggie's interest, *her* exhibitional charm, determines the view" (*P*, p. 330). James suggests that the action and the situation are much the same in the two volumes; it is the perspective that changes. The obvious difficulty with this idea is that there is a definite action, indeed a near-total alteration of the situation. In what sense, then, are the "things" in the two volumes "the same"?

The process is a more symmetrical version of the scheme of *The Wings of the Dove*, in which Kate's story is basically repeated, first by Milly and then by Densher, each of whom for a time acts as the reflector. Also as in *The Wings of the Dove* this technique of duplication gives an order to certain isolated parts of *The Golden Bowl*. In the second volume Charlotte leaves the bridge game to seek out Maggie in the garden; shortly thereafter the scene is virtually duplicated, only the roles are reversed, for Maggie has become the pursuer and Charlotte the pursued. To Maggie, as to the reader, "It was a repetition more than ever then of the evening on the terrace. . ." (XXIV, 309). It is not just that in both instances one of the women tracks down and then overwhelms the other with her power, but that she gains her advantage by telling a lie.

Another such pattern of duplication involves the appearance

of characters on balconies, though this motif extends throughout the novel. The first of these scenes takes place at Matcham, when the Prince sights Charlotte standing above him on a balcony; it is a celebratory gesture to demonstrate her freedom and availability. In the beginning of the second volume, Maggie returns with her father to Portland Place and is greeted by Charlotte and the Prince, standing together on the balcony. Nothing brings home to Maggie with more ugly clarity the confidence of the lovers in their conspiracy against her. Toward the end of the novel, as Maggie and Charlotte are in the process of exchanging their roles in relation to Amerigo, Maggie herself stands on a balcony at Fawns, overlooking Charlotte, now "beneath" her. Finally, in the last scene, Maggie and the Prince stand together on the balcony of Portland Place, bidding farewell to Charlotte and Adam. In sum the four balcony scenes are tableaux manifesting the four states of the adultery: its initiation, its triumph, its deterioration, its destruction. The various stages of the relationship are made exhibitory; the tableaux not merely crystallize the state of things, but publicly proclaim it. It is much the same as with the five balcony scenes in *The Ambassadors*. Strether's shifting attitude towards Chad and Paris is represented by the rhythm that fuses the various scenes—from the first of them, in which Strether is on the street observing Bilham on the balcony, to the last of them, in which Strether himself stands on the balcony. Strether passes from the stage of the innocent pilgrim to that of a man fully at home in Paris.[3]

Obviously the purpose of such devices is to accentuate the relation between one scene and another, compelling us to look backwards so as to measure how far we have come. In another sense, we, with the characters, continue to go over the same

3. Tony Tanner's essay, "The Watcher from the Balcony: Henry James's *The Ambassadors*," *Critical Quarterly*, VIII (Spring, 1966), 35-52, published after the completion of this chapter, further illuminates the balcony pattern in *The Ambassadors*.

ground. For an episode to be dramatized in its totality it must be dramatized more than once.

The balcony pattern must be judged a leitmotif, subsidiary to the more symmetrical and more pronounced effects gained by the over-all two-part structure, though a "compositional resource" (*P*, p. 329) of the same general order. Basic to the major plan is that in the second volume the Princess repeats the action of the Prince in the first volume. First the external evidence of the form should be noted:

Book	Principal Setting	Climactic Action
	(Volume I)	
First	London	the meeting of Charlotte and Amerigo; the marriage of Maggie and Amerigo
Second	Fawns	the creation of a permanent union between Charlotte and Amerigo; the marriage of Charlotte and Adam
Third	London	the initiation of the adultery
	(Volume II)	
Fourth	London	Maggie's conquest of Amerigo
Fifth	Fawns	Maggie's conquest of Charlotte
Sixth	London	the departure of Adam and Charlotte for Amercia

The first half concludes when the marriages reach their nadir, and the second when they have been saved. So much, however, is summary. James requires that we glance from events in the second volume to those events in the first volume which are made to correspond with them. The balancing Fawns sections indicate a pastoral harmony in the middle of each volume: in the first (seemingly) it is a harmony threatened only by Mr. Verver's loneliness and vulnerability, owing to his daughter's marriage, but the discord is to be eliminated (seemingly) by his marriage to Charlotte; in the second it is a harmony that everyone recognizes to be illusory, and no one more than Maggie suffers from "the horror of the thing hideously *behind*. . ." (XXIV, 237). Outwardly everything is much the same as before, including not only the placid country setting, but even the presence of Adam's former pursuers, Mrs. Rance and the Lutches. In the first Fawns section, the false appearances, corresponding to the imperturbable innocence of the Ververs, overwhelm reality. In the second, however, reality nearly overwhelms appearance, so that the outward calm of both setting and character seems irrelevant to the true state of things. In the second Fawns section, we are made to see not simply that appearances are false; we are made also to recognize that they have been false from the start, that the evil that all but ruptures the surfaces during the second season at Fawns has in large measure been caused by the Verver's innocent (or pastoral) assumptions during their first stay.

The method also serves James's emphasis that Maggie must change everything without ruffling the outward harmony of the group. Thus it is terrifyingly fitting that the scene at the time of her adult fears is the same as at the time of her childish fears. Something like this crosses her mind as she resumes the pattern of older times and has a long quiet chat with her father "on a sequestered bench beneath one of the great trees" (XXIV, 253) at Fawns:

The whirligig of time had thus brought round for them again, on their finding themselves face to face while the others were gathering for tea on the terrace, the same odd impulse quietly to "slope"—so Adam Verver himself, as they went, familiarly expressed it—that had acted in its way of old; acted for the distant autumn afternoon and for the sharpness of their since so outlived crisis. It might have been funny to them now that the presence of Mrs. Rance and the Lutches—and with symptoms too at that time less developed—had once for their anxiety and their prudence constituted a crisis; it might have been funny that these ladies could ever have figured to their imagination as a symbol of dangers vivid enough to pre- cipitate the need of a remedy (XXIV, 253-54).

But James is not primarily interested in drawing ironic com- parisons between the early Maggie and the late Maggie. We get a good deal closer to the appropriateness of the dualistic struc- ture when we recognize that each of the two parts concentrates on the formation of a strategy to bring about a particular kind of relationship and ends with the triumph of that strategy. Since in the first half we are mainly confined to the consciousness of the Prince, we are required to attend not only to the developing of a new relationship, the adultery, but also to the deceiving of Maggie and Adam. Amerigo and Charlotte are at first anxious to understand the odd relation that binds their marriage partners and to learn what is expected of themselves as rather neglected spouses. But they grow weary of trying to please; they even grow callous of the others' feelings and neglectful of their own responsibilities. We notice in the beginning that the secret union between the two comes to be symbolized by a golden bowl in an antique shop. Also they for a while rely upon Fanny Assing- ham to give them counsel and consolation, even to tell a lie for them; but near the end of the volume they grow indifferent to her ("Fanny Assingham didn't now matter" [XXIII, 313]) and overtly defy her ("Poor Fanny Assingham's challenge amounted to nothing" [XXIII, 350]). Finally Charlotte and Amerigo destroy all but the most superficial appearance of the original situation.

Basically the second volume carries out the same order. The Princess (in silent and ambiguous conspiracy with her father) tries to comprehend the relation of the others, recognizes the inadequacy of a policy of kindness and consideration, employs a strategy of deception, and in the end creates a new relationship, destroying all but the outer shell of the previous one. Likewise she discovers the same golden bowl in the same antique shop, and finds in it a symbol of the union she desires to produce— "The golden bowl—as it *was* to have been. . . . The bowl with all our happiness in it. The bowl without the crack" (XXIV, 216-17). Also Maggie at first leans upon Fanny Assingham for guidance and even induces her to lie for her; then she discards Fanny.

Obviously the repetitive pattern that I have sketched misrepresents the novel to an extent, for there are irregularities and disparities from one volume to the next—including, for example, the shift of point of view in the second book of the first volume from the Prince to Adam. (Thus the paralleling Fawns sections interfere with the larger parallels formed by the two volumes.) Furthermore the Prince in Volume I is considerably more passive than is the Princess in Volume II, as he concedes to Charlotte most of the control of their relationship. Yet the main outlines of the two actions are duplicated, though not so mechanically as to detract from the naturalness of the movement. It may be argued that, far from echoing each other, the two volumes are sharply opposed: the first devoted to the subversion of the marriages and the second to their restoration. But this is to alter James's emphasis, which in fact follows the same general course in each volume—a course that begins in the undermining of the existing relation and concludes with the creation of a new one. What changes from volume to volume are the actors, but our focus is regularly on the one who is the aggressor (reversing the pattern of *The Wings of the Dove*). Not until Maggie begins to take charge of the group does she replace the Prince as central consciousness.

Another rebuttal to be anticipated is that in the first volume we witness not just the formation of the illicit union, but also the preliminaries of the two marriages; though not themselves dramatized, the marriages are the major events of the first half. Yet it is surely significant that the marriages are not dramatized and that their preparations are mostly background, observed as they are from the dominant perspective of the Prince, who is mostly seen in his relation with Charlotte. Unlike his marriage to Maggie, his affair with Charlotte is rendered with fullness and immediacy. The marriages form an ironic counterpoint to the movement in the foreground. As a parallel, about half of the second volume has as its background the strengthening of the Charlotte-Amerigo tie, though our focus is insistently on Maggie's effort to destroy it and to create a very different relationship. To put it otherwise, Maggie seeks to fulfill the marriages that preceded the renewal of the illicit affair, precisely as the affair had preceded the marriages and is resumed after them.

In addition, we should not be tempted to look upon the adultery simply as the negation of the marriages. Rather we should see it as James does, as a positive contractual relationship with a social form. Certainly to Maggie the adultery is exactly the kind of "arrangement" that her marriage should have been: "Of course they were arranged—all four arranged; but what had the basis of their life been precisely but that they were arranged together? Ah! Amerigo and Charlotte were arranged together, but she . . . was arranged apart" (XXIV, 45). But in fact Maggie is arranged, for the intimacy between her and her father, though of another order, is as real as that between Charlotte and Amerigo.

How then do the volumes essentially differ? What contrast underlies the comparison? It is a facile judgment to assume that the lesson is entirely an ethical one, demonstrating the triumph of the married state over the adulterous one, or of goodness over evil. For one thing, as many commentators have demonstrated, James everywhere emphasizes that the Ververs' ethical failings (their unwillingness to give each other up, their commercialism, their indifference to the needs of their *sposi*, their childlike fan-

raises, etc.) weigh as heavily on the moral scale as the adultery.[4]

If the principle of relationship between the two halves is not a simple moralistic one, we are still left with the impression that Maggie's victory is the victory of legitimacy. It is inadequate to surmise that we applaud her because she supports marriage and opposes adultery. Since the expressed reason for her heroics is not marriage but "love" (XXIV, 116), she really competes with Charlotte on Charlotte's terms, not as the Prince's wife but as one who would be his lover. Furthermore, the power of this love is gauged by the effectiveness of the means used to secure it. Her method rather than her objective wins over the Prince. Her love is manifested in her force of will and her ruthlessness; it depends upon the intellectual qualities of self-awareness and insight into the motives of others. In practice, this amounts, first, to an ability to read appearances correctly ("if she could only get the facts of appearance straight, only jam them down into their place, the reasons lurking behind them . . . wouldn't perhaps be able to help showing" [XXIV, 52]) and, secondly, to an ability to preserve them even as she wrenches her husband from Charlotte.

In part Maggie's trouble originates in her misunderstanding of the meaning of marriage: in the beginning she seems to think of the act of marriage as the institution of marriage, an inviolable legality that can be altered by neither the conditions of time nor the vagaries of man. To both Maggie and her father, the content of marriage is the same as its form. Paradoxically this fallacy springs not from an exaggeration of the importance of form, but from a total ignorance of form. To the Americans, social forms— all surfaces and appearances—are "European," something alien and apart from themselves which they admire and wish to acquire. But their gravest mistake is their notion that form can be somehow possessed, even bought, without its being allowed to interfere with one's life. At first Amerigo thinks there is some-

4. The case against the Ververs is ably summarized by Oscar Cargill, *The Novels of Henry James* (New York, 1961), pp. 401-11.

thing amiable in Adam's aloofness from "appearances," but before long this detachment takes on less pleasant implications to him: "It was at present to come over Amerigo as never before that his remarkable father-in-law was the man in the world least equipped with different appearances for different times. He was simple, he was a revelation of simplicity, and that was the end of him so far as he consisted of an appearance at all. . ." (XXIII, 323).

One of the things that initially distinguishes the Prince from Maggie and her father is their differing attitudes toward forms, especially toward the institution of marriage. The Prince requires some vital fusion between the appearance and the reality; he desires "the maximum of immersion in the fact of being married" (XXIII, 148). The Prince is the character who is most frequently identified with architectural structures and works of art, not simply to indicate his aesthetic and historical value to the Ververs, but also to show the extent to which aesthetics are real to him, organically relevant to the living of life. Especially through the Prince, James shows that marriage, as a social form, has aesthetic properties. In the beginning the Prince is the aesthetic man unaccustomedly involved in an ethical relationship, and Maggie is the ethical woman unaccustomedly involved in an aesthetic relationship. Finally the Prince does not measure up to his wife's standards of goodness, but Maggie fails to submit herself to the new aesthetic form that her life has assumed. Her marriage remains to her something to look at rather than something to experience.

The Prince has a clearer understanding of the status of aesthetics in life than both Charlotte and Maggie. From the start Charlotte holds that appearances and realities are necessarily dichotomous. When she arrives upon the scene just before the Prince is to be married, her only real question "was to know what appearance could best be produced and best be preserved" (XXIII, 50). That is, what role should she play? During the affair with the Prince, her conscience is untroubled because her "tact" and "propriety" (XXIII, 288) have concealed the truth from the Ververs. The Prince is less comfortable with Charlotte's theory. He resists the notion that "mere formal good manners" (XXIII, 53) are a sufficient tribute to surface reality. Thus the English style of adultery appalls him. The barren rituals of country-house love affairs, epitomized by the game-like pretenses of Lady Castledean and her young man, speak to the Prince of "the fathomless depths of English equivocation. . . . They [the English] didn't like *les situations nettes* . . . even much initiation left one at given moments so puzzled as to the element of staleness in all the freshness and of freshness in all the staleness, of innocence in the guilt and of guilt in the innocence. There were other marble terraces, sweeping more purple prospects [presumably Italian], on which he would have known what to think, and would have enjoyed thereby at least the small intellectual fillip of a discerned relation between a given appearance and a taken meaning" (XXIII, 353-54). To the Prince, evidently, there can be surfaces expressive of adultery as well as of marriage. If his marriage fails to please him because its appearance misrepresents its reality, so his adultery fails to satisfy him entirely because its reality has no appearance at all.

But the Prince, weakened by passion, submits to Charlotte's policy of empty decorum. But it says a great deal about him that he even comes to think of the very falsity of their relation and their connivance in respecting the "sovereign law" of not publicly offending as giving a vague form to their affair; deceit and decency alone create "a mystic golden bridge between them" (XXIII, 325).

Until the second volume Maggie fails to realize that the form of marriage is worthless without the passion of husband and wife. When she finally recognizes how hollow her marriage has become, she at first blames the fact that she and her husband "had taken too much for granted that their life together required, as people in London said, a special 'form'—which was very well so long as the form was kept only for the outside world and was made no more of among themselves than the pretty mould of an iced pudding, or something of that sort, into which, to help yourself, you didn't hesitate to break with the spoon" (XXIV, 27-28). Maggie begins to realize that her error lay in judging the "mould" of her and her father's marriages to be identical with the fact of the marriages. She comes to see not that the form is unimportant, but that it is not enough by itself. She arrives at the Prince's understanding that the reality should be made to fit the appearances.

Therefore she sees that her task will be to win back the Prince without giving a sign of her displeasure to Charlotte or Adam, without hinting that things are not what they seem. Her successful restoration—in fact, her creation—of her marriage is from time to time attributed to a predatory aggression, an ingenious shrewdness, and a calculating empiricism. She uses all of these means, but more than anything she uses the talents of the artist. Thus she is likened to "an old woman who has taken to 'painting' and who has to lay it on thicker, to carry it off with a greater audacity, with a greater impudence even, the older she grows" (XXIII, 396); to "an actress who had been studying a part and rehearsing it, but who suddenly, on the stage, before the footlights, had begun to improvise, to speak lines not in the text" (XXIV, 33); to a playwright who looks upon a room as "a stage again waiting a drama . . . a scene she might people" (XXIV, 236); even to a circus bareback rider (XXIV, 71) and "the overworked little trapezist girl" (XXIV, 302). There are many other metaphors that relate Maggie's maneuvers to art. They are neither hyperbolic nor strained, for Maggie really is an artist, one who seeks the ideal fusion of the appearance and the content of her marriage, even to the extent that "the grave distinction between substance and form . . . signally break[s] down" (*P*, p. 115).

If one accepts these implications of the metaphorical language of the novel (in addition to the overwhelming atmosphere of art[5] that surrounds and becomes interfused with the theme of marriage), he comes to regard the institution of marriage as analogous to the form of art. It is an analogy that says as much about art as about marriage. All the principal characters are artists of a sort. The four characters who surround Maggie fail, in one way or another, to reconcile the form and the substance of marriage, and thus negatively indicate the way it should be done.

Charlotte, as we have seen, finds safety in her habit of totally dissociating surface and meaning. Her great skill with appearances far exceeds the merely conventional propriety of Lady Castledean, but it amounts in the end to nothing more than the same kind of comfortable assumption that forms are to be equated with unreality.

Adam Verver enters marriage with the same frame of mind that serves him in the purchase of works of art, even to the extent that he evaluates the Prince and Charlotte as a pair of expensive purchases. Thus "the instinct, the particular sharpened appetite of the collector, had fairly served as a basis for his acceptance of the Prince's suit" (XXIII, 140). At the time of his proposal to Charlotte, he is in Brighton to negotiate with the owner of a set of antique tiles, and the bargaining with Charlotte is of the same order as the bargaining with the dealer. Indeed the two transactions are closely related in his mind. He comes to look upon Charlotte as he looks upon the tiles—as a finished product, a work of great craftsmanship, to be treasured and not to be used: "The infinitely ancient, the immemorial amethystine blue of the glaze, scarcely more meant to be breathed upon, it would seem,

5. See Edwin T. Bowden, *The Themes of Henry James: A System of Observation through the Visual Arts* (New Haven, 1956), pp. 102-13.

than the cheek of royalty—this property of the ordered and matched array had inevitably all its determination for him; but his submission was, perhaps for the first time in his life, of the quick mind alone, the process really itself, in its way, as fine as the perfection perceived and admired: every inch of the rest of him being given to the fore-knowledge that an hour or two later he should have 'spoken' " (XXIII, 215).

If Adam brings to marriage the outlook of the art collector, Fanny is pre-eminently the art critic. With no distinct life of her own, she analyzes the relations of others with a detachment that rarely falters. She even adjusts these relations when it suits "the beautiful symmetry of [her] plan" (XXIII, 389). Her "small still passion for order and symmetry" (XXIV, 152) far exceeds whatever passion she may have for truth and goodness. Her credo—that "forms . . . are two thirds of conduct" (XXIII, 390) —amounts to a belief in life for art's sake. Finally she realizes the sterility of her social aestheticism when she witnesses the disastrous results of her scheme.

The only concept of art deserving comparison to Maggie's is the Prince's—his classical notion that human life should be absorbed in traditional forms and styles. Maggie senses in him "a life tremendously ordered and fixed" (XXIV, 66). But in the long run Maggie's experimentation succeeds and the Prince's traditionalism fails; the adultery is his confession of failure. At the end he acknowledges that his own formal "taste" has been overshadowed by his wife's inventiveness and disregard for precedent: "Taste in him as a touchstone was now all at sea; for who could say but that one of her fifty ideas, or perhaps forty-nine of them, wouldn't be exactly that taste by itself, the taste he had always conformed to, had no importance whatever" (XXIV, 345)? The incident that precipitates this insight is that Maggie has given him "an opportunity to separate from Mrs. Verver with the due amount of form"; it is a gesture manifesting that she knows everything, and ordinarily the Prince would "treat himself to a quarrel with it on the score of taste" (XXIV, 345).[6] In fact, however, it is but the last step in an operation that has regularly violated the laws of taste and the models of convention in order to preserve the only form that counts, that of the marriage.

To elicit a theory of art from *The Golden Bowl* we need not insist on an allegorical reading. As a formal institution, requiring a union of a conventional exterior order with some unique interior energy, marriage literally is an art. It closely conforms to the standards that James sets for the artist of fiction. Accordingly, Maggie Verver is the ideal Jamesian artist.[7] What most distinguishes Maggie from some other Jamesian protagonists who find themselves exploited and deceived is that her counterplot is more a detailed process than a simple gesture of assertion or renunciation. Though she has something in common with earlier heroines like Maisie and Milly, unlike them she is for a long time engaged in resisting and then in tediously converting the conditions of her life. The artist cannot remain passive. Art, for James, is "the religion of doing" (*P*, p. 347). Maggie's art, in contrast to that of the other characters in the novel, is process and act, not achieved finality. The salvation of her marriage is the struggle to preserve it.

To Maggie as to James, the outer design—*in its essentials*—is inviolable; it may bend and buckle as it responds to the needs

6. For my own present purposes, I have inevitably slighted the moral implications of this and other parts of the novel. Dorothea Krook's comments on the "touchstone of taste" passage are judicious and, I would hope, not inconsistent with my own: "When he repudiates the touchstone of taste, [the Prince] does so because he has perceived at last not only the goodness of Maggie's love but also the beauty of that goodness" (*The Ordeal of Consciousness in Henry James* [Cambridge, England, 1962], p. 275).

7. As Laurence Bedwell Holland, *The Expense of Vision: Essays on the Craft of Henry James* (Princeton, 1964), points out, metaphors of marriage abound in James's critical writings (pp. 57-58). Walter F. Wright, *The Madness of Art: A Study of Henry James* (Lincoln, Nebraska, 1962), comments briefly on Maggie Verver as artist (pp. 253-54).

of the subject, but it may not crack. If the chosen form contains elements that are merely ornate or for some other reason un- workable, these must be eliminated. In *The Golden Bowl* Maggie's and Adam's four-sided scheme not only constitutes a superficial order, entered into for its "beautiful harmony" (XXIV, 74), but it precludes any vital order that may grow from within. One is reminded of James's comment on Scott's *The Bride of Lammermoor*: "The centre of the subject is empty and development pushed off, all round, toward the frame—which is, so to speak, beautifully rich and curious" (*P*, p. 68). To recast the "beautifully rich and curious," but merely decorative, form of her marriage into something new, Maggie has no choice but to sacrifice Adam and Charlotte. She cannot ignore the intimate connection between the "centre" and the "frame," and only in grasping the demands of the center does she perceive the weak- ness of the frame. Building precedes destruction, but finally requires it. The ideal unity which Maggie strives to achieve is at odds with the preconceived design that in effect is a parody of marriage.

The analogous relation between Maggie's process of restoring her marriage and James's art is nowhere better suggested than in the preface to *The Wings of the Dove*. The passage deserves full quotation:

One's plan, alas, is one thing and one's result another; so I am perhaps nearer the point in saying that this last strikes me at present as most characterised by the happy features that were, under my first and most blest illusion, to have contributed to it. I meet them all, as I renew acquaintance, I mourn for them all as I remount the stream, the absent values, the palpable voids, the missing links, the mocking shadows, that reflect, taken together, the early bloom of one's good faith. Such cases are of course far from abnormal—so far from it that some acute mind ought surely to have worked out by this time the "law" of the degree in which the artist's energy fairly depends on his fallibility. How much and how often, and in what connexions and with what almost infinite variety, must he be a dupe, that of his prime object, to be all measurably a master, that of his actual substitute for it—or in other words at all appreciably to exist? He places, after an earnest survey, the piers of his bridge—he has at least sounded deep enough, heaven knows, for their brave position; yet the bridge spans the stream, after the fact, in apparently complete independence of these properties, the principal grace of the original design. *They* were an illusion, for their necessary hour; but the span itself, whether of a single arch or of many, seems by the oddest chance in the world to be a reality; since, actually, the rueful builder, passing under it, sees figures and hears sounds above; he makes out, with his heart in his throat, that it bears and is positively being "used" (*P*, pp. 296-97).

In this study I have tried to describe some instances of James's recasting of traditional literary forms. Earlier chapters have re-counted variations of his general technique of beginning with a blanket exploitation of some more-or-less standard genre or con-vention—such as the comedy of manners, the three-act play, and the naturalistic novel—and then radically transforming that model as he allows his subject to find its own shape. Often it is not a conventional form with which James begins, but his own highly arbitrary and highly symmetrical ideal of order. Like Maggie, James seeks not simply to infuse some life into the abstract forms, but to discover what is viable in them. The "patches" and "parts" which are distinct from "the achieved iridescence from within" (*P*, p. 262) obscure the iridescence and so must be discarded. Though a writer who both demanded "decent symmetries" (*P*, p. 100) and encouraged the organic growth of the subject, James is basically more pragmatic and experimental than he is conventional and formalist, though his regular effort is to be all of these. Predetermined schemes, whether conventional or of his own creation, at most contribute a provisional form that retracts or expands to accommodate the subject. Furthermore, "the high price of the novel as a literary form [is] its power not only, while preserving that form with closeness, to range through all the differences of the individual relation to its general subject-matter, all the varieties of outlook on life, of disposition to reflect and project, created by conditions that are never the same from man to man . . . but positively to appear more true to its character in proportion as it strains, or tends to burst, with a latent extravagance, its mould" (*P*, pp. 45-46).

Maggie Verver also discovers that a form is preserved only as it is strained. The strain nearly overwhelms her as she watches the outwardly placid card game at Fawns; she fears that "she might sound out their doom in a single sentence," in which case "all this high decorum would hang by a hair" (XXIV, 233). Maggie is never "more true" to the form of her marriage than when she presses the hardest against the frail restraints of propriety that weakly bind it together. The form noticeably "tends to burst" when she confronts the Prince with her evidence of his intimacy with Charlotte and when she boldly lies to Charlotte at Fawns.

Though *The Golden Bowl* probably has more to say about James's compositional principles than any of his other novels, we also find the subject glanced at elsewhere. The early international fiction, for example, offers analogous insight into the artistic synthesis between classical order and free organic growth. The aesthetic tension between fullness and economy is a reconstitution of the moral problem faced by Isabel Archer. *The Portrait of a Lady* works toward a union between the restraining order of a civilization and Isabel's freedom of mind and spirit—"the union of great knowledge with great liberty; the knowledge would give one a sense of duty and the liberty a sense of enjoyment" (IV, 198). Isabel's free intelligence, tragically unmindful of the reality of appearances, is sharply contrasted to the absolute formalism of Madame Merle and Osmond, who regard the self too lightly. As Frederick C. Crews observes, the novel moves toward a reconciliation of these opposites.[8] In the end Isabel acquires considerably more respect for worldly prudence than she had originally possessed.

Some of James's works approach the problem from another direction. *The Sacred Fount* and "The Altar of the Dead," among other novels and tales, dramatize tensions between the desire to impose rigid symmetries upon life and the acceptance of the disorder of experience. *The Sacred Fount*, bewilderingly, is unresolved: we have no certainty whether the narrator's schematic analysis of the events he witnesses is a solipsistic irrelevance or a true accounting of the facts. In any case, he has much in common with the early Maggie and Adam Verver, who are equally enthralled by their own symmetrical design. Though it contains none of the overt speculation on the relation between art and life that we find in *The Sacred Fount*, "The Altar of the Dead" is a particularly instructive commentary on James's aesthetic. George Stransom's "masterpiece of splendour" (XVII, 15), his altar with its precise arrangement of candles, is his great compensation for the brutalities, confusions, and dissatisfactions of life. His altar becomes his art, his contrived symbol of "his dead." Yet its very clarity and beauty make the tangle of life increasingly repellent to him: "There were hours at which he almost caught himself wishing that certain of his friends would now die, that he might establish with them in this manner a connexion more charming than, as it happened, it was possible to enjoy with them in life" (XVII, 19). Accordingly, he becomes obsessed with the idea that his own death will make his beautiful altar complete:

8. *The Tragedy of Manners: Moral Drama in the Later Novels of Henry James* (New Haven, 1957), p. 17: ". . . Isabel, the unimpeachable heroine, moves reluctantly toward an acceptance of the very attitude of her enemies, or at least to a significant part of that attitude. . . . she has cast doubt on her original philosophy of the soul's invulnerability. . . ." A general interpretation of the international theme along similar lines is to be found in Christof Wegelin, *The Image of Europe in Henry James* (Dallas, 1958).

There came a day when, for simple exhaustion, if symmetry should demand just one he was ready so far to meet symmetry. Symmetry was harmony, and the idea of harmony began to haunt him; he said to himself that harmony was of course everything. He took, in fancy, his composition to pieces, redistributing it into other lines, making other juxtapositions and contrasts. . . . Finally, in this way, he arrived at a conception of the total, the ideal, which left a clear opportunity for just another figure. "Just one more—to round it off; just one more, just one," continued to hum in his head (XVII, 53).

In this manner art—defined as 'ideal composition'—cancels out life. The altar of the dead has lost its connection with the experience of the living. Its austere geometry is disturbed only by its worshipper's not being himself dead. Stransom has believed that the inclusion of a candle for Acton Hague, his betrayer, would violate or repudiate the harmony of the altar. But not until he forgives Hague through the gesture of inserting a candle for him does the altar attain its perfection. Stransom changes from one who would possess and control the dead to one who loves and forgives them; the deed which is the expression of this maturing suddenly infuses reality into what had been a sterile symmetry. The situation in the tale is analogous to that in *The Golden Bowl*: Maggie's submission to the fantasy that the design of the marriages counts for everything and her gradual recognition that the old order must be violated for a living order to be gained. This also is the rule of James's fiction: the perfection of form consists in the violation of form.

INDEX